ENQUIRIES IN MEDIEVAL INDIA
Religion, Society, Culture, and Polity

ENQUIRIES IN MEDIEVAL INDIA

Religion, Society, Culture, and Polity

Rattan Lal Hangloo

PRIMUS BOOKS

PRIMUS BOOKS
An imprint of Ratna Sagar P. Ltd.
Virat Bhavan
Mukherjee Nagar Commercial Complex
Delhi 110 009

Offices at CHENNAI LUCKNOW
AGRA AHMEDABAD BENGALURU BHOPAL COIMBATORE
DEHRADUN GUWAHATI HYDERABAD JAIPUR JALANDHAR KANPUR
KOCHI KOLKATA MUMBAI PATNA RANCHI VARANASI

First published 2022

ISBN: 978-93-5572-183-9 (hardback)
ISBN: 978-93-5572-184-6 (POD)

Published by Primus Books

Laser typeset by Mithu Karmakar
mithu.karma@gmail.com

To my parents

SMT. RUPA PANDITA HANGLOO

and

SH. RADHA KRISHAN HANGLOO

Contents

Acknowledgements

THIS BOOK IS THE result of persuasion by my friends who were very unhappy with me for having accepted administrative assignment for the past seven years. They always wanted me to get back to research on our fascinating subject of medieval Indian history. Therefore, my thanks go to Professor Paramjeet Singh Romana, a reputed scholar and linguist of Punjab, Mr Pare Lal Pandita, Shree Sudesh Bhat, Shree Ashok ji Bhat, Shree Bhushan Lal Dhar, my sister Amriteshwari and her husband Mr Sandeep Bazaz, Shree Madan Lal Kaul, Shree Soom Nath Malla, Professor Saleem Khan, Prof Altaf Hussain Para, Dr Ashraf Dar, Dr Javed Wani and Mr Sudarshan.

I also thank my great teacher, Professor Harbans Mukhia ji, for always providing me with excellent suggestions and knowledge in the pursuit of learning. One of the great advantages of being his student is that at points of difficulty, I can always turn to him for reliable advice. My fundamental intellectual debt goes to him. I have benefitted hugely from the writings of Professor Irfan Habib, who was generous in presenting me with a complete set of his books during my visit to Aligarh Muslim University on 15 April 2016 on the occasion Sir Syed Ahmed Khan's bicentenary celebration for delivering Sir Syed Memorial Lecture.

I also express my thanks to my students who always asked critical questions and brought to my knowledge varied sources while they worked for their respective research themes. Some of these include Professor S. Victor Babu, Professor Salma Ahmad, Dr Naga Sridhar, Dr Yaseer Arafat, Dr Anjaneya

Swami, Dr K.V.N. Raju, Dr Fayaz Ahmad, Dr P. Sihabudeen, Dr Asif Ahmad Khandey, Dr H. Vanlalhruaia, Mr Salil Kader, Ms Praveena, Dr Rao Shashi Kant Das, Dr Ch. Srinivasa Reddy, Dr Rama Krishna, and Dr Phenish Babu. My thanks also go to Dr Mamta Nanda and Dr Nazneen Farooqi for reading the draft.

I also wish to acknowledge the support of my family. My brothers Shree M.L. Hangloo, Shree P.L. Hangloo and Dr Nanaji Hangloo, and my children Arkaprateem, Akanksha, Dr Arkapravah and Akhil ji who always enjoy my involvement with the subject. I appreciate their close attention to detail.

I am also grateful to Professor O.N. Kaul for countless enlightening conversations and his valuable feedback and suggestions.

Lastly I thank my wife Sharika Kaul Hangloo for walking with me every step of this journey. She worked very diligently to improve my devotion to the subject. I always find her insatiable curiosity and her encouragement of new ideas exemplary.

Jammu RATTAN LAL HANGLOO
October 2021

Introduction

> The analysis of myth, the unravelling of the language, the probing of individual, and even more important, the collective unconscious, these are but some of the ways in which the past can be put together as a whole and therefore better understood. In fact there is nothing that is alien to historical study. In consequence no historian can today afford to be a narrow specialist. He has, of course, to have a thorough grasp of his particular field but the field has many layers.[1]
>
> —BIPAN CHANDRA, ROMILA THAPAR and S. GOPAL

HISTORY IS NOT merely about what happened in the past, but also about how that past is interpreted from time to time. Since no field has been completely researched, there will always be limitations for historians and gaps for people to access knowledge of our past. In addition to written information, there are numerous scientific techniques for analysis of empirical evidence that is available to us in various repositories of knowledge. Every available source about the past has its own specificities, priorities, compulsions, and prejudices because each source was written with a definite purpose and idea. Whatever has survived in terms of evidence is a fraction that, therefore, needs to be interpreted very carefully. Reconstruction of the past and study of the present is more important than putting many facts together. For historians, collecting and weighing extant evidence is only a limited part of their work. A historian's ultimate purpose is not only to indulge in a dispassionate study of the past, but also to objectively reconstruct it, lest it be a simple repetition.

Construction or reconstruction of any historical event is a cumulative process leading to various formulations, which further lead to creations, modifications, and eliminations of certain items associated with our historical past.

There is a need to transcend the limitations of our ideological positions to understand the medieval period in order to help scholars to go beyond the narrow confines of their own understanding and, thereby, enhance people's intellectual curiosity about the era.

How much of antiquity got overwhelmed by medieval developments and how much of modernity incorporated medieval institutions are questions that deserve the attention of future scholars. All ideas and institutions of medieval India were not obsolete; that is why they gave way to the modern. The same is also true of ancient India. Both internal and external forces have played a significant role in the entire process. External forces played a positive role in the evolution of the medieval period by building institutions that assimilated and Indianized the foreign influences. However, the transition to modernity was also thrust upon India by colonialism with no respect for Indian values and traditions.

Today, efforts are made to observe medieval history from a specific ideological lens. In the process, an objective understanding of the nature and role of ideas and institutions in that period gets compromised. Therefore, a discussion of such aspects becomes necessary. We have looked into questions of periodization and illustrated how multiple strands of history writing influenced it and made different criteria relevant and irrelevant with the progress of history writing in India vis-à-vis spatial and temporal dynamics. We have managed this without losing sight of the fact that the medieval period facilitated a better understanding of the ways in which religions grew and disseminated art and ideas and borrowed from different regions and people, and of the aspirations behind the adventures and conquests that ultimately shaped the larger kingdoms and empires that rose and fell.

Today, the decline of history teaching in our institutions is reflected in the attitude of the public and politicians towards the subject. We find that certain aspects of medieval history become strong reference points in politics in order to overshadow or replace others. The lack of objective history writing and teaching has grave consequences for the image of India, which is constantly evolving, changing, and transforming. The medieval period in Indian history is important because it provides the chance to study how communities evolved and confronted the challenges in their respective societies, or how the mosaic of plurality and the basis of common citizenship that evolved in Akbar's period (1556–1605) is essential for understanding history.

A commitment to common goals is fast disappearing today. Some may disagree, but a common view of our past is contested and a dominant cultural ethos is imposed. Under such circumstances, a new way of perceiving and writing our history is emerging from sections that are biased but are central to India's identity. We find certain perspectives are preferred over others because of which the nature of explanation for any past event depends on who is interpreting it and on which side the historian places himself or herself. Whatever the level of historian's analytical skills may be, a historical study can never be carried out in vacuum; there should be interaction and parallel discourses and exchanges with different approaches if we want to comprehend the intricacies of medieval Indian history.

India's history, which is spread over thousands of centuries, from earlier times till date, has been organized and reorganized into periods, phases, and timespans that are specific to different dynasties that ruled this country from time to time. Each of these divisions is based on a variety of reasons. To distinguish one period from another, some use religion of the rulers as the basis, while others use the name of the dynasty, while some talk of the forces that brought transition and transformation in Indian society, economy, politics, and culture from time to time.

The period generally referred to as medieval roughly starts from the eighth century AD and goes up to the mid-eighteenth century. Various rationales are put forward by both Indian and non-Indian historians for the classification of this period, but the group of historians that provides reasonable ground for dating the medieval period to this particular epoch believes that there was a transition and transformation from the early medieval period that commenced around the eighth century AD and had a strong influence on the nature of India's economy, society, polity, culture and religion, and continued up to the mid-eighteenth century when the British gradually incorporated the Mughal Indian State into their empire.

According to my own research as a historian, this period indeed stands out distinctly with its particular characteristics. (This is not to suggest that the eras preceding and succeeding the medieval period were static.) The Turks, Afghans, and Mughals vanished from the dominant political scene after the collapse of Mughal period, the perceptions which were uninterruptedly nurtured will remain with public from generation to generation and will continue to provide a rich and varied source for creative historian and allow people to assess long term meaning in history of their country. Each of us should remember that our way of life, our consciousness, and our knowledge are directly built out of our past. After the Sultanate period, the advent of Afghans and Mughals enlarged the scope of characteristics of the medieval period. The polity got transformed from a loosely knit tribute-paying relationship of Delhi Sultanate to a more organized and directly administered subas, giving birth to the colossal Mughal state with its huge paraphernalia of institutions.

Numerous changes during this period facilitated the organization and reorganization of land and land-based relationships, both from above and below, which gave great allowance to the development of land as property, peasantization, expansion of areas under cultivation, agricultural techniques and technology, establishment of new villages, artisanal production, and development of towns and cities. New art forms, new music, cultural practices, and new literary forms also evolved during this period. People migrated from one region of India to another, while foreign immigration to India also took place on a large scale. The hateful Indian institution of caste was also impacted by these developments. This institution proliferated and grew by bringing in new technology, new social categories, tensions, and resilience. The new communities of various professions of smithy, carpentry, gold beating, tailoring, stylish masonry, calligraphy, language expertise, construction expertise, teaching, *hakeemi* (medicine), *muhasabat* (accountancy), among many more, grew with the coming of Turks, Uzbeks, Mughals, and many other emigrants from Persia (which included various parts of Central Asia) and the Arab world. Turks brought their share of new ideas, institutions, technology, knowledge, and politico-ideological mechanisms to legitimize their rule. The new institution of ceremonies grew alongside the new political system. The medieval Indian state evolved as a robust institution with its new bureaucratic apparatus, new perception of territoriality, new towns and cities, an army with new warfare technology, new methods of persuasion, new elements of coercion, new sources of revenue, new nobility and new royalty, new social basis of power, new processes of adjustment and assimilation, new political ideologies, new legitimational tools and, above all, new strategies of subjecting people.

These changes also contributed to society and culture in medieval India. The response got reflected in the Bhakti movement and Sufism. These developments challenged the traditional religio-cultural monopoly and hegemony and, as a result, both these religious forces (Bhakti and Sufism) spread across the length and breadth of the country through various institutional and ideological mechanisms. A number of marginalized and subjected communities began to interact on a large scale and across varied social stratifications, throwing up forces of social change and dynamism with respect for pluralism and social and religious harmony. These items became a symbol of unifying force for medieval India.

Dynasties came, ruled, and perished, but the institutional bases formed a bedrock for the entire medieval period and beyond.

There were intervals of crises on all fronts, but the new order thrown up by those crises strengthened the basic structure of medieval period on every occasion, making the idea of India more cohesive and strong. As a result, the evolved medieval Indian culture became internally plural and, in due course, reflected a continuing conversation between India's different traditions and strands of thought. It grew after conscious as well as unconscious interactions among various social groups. Today, we may not agree, but from antiquity, Indian culture has always been subject to external influences which it has assimilated in its own autonomous ways.

The agrarian economy became more organized and viable. The new political elite grew in number, with new social classes enhancing the volume of economy and opportunities, and also revenues for the government. The new military administrative apparatus of mansabs, jagirs, and zamindars dotted entire India. The transferable nature of this administrative machinery strengthened the unifying characteristics of medieval India by bringing all regions under one political umbrella—both through tribute mechanism and direct administrative interference. However, there were zones of confrontation, too, between the Mughal state and some other regional polities, such as in the Deccan, but that did not hinder the Mughal state from registering its achievements for public good.

The different cultures and traditions representing different systems of meaning and visions of the good life merged. Since each culture realized a limited range of human capacities and emotions, and grasped only a part of the totality of human existence, it gradually began to understand other cultures to expand its intellectual and moral horizon. People felt that a culturally self-contained life was virtually impossible for most human beings in an interdependent world. They tried to find ways of reconciling the legitimate demands of unity and diversity, of achieving political unity without cultural uniformity, and of cultivating among themselves both a common sense of belonging and a willingness to respect and cherish deep cultural differences. Therefore, political theories, institutions, vocabulary, virtues, and skills that developed in medieval times in the course of consolidating and conducting the affairs of a pluralistic society remained the characteristics of a positive development and strength. Akbar was more concerned with building a stable Mughal state because for him the well-being of medieval India depended upon deep attachment, affection, love, sense of justice, and the idea of protecting its people, irrespective of their religion.

Guided by such loyalty, no one dared to criticize the form of Mughal government, its institutions, policies, values, ethos, and the dominant perception of Akbar himself. He thought that disloyal people would harm the state's survival and well-being and made people conscious that external as well as oppositional forces should be loyal to their community just as much as they were committed to their state in India.

During the medieval period, literature, art, culture, science, geography, discovery and exploration of oceans, knowledge of nautical techniques, ship building, maritime and inland trade, and cartography also made great progress by receiving political patronage. India got symbols that are named among the wonders of world even today. The institutional basis of the medieval state became strong enough to woo multiple ethnicities, cultures, and social groups from various regions. The trade between medieval India and rest of the world grew to such an extent that the world began to envy India's wealth. The flourishing of commerce provided further revenues that allowed the rulers to fund expeditions targeting locations that brought more resources and opportunities. This also resulted in new cultural trends and urbanization. New cities grew with new urban culture, inventing amenities for habitants which became the theme of many, Urdu, and Persian poets' *ghazals*.

After Akbar, the growth and expansion of the medieval Indian state could not maintain the compatibility between the resources and the administrative efficiency on one hand, and the medieval state's structural expectations on the other.

As a result, medieval India was confronted with challenges at every level—both internally and externally, particularly from Europe—which again transformed it by bringing new ideas, ideology, knowledge, technology, and tools for seeking political legitimacy.

The march of history will go on as usual despite weak or powerful regimes because un-changeability is not a characteristic of any society. The medieval period will always be remembered for all these distinct characteristics that shaped it from the eighth to the mid-eighteenth century. It is not possible to illustrate in detail all aspects of this period in this volume. However, this book attempts to bring to the notice of readers certain aspects, the specificities of which shall further enhance their understanding about this period. For this purpose, I choose to look at the questions that pertain to periodization of medieval India, the nature of linkages between India and Central Asia, the tools of legitimacy and territoriality through medieval towns, and the process of assimilation during the Mughal rule. All these aspects are embedded in medieval Indian society, culture, economy, and represent a particular vision of the medieval Indian state's personality which, today, is influenced more by political forces than by its own laws of development.

Today, efforts are made to project medieval Indian ideas and institutions from a specific ideological lens and, in the process, the objective understanding of the nature and role of ideas and institutions in medieval India gets clouded. Therefore, the discussion of such aspects becomes necessary. While looking into these, we illustrate how multiple strands influenced these themes and made different criteria relevant and irrelevant with the progress in history writing in India and in terms of space-time dynamics. Without losing sight of the fact that medieval period facilitated better understanding of the ways through which varied ideas and institutions grew and disseminated their influence which were also borrowed from different regions, people and the aspirations behind adventures and conquests that ultimately shaped the larger kingdoms/empires that rose and fell.

NOTE

1. General Introduction to Harbans Mukhia, *Historians and Historiography During the Reign of Akbar*, Delhi: Vikas, 1976; repr., Delhi: Akar, 2017, p. xii.

CHAPTER 1

Periodizing Medieval India

All historical writing periodizes the past, and makes choices among chronological realities, based on positive or negative preferences that are more or less conscious. Traditional history, which is oriented to brief time spans, to the individual, to the event, has long accustomed us to an account that is precipitate, dramatic, and breathless.[1]

—FERNAND BRAUDEL

THE HISTORICITY OF the medieval period in Indian history is richly layered and complex. This period is the gateway through which our past and present interact to define their characteristics and gain an identity in Indian history. Medieval Indian history reverberates through contemporary Indian society, as can be evidenced in the Rama Janmabhoomi–Babri Masjid issue or in the reinforcement of the medieval past as reflective of manifold social, economic, cultural, and political dimensions—slices of which are sold at various platforms of tourism and cultural heritage.[2] The teaching and research of medieval history contributes significantly to a strength that is rooted in our multiculturalism, tolerance, and unity in diverse values and traditions that the collective soul of our civilizational nation embodies.[3] The preface to this teaching is actually encoded in school textbooks which impart an understanding of the medieval and from there multiple ideas branch out. Today, a neo-imperialist culture has increasingly overwhelmed the Indian society and, consequently, the study of the medieval period has suffered a serious neglect. This is reflected more so in the presentist bias that surrounds grand narratives and even more with regard to local narratives.[4]

The period from the eighth century AD up to the twelfth century is considered the early medieval period. From then onwards up to the middle of the eighteenth century is generally accepted as the late medieval period. But in some regions like north-east India, Kashmir, Ladakh, the upper reaches of Himachal Pradesh, and parts of Uttarakhand, the medieval period may not exist at all, or it extends even to the nineteenth century, keeping in mind the nature of tribal and other socio-economic and state formations prevalent in these areas until that century.

Is the 'medieval' a slice of time or is it a period which saw new, distinctive trends emerging that distinguished it from the preceding ancient period? There is no coherent framework that works well for all regions. The 'medieval' is understood to be chronologically inconsistent and spatially disparate. Islam came from diverse parts of the globe to India—from Central Asia and from Arabia.[5] As David Ludden writes:

> It came to Sind in the seventh century, to Kashmir from eighth/ninth/tenth century, to Kerala in the shape of traders[6] from the eighth century and spread thereafter, largely peacefully in the south culminating in the Bahmanis in the first half of fourteenth century.[7]

The military, commercial, and technological prowess of the *Turushkas* (Turks) in northern and eastern India and Kashmir was admired by contemporary rulers of various Sultanates from the eighth century AD.[8] By contrast, Islam arrived in northern, western and eastern India in the thirteenth century as a result of conquest.[9] Peter Hardy observes:

> The entry of Muslims into South Asia by so many and separated doorways and their spread over the subcontinent by so many different routes, over a period of centuries, ensured that Islam would present itself to the peoples of South Asia in many different epiphanies seen from many angles. Neither to its own adherents nor to non-Muslims in South Asia has Islam seemed monochromatic, monolithic or indeed mono anything.[10]

If the 'medieval' as we know it is conceptually inconsistent, the notion of the 'early medieval' also presents a problem. Taking out a slice from the 'medieval' does not make sense, insofar as the early medieval is also part of the process of transition to change that signifies the medieval.[11] This change, and its allied transition, was part of a gradual process that emerged with new political and administrative ideas and institutions, trading patterns, long distance trade, and social and ideological institutions that manifested themselves in technological vigour, urban renewal, and more nuanced institutions of governance. Islam did not just arrive with the Koran and the sword as is conventionally perceived.[12] Thus, the region as a physiographic construct is incomplete without seeing it as an ethno-historical category. For example, Tamilagam was the Tamil region, but with the medieval western Tamilagam or Chera Nadu, it became Cheralam and was transformed into Keralam. Thus, we saw the emergence of Kerala.[13] Similarly, in Kashmir, it resulted in the evolution of the identity of the Kashmiri Pandit community when a majority of the people abandoned Buddhism and Hinduism, and accepted Islam as its religion.[14]

In India, the term *medieval* was not used in the medieval times. Before the application of the Marxist model of periodization, from which stemmed feudalism/state formation, debates on the eighteenth century in Indian history, the characterisation of the 'medieval' is essential, but was not the result of an objective periodization of Indian history. Marcus Bull writes:

> Periodization is an inescapable part of the study of history at all levels. It involves two related processes. First, we slice up past into pieces of varying sizes, and then we allocate special names, labels that help us to demarcate each slice as something distinct and unique. Periodization is embedded in the structure of school and university syllabuses, the titles of academic organizations, even job titles. We like to think that we can rise above the constrains of periodization, but no individual can hope to gain in-depth knowledge of anything more than a tiny fraction of the totality of human experience, and so slicing history up into manageable portions makes studying the past a more focused, realistic and ultimately exciting prospect. To this extent, at least, periodization serves a positive end.[15]

The main pillar on which colonial scholars based their arguments was guided by religious reference points such as the evolution of Islam and its aggressive expansion, a view that is reflected in policies in Europe even today,[16] while ignoring the political, economic, and financial innovations introduced by the various sultans and emperors, as exemplified by Balban's (1266–87) political acumen, Alaud-Din Khalji's (1296–1316) many innovations, the political and economic vision of Muhammad bin Tughlaq (1325–51), and the firm foundations established by Akbar (1556–1605), centralizing and perpetuating the medieval Indian state and society.[17]

This particularistic view of Islam was the result of Europe's long and ultimately inconclusive battle against Islam since the Crusades, dating back to the eleventh century.

> The rise of Islam was perceived as a threat by medieval Christianity is recorded well in history, and is clearly evidenced by the 'scurrilities of medieval polemic and lampoon' and Muhammad's demonization as a 'false god' and a 'false prophet' and a 'cunning and self-seeking imposter'. One widespread medieval legend even presented him as 'an ambitious and frustrated Roman Cardinal' who 'sought an alternative career as a false prophet.[18]

Interestingly, Europeans found the same enemy in Asia when they arrived, but with a difference. The enemy was not just viewed through the lens of religion. The material dimensions of the previous encounter had resulted in the waning of feudalism and the beginnings of mercantile ambitions in Europe. But once in Asia, the associated material conditions were different, while the old enemy remained. Islam was not just in control of the eastern Mediterranean and Constantinople; it was a driving force almost in every state in India. It was, perhaps, time to move on to a stage beyond mercantilism, because mercantilism would not work in a holistically conceived organic economy and polity that functioned through consent. This is clearly reflected in Kerala where there were good relations between the Muslims, the Hindus, the Christians (the only indigenous Christian community of India), and the Jews.[19] All this changed rapidly after the rise of the Portuguese when they started an anti-Muslim tirade, making the local Christian community anti-Muslim in the process.[20]

Akbar, perhaps the greatest of the Islamic rulers, conceived of a multi-ethnic and multi-religious state and society, to be governed by a mutual contract and satisfying to almost all classes, communities, and interest groups.[21] Islam as the driving ideology had given way to a centralized, all-powerful state, not necessarily owing allegiance to any particular religion. However, in India, society and state were deliberately perceived by the English to be 'Islamic'—a label that satisfied the innate craving of the English to be rid of the Islamic spectre that had haunted them in Europe.[22]

This vision helped to justify the English standpoint, elaborated later in history writing, that the Muslim/Mughal rule in India was authoritarian, autocratic, and anarchical, and, therefore, this needed to be followed by a more humane, civilizational, European rule—a view endorsed by James Mill.[23] This view had already been imbibed insidiously by the regional forces of Marathas, Jats, Satnamis, Sikhs, and Rajputs while opposing the Mughal rule in the eighteenth century.[24] The foundations of the moral economy of future British rule, thus, stemmed from this unique English view of Indians against Islam, as projected by James Mill. Akbar's multi layered world, his multi-cultural vision, was buried forever.

The new political order was, thus, envisioned, along with putative Indian allies, long before the actual conquest in 1757 took place. Those who consistently challenged the Mughal rule, such as the Marathas, were not recognized. They were smashed soon after in 1761 in the Third Battle of Panipat.[25]

However, the change introduced by the English assumed a new and more malignant form—not of a true multi-cultural and autonomous society, but that of a colonial colossus. To the delightful surprise of the English, the mighty Islamic rulers were ultimately defeated and the Mughal Empire was reduced to a shadow of its former self.[26]

We now see that the innate vitality of Islam was sapped in the new periodization the English proposed as 'Muslim', supposedly the 'medieval'. They divorced Islam from its positive and regenerative aspects and presented medieval

India as a frozen tableau on which colonialism imposed and inscribed itself.[27] But while attributing negative aspects to Islam in Asia, they forgot that the rise and expansion of Islam had been praised by no less a scholar than Henri Pirenne who wrote, 'Without the Prophet Mohammad, the founder of Islam, it would be almost impossible to evaluate the role played by Charlemagne, the King of Franks between 768 and 814, and the first western ruler since the fifth century to revive the title of emperor. Charlemagne became the model par excellence for future generations of rulers in Europe.'[28]

The coming of institutional Islam as a governing mechanism and the challenge of monotheism saw the beginnings of a transition that gradually influenced Hindustan's society, economy, politics, and culture, evidenced, for example, in the search for new religious idioms such as Bhakti.[29] The urgency to systematize the Upanishads and plead for a reassertion of monotheism came to symbolize the beginning of medievalism in southern Hindustan. This was the result of increasing contact with the Arabs who had accepted Islam and were marching with their new ideas of allied institutions backed by a new religious fervour.[30] These new institutions, and their underlying philosophy, laid the foundations of a new political order—that of a capable ruler capturing power. However, this new political order was not confined to the political domain alone; it also threw up new social activities and identities, administrative ideas, institutions, technology, and economic opportunities for the vast mass of common people.[31]

The increasing proliferation of *jatis* went along with new societal patterns emerging vertically and horizontally. New crafts emerged, as did a peasantization not seen on such a scale earlier. New towns emerged, as did new technologies, new occupations with specialized labour, increased productivity of land, new military ethics as well as new rules of engagement.[32] Ludden writes:

> Medieval social environments evolved over the centuries in the context of two long term economic trends: sedentary farmers increased the productivity of land with specialized labour and technology, and mobile

groups extended transportation and communication by land and sea from south Asia to Central Asia, China and the Mediterranean.[33]

Therefore, this boundary between the ancient and the medieval period emerges as real and not artificial, but not for the purpose and the way colonial administrators conceived of it intentionally.[34]

The entrance of Muslims on to the political stage of Hindustan must have been one of the most important and explosive events in history. Most historians do not like to establish terminal points while characterizing periodization because the movement of populations and the way that exercised influences on host societies occupied long stretches of time, space, and action that cannot be attributed to a single year or a single moment. The establishment of the Delhi Sultanate in AD 1206 was predated by a long period of Islamic presence on India's shores—a period in which the Turks and other foreigners coming from different parts of Persia and Central Asia had already indigenized themselves. It would have otherwise been most unusual for the Ghorids to have succeeded in handing over the reins of government to their loyalists, so abruptly in 1206.[35] We need to keep in mind that no significant historical change occurs abruptly.

Persian chronicles which were produced from the thirteenth century (Minhaj-us-Siraj's *Tabaqat-i-Nasiri* or *Kamilat Tawarikh*) to the seventeenth or early eighteenth centuries (Khafi Khan's *Muntakhab-ul-lubab*) remained the most reliable sources for those who worked on the medieval period. Why is this so? I would suggest that this obsession with the hegemonic political stems not only from the blueprint laid down by our former colonial masters, but also remains an abiding lacuna in the face of our inability to source adequate regional literature in the absence of a nation state as such, prior to 1947.

However, there was then no notion of an India as such, nor was there a notion of regions comprising the nation, except the notion of Hindustan in the Persian chronicles at the court of Delhi Sultans and Emperors of Hindustan, or the loosely structured Bharat of ancient times, details of which are sketchy at best. We have been, therefore, complicit in our idea of the 'Indian' nation as being one confined to the Upper Gangetic plains, as seen in the dominant discourse on medieval India.

Two significant features dominated historical writing on medieval India during the nineteenth century: the translation and interpretation of various Persian texts, and the effort to periodize medieval Indian history with a specific intention.[36] Both these tasks were, by and large, state-sponsored and were accomplished by European adventurers and administrators at a time when colonialism was steadily expanding its tentacles in India.[37] Warren Hastings' colonial rule contributed to many of the malicious trends that exist till date, such as facilitating history writing in India which characterized Indian history on communal lines or the division of the Gangetic valley.[38] It is essential that we study the entire medieval period and its linkages throughout the length and breadth of Hindustan for a proper evaluation of the colonial period.

Among those who took keen interest in this effort, the name of Sir William Jones (1675–1749) figures very prominently. He applied the notion of Hindu for the ancient, Muslim for the medieval, and British for the modern period.[39] While the application of Hindu and Muslim labels to ancient and medieval periods, respectively, was purely religious, the British period was referred to as British and not Christian because 'British' indicated nationality. According to Ronald Inden:

> Partly shadowing the master narratives of European and world history, but with an orientalist twist, the historians of India divide its history into that most widely normalized scheme of periods—ancient (or classical), medieval, and modern. Whatever labels they give to them, historians have tended to equate ancient with Hindu, medieval with Muslim and modern with Christian, British, or Western. How are events related to one another within these periods, and more importantly how are these periods related to one another? Historians use notions of repetition, influence, development or growth, and the unique, apocalyptic event move their narratives along. Historians of South Asia have been fond of

the apocalyptic event, in the form of invasion or conquest, as marking the shift from one period to the next. That is, the narrative is a story of the conquest of one civilization by another where each civilization is assumed to be a monolith.[40]

Jones upheld the achievements of the Hindu rule and bemoaned the Muslim period as a period of decline, anarchy, and barbarianism. He tried to portray as if every development in India was inspired by the British.[41]

From 1817, this sectarian, communal notion was deliberately reinforced by James Mill when he wrote *The History of British India*. The first two periods, ancient and medieval, were labelled with religious identities, and the third one with a secular 'national' identity.

For the entire nineteenth century, Mill's book remained the most important textbook on Indian history. Harbans Mukhia rightly argues that this application of a religious identity to characterize periodization in Indian history generated consciousness of a religious solidarity of Hindus and Muslims on communal lines and made clear the intentions of colonial historians.[42]

Among those British adventurers and administrators who legitimized and carried forward these notions to drive a wedge between the Hindus and the Muslims in India by deliberately misinterpreting the collected evidence from numerous Persian chronicles are Sir H.M. Elliot and Professor John Dowson. The evidence which they chose from the Persian chronicles was titled *The History of India, as Told by Its Own Historians: The Muhammadan Period*.[43] Tellingly, instead of mentioning the period from the thirteenth to the eighteenth century, the title refers to it as the 'Muhammadan period'.

The project was supported by the Secretary of State for India (1867–77). The title was also suggested by the colonial masters; the authors otherwise wanted to title it *Selection of Papers from Persian Chronicles* by H.M. Elliot.[44]

The quality and nature of this work can be understood from Dowson's own statement: 'Living far away from great libraries, I have had access to few books beyond my own limited collection and I have seldom enjoyed the advantage of taking counsel with others upon doubtful passages and obscure allusions.'[45]

Here, it should be pointed out that *The History of India as Told by Its Own Historians* was published in 1867–77 and, by this time in Europe, particularly Britain, John Ruskin's term 'medieval' was frequently used to distinguish the social and cultural situation of one period from another even at a popular level.[46]

This proves that the usage of terms such as 'the Muhammadan period' or 'Musalman history' of 'Musalman India' was not unintentional on the part of the colonial historians. Most of them, like Mountstuart Elphinstone, Rushbrook Williams, Heinrich Blochmann, William Irvine, and Henry George Raverty, deliberately overlooked the specificities of social, cultural, and economic aspects and, in the words of Mukhia, 'tried to portray as if historical causation lay in their theological conception'.[47]

The entire effort of these translators and historians resulted more in rousing communal passions than in an objective reconstruction of medieval Indian history in the nineteenth and early twentieth centuries.[48]

In the twentieth century, when Indian historians started reconstructing Indian history, particularly of the medieval period, they began to contest the colonial historians' version of the Muslim rulers' oppression of the Hindu subjects and the heroic resistance by the Hindus which, according to the British, culminated in the collapse of the Mughal Empire.[49]

Many within the community of Indian historians became polarized along religious lines not only in their view of the fall of the Mughal Empire, but also in their perception of the entire span of medieval history itself. If, on one hand, the Hindu communalist historian visualized the medieval period as one of alien Muslim domination over the Hindus, who were also termed 'natives' by the British historians, on the other hand, Muslim communalist historians treated the medieval period as the period of assertion of Islamic identities as a part of Islamic glory.[50] This further helped colonial historians to illustrate Hindus and Muslims perpetually in conflict, basing their analysis on dynastic and political history which was already misinterpreted by European translators and the colonial administrators.[51]

From the early twentieth century, when the support base for the nationalist movement grew, historians influenced by the nationalist consciousness tried to contextualize the religious motivations of the Muslim rulers of medieval India. They brought forth evidence to suggest communal harmony instead of communal divide in medieval India. Some of them tried to explore the social and economic aspects of the Indian society and gradually shifted the focus of research from communalization to secularization of medieval Indian history, even though the framework of communal historians remained vibrantly intact.

The important works which appeared at that time were: *The Commercial Policy of the Moguls* by D. Pant (1930), *Commercial Relations between India and England* by Bal Krishna (1924), *Economic Condition of India during the Sixteenth Century* by H.L. Chablani (1929), and *The East India Trade in the 17th Century, in Its Political and Economic Aspects* by Shafaat Ahmad Khan (1923).

However, W.H. Moreland quickly responded by treating European sources on India as more reliable.[52] He attempted to institute a comparison between the economic aspects in Akbar's India and those prevailing under the British. Moreland, like many other colonial historians, wanted to attribute better conditions of the Indian peasantry to the British, though they were probably a shade better under Akbar than under the British. Moreland even denied the existence of ownership of land to the peasant and tried to establish that it was the British rule which had conferred ownership rights on Indian peasants for the first time, denying the fact that the Indian peasant had the right to sell and mortgage his land holding even from early ancient times. In 1929, Brij Narayan wrote *Indian Economic Life: Past and Present* and tried to disprove what Moreland, as a colonial historian, had intentionally misinterpreted about Indian history. However, this period saw the growth of political and administrative history, and hardly any attempt was made to understand or study the overall Indian society and its transition from one epoch to another.

Although the period up to the late 1930s did not see any new methodological approaches, such writings did help in unveiling social and economic relations. Only disjointed pictures were developed by studying people's lifestyles, fashions, and food habits where the upper strata figured prominently, and the study remained purely of a descriptive nature. The themes of food, customs, and manners were the criteria for social stratification. Although these aspects were part of the process of the overall characterization of social stratification as per the Annales school, it was not the sole criterion.

From late 1930s to the 1950s, even though lot of literature grew on the subject of medieval history with new sources coming to light, the major focus of medieval India was dynastic history and aspects such as the rulers' religious policies. For instance, while the nationalist historians admired Akbar's policies, their writings displayed a woeful neglect of other facets of the medieval period.

It is interesting to note that in this process of glorification of the rulers' religious policies, the language of the communal and the nationalist historians became interchangeable; at times, the writings of the same historian reflected both the approaches. The classic example is that of Mohammad Yasin who wrote *Akbar and Indian Nationalism* and *A Social History of Islamic India*. In a similar vein, R.K. Mukerjee wrote *The Fundamental Unity of India* wherein he stated, 'The religious unity and spiritual fellowship among Hindus all over India was held to be the basis of Nationalism which overrode barriers of language and distance; the ideals of an all India Empire and full or partial realization of it in the past were stressed in justification of its demands for the present.'[53]

With such endeavours of nationalist historians, the historical methodology which evaluated rulers in terms of their religious attitudes was validated. However, despite all their efforts, the historians' vision was limited. As a result, they sought support from contemporary historical explanations and immediate solutions to dilemmas they faced while writing history. Hence, the scope of historical writing itself was neither enlarged nor enriched.

It was, finally, 1950 onwards that new methodologies evolved and sought guidance from the Marxist method. The historians working on medieval Indian history widened their horizon of analysis and the scope of source materials. They raised critical conceptual questions which they felt had been ignored by colonial, communal, and nationalist historians until then. They began to explore the basis of the chronological order of the medieval period AD 712–1206 and 1206–1707, and 1206–1526 and 1526–1707, along with the validity of the labels of Hindu, Muslim, and British, as well as Ancient, Medieval, and Modern.[54]

They also looked at the dynastic criterion of periodization such as the Mamluk Sultanate, Khalji Sultanate, Tughlaqs, Sayyids, Lodhis, and Mughals. They discovered that there were no special or specific historical attributes of these labels because given the obvious elements of change, which spread over long periods and cut across dynastic diversities and divisions, there were important features which needed their attention. In all these fields of history writing they introduced new evidence from the underside, shifted the focus, and opened new areas of inquiry by challenging old assumptions, and brought recognition to varied groups of marginal categories such as women, labourers, and tribals which were ignored until then. They further questioned how far the earlier labels signified the process of change in society, economy, polity, and culture of their periods. The process of writing history changed along with content and broke through the barriers between chroniclers and their audience. It tried to give back to people who made and experienced history a central place that they had deserved for long time. It was then that the ordinary people understood the upheavals and changes which they experienced in their own lives such as wars, socio-economic and political transformation, and their own changing position in society. According to Mukhia:

Historical Writing has remained alive and creative because it is perennially assuming new forms, opening up new avenues of Knowledge, and adopting itself to the changing needs of society. A desire to understand the past and make it relevant to the present, a commitment to shed, as far as is humanly possible, prejudices and preconceptions in the course of this quest—these are common to all the great practitioners of the discipline; but otherwise there is very little in common between them, and this is what gives the subject its zest and its drive. Historians have of course been influenced by each other, but historical writing has not so much evolved as spread. Like a great river, it flows across the country side, submerging new areas, picking up tributaries, drying up in old beds, but never petering out into the sands, and unlike the great rivers, never reaching the sea.[55]

Accepting these labels blindly would mean recognition of long periods of un-changeability. This was one way of looking at these periods, but soon the question emerged: How far did this approach facilitate the right understanding of medieval Indian history in the light of immense regional variations? It involved methodological problems of causation. Therefore, Mohammad Habib and K.M. Ashraf stressed on the urgent need for the study of social and economic history of various regions of India in the light of the application of the theory of modes of production. They provided a perspective for the medieval period and showed how the characterization of Indian society on religious basis served the interests of the ruling class and how it affected the country's economy.

Irfan Habib rightly remarks that Ashraf, in his book *Life and Conditions of the People of Hindustan*, made the first attempt to analyse the society and economy of the Delhi Sultanate; his obvious nationalism does not cloud his critical prowess. Works like these have laid the basis for objective historical writing in India.[56] As a result, two important debates stemmed from this application of the Marxist method: one related to the characterization of the country's economy and society, and the other related to the nature and processes of state formation which they felt were necessary for a comprehensive understating of India's medieval and modern society. (For that would provide important clues and avoid any entanglement with wider interpretations and insist only on the pursuit of knowledge for its own sake.)

Themes like nobility, class structure, agrarian economy, trade and commerce, the institutions of zamindari, jagirdari, mansabdari, and the conditions of peasantry—forms of exploitation, basis of social stratification, technology, etc.—were taken up to establish the nature of medieval Indian society.[57]

Apart from the studies of Ashraf and Mohammad Habib, A.C. Banerjee brought out *Medieval Studies*, Saiyid Nurul Hassan wrote *Thoughts on Agrarian Relations in Mughal India*, and Satish Chandra wrote *Parties and Politics at the Mughal Court: 1707–1740*. In these studies, the foreign character of nobility was questioned and factionalism was related to the growing crisis in the agrarian sector with significant historical evidence. Not only did this validate the application of Marxist methodology in Indian historiography, but also helped to delegitimize the relevance of the Hindu and the Muslim communalist historians' notions of Indian history and society. The research pertaining to various other aspects of socio-economic history of India was also taken up by many scholars among whom Athar Ali, Irfan Habib, Harbans Mukhia, Iqtidar Alam Khan, Iqtidar Hussan Siddiqui, Noman Ahmad Siddiqui, Aniruddha Ray, Ashin Das Gupta, Sushil Chaudhary, and Dilbagh Singh occupy a prominent position. These scholars further suggested through their studies that the fall of the Mughal Empire was largely a result of growing social and agrarian crisis. This, in turn, was traceable in the 'class, ethnic and regional tensions prevailing in medieval Indian polity and society'.[58]

Here, it should be noted that this approach was part of the multiple ongoing processes to reconstruct medieval Indian history along scientific lines. It shifted the focus from mere politico-religious to social and economic issues and to the nature of contradictions that existed in medieval Indian system in general.

In a detailed study, Athar Ali, in *The Mughal Nobility under Aurangzeb* and *The Apparatus of the Empire: Awards of Ranks, Offices and Titles to the Mughal Nobility (1574–1658)*, adopted a statistical approach to analyse the positions of different ethnic and religious groups as well as hereditary elements in the incorporation of nobility and zamindars.[59]

This approach minimized the importance of religions and sectarian considerations in the reconstruction of medieval Indian history. One of the significant results of this approach was that the historians working on medieval India opened up the possibilities of seeing what Mukhia calls 'an extensive continuum of social and economic formations from the seventh or eighth to the thirteenth century'.[60]

Apart from rejecting categorization on communal and dynastic lines, the theory of mode of production and social formation became the basis for identifying a historical process at the hands of various scholars in India. In establishing the relevance of this methodology, the Centre for Historical Studies at Jawaharlal Nehru University played a significant role by training young scholars from Kashmir to Kanyakumari and abroad. This led to the growth of reconstruction of regional history in various parts of India and also opened up the debate of the characterization of Indian society and economy with particular reference to the medieval period of Indian history.[61] The applicability of the concept of feudalism in the Indian context was questioned and a new application of medieval Indian economy and free peasant production was put forth as a more appropriate characterization for medieval Indian society.

Whatever the nature of controversies and contradictions among Indian scholars—particularly R.S. Sharma, Mukhia, and Irfan Habib—the debate did not move out of the theory of modes of production. The debate brought into focus many important issues and succeeded in diminishing the attention that the communalist historians paid to the reconstruction of Indian history. The other debate that continued to dominate Indian historiography is related to the nature of the eighteenth century. While differing on the nature of the developments of eighteenth century India, the scholars did not transcend the basic premise of the progressive methodology. This provided a fresh perspective for viewing the eighteenth century from a wider angle, taking into account a comprehensive knowledge base provided by various sources of information.

However, it was only with the collapse of the Soviet Union and with the growth of new trends in Hindu and Muslim communalism in South Asia, particularly in India and Pakistan from the late 1980s, that the communal political elements surged, and with them grew their patronage to the communal social scientists. The more the Hindu communalist politics made headway towards the centre of political power and various state institutions, the more the social scientists with a communal ideological bent became assertive in reconstructing and reinterpreting the Indian state, society, and culture. Same thing happened in Pakistan: the radicalization of Islam not only led to terrorism, but also defaced the history of South Asia. The politicians from secular parties also indirectly served their interests by picking up the agenda of sectarian and caste issues because it could potentially facilitate the failure of an oppositional, Hindu fundamentalist ideology. The issues of Babri Masjid-Rama Janmabhoomi, the migration of Kashmiri Pandits, Godhra riots, and burning the bogies of Samjhauta Express resulted in giving additional allowances at frequent intervals to such sectarian and communal politics. This helped the communal historians to expand their agenda and reinterpret and misinterpret the issues concerning the Indian society on a far broader scale. They also integrated regional political problems into a national communal framework to suit to the perpetuation of the power of their patronizers. Hence, the link that was overshadowed and weakened by the debates mentioned earlier, which stemmed from the application of Marxist methodology, began to get a new lease of life by attacking the historical reconstruction and interpretation of secular and progressive type and by producing history (weather false or true) which has found eager and faithful supporters.

Interestingly, the faulty process which was released by the forces of globalization, caste-based regional politics, corruption, excessive bureaucratization, oppressive legal system, the US-Iraq conflict over Kuwait, and the evolution and decline of Taliban gave an allowance to both the communal approaches to revive their efforts. On one hand, the Muslim communalists began to seek refuge in religion and attributed the crisis that the society was undergoing to American imperialist tendencies and to disunity among Muslims on a global scale. On the other hand, the State's sponsorship of Hindu communalist interpretation facilitated the reassertion of the old agenda of Hindu nationalism and divisive religious tendencies. The establishment of Shivaji's statue in Agra and the efforts to articulate the reconstruction of Ram temple are pertinent examples. The opening up of such issues not only deviates from the basic principles of objective historical method and analysis, but also misinterprets the debates in Indian history, like the ones on socio-economic formations and the eighteenth century, which are crucial and relevant to entire South Asia.

In this discussion, we deal with some of the trends that emerged in the processes involved in construction and reconstruction of medieval Indian history and the way they impacted the actual situation. Historians have to guard against these tendencies even in times of political and social upheaval in order to provide better insight to future generations.

According to Dr R.C. Majumdar:

> The plain duty of a historian of India is to reveal the truth about the communal relations in the past, without being influenced in any way by any extraneous factor. It is the binding duty of every historian to guard himself against the tendency and fight it with the only weapon available to him, namely by holding on just to truth in all his writings, irrespective of all consequences. A historian should not trim his sail according to the prevailing wind, but ever go straight, keeping in view the only goal of his voyage—the discovery of truth.[62]

NOTES

1. Fernand Braudel 'History and Social Sciences. The Long Duree', *Review: A Journal of the Fernand Braudel Centre for the Study*

of Economies, Historical Systems, and Civilizations at Binghamton University, State University of New York, vol. 32, no. 2, 2009, p. 173.

2. Javed Alam 'The Composite Culture and its Historiography', in *Islam in History and Politics: Perspectives from South Asia*, ed. Asim Roy, New Delhi: Oxford University Press, 2006, p. 43. See also Aijaz Ahmad, *Lineages of the Present: Political Essays*, Delhi: Tulika, 1996, p. 274. Ahmad observes, 'The true object of its (Sanghparivar's) desire is not mere Muslim Submission but State power and the remaking of India as a whole—politically, ideologically, historically: and, true to form, this project of remaking India in its own image involves a great deal of unmaking, both through selective appropriation as well as outright rejection of very large parts of our past and present histories.'
3. Jagadish Narayan Sarkar, *Thoughts on Trends of Cultural Contacts in Medieval India*, Calcutta: OPS, 1984, 'Introduction'.
4. In every region of India there are large number of sources in Persian and other languages that pertain to medieval period but not many have been studied and utilized for reconstructing Indian history as a whole.
5. J.D. Rees, *The Muslim Epoch*, London: Longamns, Green, 1894; repr., New Delhi: Asian Publication, 1978, p. 2. See also David Ludden, *India and South Asia: A Short History*, London: Oneworld, 2006, p. 6.
6. Tara Chand, *Influence of Islam on Indian Culture*, 2nd edn., Allahabad: The Indian Press, 1976, p. 28.
7. Ludden, *India and South Asia*, p. 15.
8. Kalhana, *Rajatarangini*, tr. M.A. Stein, under the title *River of Kings*, 3 vols.; repr., Delhi: Motilal Banarasidas, 1979, vol. 2, book vii, verses 56, 70, 118, 1149, 3412.
9. Ludden, *India and South Asia*, p. 15.
10. Peter Hardy, 'Islam and Muslims in South Asia', in *The Crescent in the East: Islam in Asia Major*, ed. R. Israeli, London: Humanities Press, 1982, pp. 39–40.
11. For details see B.D. Chattopadhyaya, *Making of Early Medieval India*, Delhi: Oxford University Press, 1994; repr., 2012, pp. 1–8.
12. Rattan Lal Hangloo, 'Mass Conversion in Medieval Kashmir: Academic Perceptions and Peoples Practies', in *The Valley of Kashmir: The Making and Unmaking of a Composite Culture?*, ed. Aparna Rao and T.N. Madan, Delhi: Manohar, 2008, pp. 97–138.
13. Ludden, *India and South Asia*, pp. 49–50.
14. Rattan Lal Hangloo, *The State in Medieval Kashmir*, Delhi: Manohar, 2000, Chapter 2.

15. Marcus Bull, *Thinking Medieval: An Introduction to the Study of the Middle Ages*, New York: Palgrave Macmillan, 2005, pp. 42–3.
16. K.N. Panikkar, *Communal Threat and Secular Challenges*, Chennai: Earthworm, 1997, p. 77.
17. Ibn Hasan, *The Central Structure of the Mughal Empire and Its Practical Working up to the year 1657*, London: Oxford University Press, 1936; repr., Delhi: Munshiram Manoharlal, 1970, pp. 30–77.
18. Bernard Lewis, *The Arabs in History*, 4th edn., London: Oxford University Press, 1966, pp. 47–8. See also Roy, ed., *Islam in History and Politics*, 'Introduction', p. 2.
19. Chand, *Influence of Islam*, p. 28.
20. Vijayalakshmi Teelock, *Mauritian History from Beginning to Modern Times*, revd. edn., Moka, Mauritius: Mahatma Gandhi Institute, 2009, pp. 9–11.
21. Ishwari Prasad, *A Short History of Muslim Rule in India: From the Advent of Islam to the Death of Aurangzeb*; repr., Delhi: Surjeet Publications, 2016, p. 258.
22. Peter Hardy, 'Some Studies in Pre-Mughal Muslim Historiography', in *Historians of India Pakistan and Ceylon*, ed. C.H. Philips, New York: Oxford University Press, 1961, pp. 115–27.
23. James Mill, *The History of British India*, London: Baldwin, Cradock and Joy, 1817, vol. 1, pp. 219–20, 417–18.
24. J.S. Grewal, *The Sikhs of Punjab*, The New Cambridge History of India, vol. 3, Cambridge: Cambridge University Press, 1990, pp. 70–90. See also M. Athar Ali, 'Recent Theories of Eighteenth-Century India', *Indian Historical Review*, vol. 13, no. 1–2, 1986–7, pp. 102–8. See also Irfan Habib, 'The Eighteenth Century in Indian Economic History', in *The Eighteenth Century in India*, ed. Seema Alvi, Delhi: Oxford University Press, 2002, pp. 57–83.
25. G.S. Sardesai, *The Main Currents of Maratha History*, Bombay: K.B. Dhalve, 1933, p. 183.
26. William Dalrymple, *The Last Mughal: The Fall of a Dynasty: Delhi, 1857*, Delhi: Viking, 2006, pp. 305–486.
27. Gerald James Larson, *India's Agony over Religion*, Delhi: Oxford University Press, 1997, pp. 123–4.
28. Henri Pirenne, 'A Problem of Transition', *Mohammed and Charlemagne*, Allen & Unwin, (in) *Economic History Review*, vol. 10, no. 1, 1939, pp. 60–2.
29. Genevieve Lemercinier, *Religion and Ideology in Kerala*, Delhi: D.K. Agencies, 1984, pp. 106–26.
30. Maulana Syed Sulaiman Nadvi, *Arab-o-Hind Ke Talluqat*, Allahabad: Hindustan Academy, 1930, pp. 4–5.
31. Ludden, *India and South Asia*, pp. 45–95.
32. Irfan Habib, *The Economic History of Medieval India*, Delhi:

Tulika, 2001, pp. 1–20. See also by the same author, *Essays in Indian History: Towards a Marxist Perception*, Delhi: Tulika, 1995, pp. 59–108 and 161–79.

33. Ludden, *India and South Asia*, p. 43.
34. Mill, *The History of British India*, pp. 220–2.
35. Richard M. Eaton, *Essays on Islam and Indian History*, Delhi: Oxford University Press, 2000, pp. 11–44.
36. Peter Hardy, 'Modern Muslim Historical Writing on Medieval Muslim India', in C.H. Philips, ed., pp. 294–309. See also Romila Thapar, Harbans Mukhia, Bipan Chandra, eds., 'Communalism and the Writing of Indian History', *Economic and Political Weekly*, vol. 5, no. 19, May 1970; also published as a book, Delhi: People's Publishing House, 1969.
37. C.H. Philips, 'James Mill, Mountstuart Elphinstone and The History of India', in *Historians of India, Pakistan and Ceylon*, London: Oxford University Press, 1961, pp. 217–29.
38. W.W. Hunter, *A Brief History of the Indian People*, London: Trübner, 1882; 23rd repr., Delhi: Vikram Jain Books, 1990, pp. 187–92.
39. Sir William Jones, 'A Dissertation on the Orthography of Asiatic Words in Roman Letters', *Asiatic Researches*, no. 1, pp. 1–56. See also *Dissertations and Miscellaneous Pieces: Relating to the History and Antiquities, the Arts, Sciences, and Literature, of Asia*, 4 vols., London: G. Nicol, J. Walter, and J. Sewell, 1792.
40. Ronald Inden, 'Introduction: From Philogical to Dialogical Texts', in *Querying the Medieval: Texts and the History of Practices in South Asia*, ed. Ronald Inden, Jonathan Walters, Daud Ali, New York: Oxford University Press, 2000, p. 16.
41. S.N. Mukherjee, *Sir William Jones: A Study in Eighteenth-Century British Attitudes to India*, Cambridge: Cambridge University Press, 1968.
42. Harbans Mukhia, Perspectives on Medieval History, Delhi: Vikas Publishers, 1993, pp. 42–51. See also Thapar, et al., *Communalism*.
43. H.M. Elliot and John Dowson, eds., *The History of India, as Told by its Own Historians*, in 8 vols., London: Trübner, 1867–77; repr., Delhi: D.K. Publishers, 2001, vol. 1, p. xvii.
44. Ibid.
45. Ibid.
46. Harbans Mukhia, 'Medieval India: An Alien Conceptual Hegemony', *The Medieval History Journal*, vol. 1, no. 1, January–June 1998, pp. 91–106.
47. Ibid.
48. R.C. Majumdar, ed., *The History and Culture of the Indian People: The Delhi Sultanate*, vol. 6, 4th edn., Bombay: Bharatiya Vidya Bhavan, 1990, p. xxiv.

49. Ibid.
50. B.L. Grover, Alka Mehta, eds., *A New Look at Modern Indian History: From 1707 to the Modern Times*, revd. edn., New Delhi: S. Chand, 2011, pp. 428–9.
51. Mukhia, *Perpectives on Medieval History*, pp. 33–51. See also Thapar, et al., *Communalism*,
52. W.H. Moreland, *India at the Death of Akbar: An Economic Study*, London: Macmillan, 1920, pp. 90–177.
53. R.C. Majumdar, 'Nationalist Historians', in C.H. Philips, ed., pp. 416–23.
54. Mukhia, 'Medieval India', pp. 91–106.
55. Mukhia, *Historians and Historiography During the Reign of Akbar*, Delhi: Vikas, 1976; repr., Delhi: Aakar, 2017, p. 1.
56. Irfan Habib, *Interpreting Indian History*, Shillong: North Eastern Hill University Publication, 1986, p. 33.
57. Mukhia, *Perspectives on Medieval History*, Delhi: Vikas, 1993, pp. 214–44.
58. Habib, *The Agrarian System of Mughal India, 1556–1707*, Bombay: Asia Publishing House, 1963; repr., Delhi: Oxford University Press, 2013, pp. 298–342. See also Habib, *Essays in Indian History*, Delhi: Tulika, 1995, pp. 161–80.
59. Athar Ali, *Mughal Nobility under Aurangzeb*, Delhi: Asia Publishing House, 1966 (for the Department of History, Aligarh Muslim University). See also Ali, *The Apparatus of Empire: Awards of Ranks, Offices, and Titles to the Mughal Nobility (1574–1658)*, Delhi: Oxford University Press, 1985.
60. Mukhia, 'Peasant Production in Medieval India', in *Feudalism and Non-European Societies*, ed. Harbans Mukhia and Terry J. Byres, London: Frank Cass, 1985, pp. 228–52.
61. Prasanta Kumar Nayak, *Periodisation of History: Arunachal Pradesh*, Delhi: Kalpaz, 2017, pp. 32–54.
62. Majumdar, *The Delhi Sultanate*, p. xxx.

CHAPTER 2

Contacts between India and Central Asia

DESPITE THE IMMENSITY of distances, the history of India's contacts with Central Asia goes back to antiquity. The earliest evidence of contact between the two civilizations is located in the early Bronze Age, when the invention of bronze improved the techniques of production of metal objects, which enabled Persia to increase the export of copper, lead, tin, etc., to neighbouring regions including India.[1] As these transactions grew, the movement of people and materials on routes which connected India to Central Asia became more frequent. Among those who worked extensively on these early Central Asian contacts with the outside world, the work of Masson and Sarianidi has served to establish the key role that this trade played in maintaining these contacts:

> It seems likely that trade was the motivating force behind connections between India and Central Asia, which became much more marked in Middle Bronze Age. . . . We see then that the settled agriculture communities of Southern Turkemenia in the Middle Bronze Age comprised societies with a complex and highly developed economic structure, with craft as a special sphere of production on one hand, and agriculture on the other, the very existence of this division suggesting an internal exchange system growing into trade as an essential link in the economic system as a whole.[2]

Contacts like this occurred in every part of the world, but they followed different patterns and ended in diverse ways. Unfortunately, history never reveals the basis of such contacts in a pure state because the cultures mingle and interpenetrate. They also display specificities and complexities that result both from variations of time and place, and also from differing mentalities of the participants in these contacts.[3]

Initially, the course of Indo-Central Asian contacts was crucially determined by the geophysical situation of Central Asia, which led to major migratory movements out of this region.[4] From very early times there were frequent migrations from Central Asia to other parts of the world. Marija Gimbutas recorded three major migratory movements: between 4300 and 4200 BC, between 3400 and 3200 BC, and between 300 and 280 BC from Central Asia to the Western world.[5] Around the first millennium BC, when the eastern branch of Iranians came from Transoxiana (Mavara-un Nahar), they were unable to move towards the south of the Hindu Kush, because by that time the entire region of Arachosia and Punjab had already passed into the hands of a sister branch of the Aryans.[6] Between the seventh and fourth centuries BC, when the Achaemenids extended their area of influence, they incorporated a part of India into their dominion wherein they introduced Aramaic as an official language.[7] Apart from the Indian portion, the territories which constituted their dominion included Mesopotamia, Syria, Egypt, Greek cities and Asia Minor. About their Indian contacts, Roman Ghirshman says: 'Abandoning narrow nationalism, the Achaemenians as a concession to imperial interest introduced it (Aramaic language) to India when under its influence *Kharosthi*, the oldest known alphabet, was developed.'[8] By the end of the first century BC, a group of Kushans, under their king Kujula Kadaphises, conducted a series of conquests and after crossing the Hindu Kush discovered that the wealth of India was much more tempting than the region of eastern Iran. Subsequently they established the Kushan kingdom in India.[9] When the Sasanians came to power, they maintained friendly relations with the Gupta rulers in India for a long time. They also blended the western influences penetrating into Central Asia with those from India.[10]

The focus of this evidence is not only the simple assertion of the existence of contacts between Central Asia and India, but rather is more concerned with the operational reality of these contacts and the attitudes and responses of people from both the regions, which contributed to their stability to the extent of allowing them to establish ruling dynasties one after the other. The hypothesis underlying this argument at this stage is that unless there is a correlation between any given society and the forms and the effectiveness of social domination or control that penetrates from outside, the contacts do not grow on a more stable basis and for a longer duration. For example, the medieval Indian civilization was preceded by a variety of material cultures within the Indian environment (prehistoric, proto-historic, early historic, and ancient), the nature of which is clearly identifiable.[11] There is little doubt that this pre-medieval culture was essentially a mechanism for the manifestation of the civilization that followed. Like any other material culture, it constituted foundations and anticipated some social arrangements, but could this material culture have supplied the necessary impetus that the transformation seems to have required?

While those preceding material cultural formations located within the pre-medieval Indian context were a necessary pre-requisite for its emergence, that material culture alone was not reason enough for a transition to take place. Therefore, the real breakthrough came because of India's contact with the outside world whence also came new ideas, institutions, technology, and values. The evidence provided by Andre Gunder Frank and Denis Sinor lends credence to this argument here:

> The domestication of horses began in Czechoslovakia, the Ukraine and Southern Russia about 6,000 years ago, but the most important development occurred further east in Central *Asia* in the second millennium BC. For thousands of years these animals were the main source of human overland transportation, military superiority, animal protein, warm clothing, tenting, etc. Moreover these developments were complemented by others in transportation, military technology and metallurgy (especially in Caucasus) much of which also came from Central Asia. The incursions of Central Asia into more civilized outlying areas in the period 1700–1500 BC were victorious largely on account of horse drawn, spoked war chariots, which were developed or improved in Central Asia. They must have also brought with them a

social organization, which was effective enough to organize their military campaigns and to make them victorious against their 'more' civilized neighbors. As noted earlier, around 1000 BC, Central Asian incursions were again victorious. They had again made important advances in transportation and military technology, including metallurgy to bring on the Iron Age. This time they rode larger, domesticated horses and came armed with weapons made of iron. The fact that Central Asians were again victorious suggests that they had developed something of a value in a competitive world. Their near sedentary neighbors also developed a technology and social organization in response to their relations with Central Asians and of course with each other. This organization includes the formation of states and the organization of political power.[12]

It is certain that these developments accompanied Central Asians during their Indian occupation. In fact, a rich spectrum of variants can be observed, from extreme indifference to overwhelming displays of friendship with which the new corners from Central Asia would have been welcomed. Sometimes the presence of Central Asians in India can be regarded as a special form of collision, in which the subjugated population of India survived liquidation, albeit in circumstances which largely precluded the survival of their political institutions.[13] The establishment of Kushan rule, Turkish Sultanate, Bahmani Sultanatein the Deccan, Shahmir Sultanatein Kashmir and even Mughal occupation are the best examples to illustrate this point.[14] The advanced Central Asian culture with adequate military equipment, transportation, metallurgical developments, and craft production technology was bound to dominate the societies that came in contact with it.[15]

Many scholars who worked on some aspect of these Indo-Central Asian contacts during medieval times have provided interesting analysis of the information on the subject, but their work has, by and large, remained an appendage without linking the discussion to larger geographies in which the specific typologies of these two civilizations interacted.[16] As Fernand Braudel puts it, 'All the social sciences must make room for an increasing geographical conception of mankind.'[17]

However, one of the problems raised by the larger geographical complexity is rooted in the very characterization of what is termed as Central Asian.[18] For, while studying the structures, institutions, and roles as determinants in medieval Indian social life, many scholars have tended to clothe the social production of these contacts with generalizations like Indo-Islamic, Islamic, and Indo-Persian.[19] Even the most celebrated historians such as K.M. Ashraf and M. Athar Ali, whose writings played a significant role in establishing and reinforcing the progressive or secular nature of Indian historical writing, do not seem to have (consciously or unconsciously) hesitated while doing so. Ashraf remarks: 'As a result of Muslim impact, the ancient Hindu order was almost completely destroyed. Political and social institutions were leveled, caste was modified, religious tendencies took a new direction and force and finally the conception of India as a whole was made possible.'[20]

Similarly, Athar Ali also attributes the changes that took place in India between the thirteenth and fifteenth centuries to the intrusion of Islam.[21] I do not intend to undermine the role that Persian or, more particularly, various Central Asian communities played in structuring Indo-Central Asian contacts during medieval centuries, but the problem is to consider how to return our attention to more specific issues within that larger geographical complexity in which participation from both regions was registered.

Evading the legacies of these contacts and attributing everything solely to Persian, Indo-Islamic, and Islamic narrows down the very definition of Indo-Central Asian contacts. This results in over-theorization and also compounds the difficulty in perceiving Central Asian beyond 'Persian' and 'Islamic'.[22] There were Turkemenians, Kazakhs, Badakhshanis, Yarkandis, Afghans Turks, Kashgaris, Tajjiks, Mongols, Armenians, Azerbaijanians, Uzbeks, and variety of others. Therefore, something was lost by this unfortunate neglect of larger complexities and, conversely, there is something of value to be gained by stretching the discussion and its conceptual links across the abyss that exists between the Indo-Central Asian contacts. Any effort, therefore, that intends to provide even a cursory glance of such contacts, which are spread over thousands of years, cannot ignore the fact that the whole social world from both India and Central Asia has entered into these contacts at some point in time. Such contacts have been both temporarily and geographically structured in a number of different ways because the social world always is comprised of space and time, and these entities have causal powers which may or may not be realized, depending on the patterns of interdependence between such entities.

Hence, we need to understand the nature of these processes which produced people who constituted the social world at different levels in these contacts as occupants and users of particular space within the temporal and geographical system. This can be readily observed in the medieval Indian context through an examination of a host of collision and cooperative efforts from which stemmed the reinforcements of these contacts from time to time at the hands of various Indian and Central Asian elements. In general, it can be firmly stated that in the course of medieval Indian history, the Central Asian culture was never adopted as a seamless whole. Its individual components always met with very different degrees of receptivity in different regions of India, but the nature of response does not reflect an outright rejection or opposition to it, but a synthesis.

In order to clarify this point, I have specifically chosen the role of Turkomans as a representative instance from Central Asia in reinforcing these contacts between India and Central Asia during the Sultanate period (thirteenth to fifteenth century). This is done not only because our sources are fragmentary to permit a generalization covering all the ethnic groups spread across the entire Central Asia, but also because it becomes a historically unintelligible and geographically diffused enactment of the complex variety of ethnic, regional, and religious groups inhabiting such a wide world of centrality between the east and the west amid enduring conflicts.[23] Historians and Arab geographers were the first to introduce the terms Turks and Turkoman in the history of Central Asia. The term 'Turkoman' appears for the first time in the works of Arab geographer al-Maqdisi in the second half of the tenth century AD. At that time, the Turkomans were located on the eastern frontier of the Arab Empire in the vicinity of present day Chimkent and Tashkent. The Arabs referred to them as Oghuz. They mention that there were 22–4 tribes of Turkomans who always sold their services as warriors to the Persian Khans of Khiva or Amirs of Bukhara and, at times, even to Indian rulers. This is how they came in contact with the outer world.[24] Therefore, I have attempted to analyse how a particular group associated explicitly with military campaigns gradually built its influence and then shaped a wide variety of elements within the Indian society corresponding to them before and after the establishment of their power.

In the post-Gupta period, the contacts between India and Central Asia were promoted by various ethnic groups, but the role of the Turkomans stands out as the most significant and central to this relationship.[25] From the eighth century AD onwards, we get more organized and consistent information on this aspect. *Rajatarangini*, the earliest authentic historical record composed by Kalhana (a Sanskrit chronicler of Kashmir) in AD 1149–50, provides indisputable evidence about the Turkoman presence in India from earlier times, which helps us structure our argument with a little more clarity. Kalhana writes: 'It is by his [i.e. King Lalitaditya's (AD 725–53)] command to display the mark of their bondage that the *Turshukas* carry their arms at back and shave half their heads.'[26]

In AD 883–903, King Lalliya Sahi perceived the *Turshuka* rulers as a great threat to his authority.[27] In the early eleventh century, Trilochanapala, the last ruler of the Sahi dynasty sought military help from Kashmiri King Sangram Raja (1003–28) against the *Turshukas*.[28] When King Kalasa (1063–89) of Kashmir wanted to put a gilt parasol over the temple of Shiva, he sought the help of *Turshuka* artists from *Turshuka* country (Central Asia).[29] At another place, Kalhana refers to

Turshuka girls being brought to the seraglio of King Kalasa.[30] King Harsha (1054–1101) of Kashmir employed hundreds of *Turshuka* captains in his army for their military skill and strength.[31] Many Indian and Central Asian towns owed their existence to the caravan trade on the Silk Route, linking various parts of Central Asia to India. The traders from places like Kashgar, Khotan, Yarkand, Herat, Bokhara, Khurasan, Turkistan, Balk, Urumchi, Andijan, Kokand, Aksu, Tashkent, Mery and many other parts of Central Asia were actively engaged in the Silk Route trade with Indian merchants from Ladakh, Kashmir, Punjab, and other Indian regions.[32]

Interestingly, the profession of arms was a supreme aristocratic vocation of Central Asian society in general and the Turkomans in particular from very early times.[33] Discomforting though the thought might seem to some people, the Ghaznavid rulers whose armies occasionally invaded India owe their origin to the Turkomans.[34] Even though the contacts between India and Central Asia were irrevocably set on a collision course by some invaders, including Mahmud Ghazni, this collision never meant the end of the contact between the two cultures. Instead, it resulted in enlarging the range of Indo-Central Asian contacts and also in increasing the volume of Indian response to it. Since the variety of contacts were there for a long time, the Turkoman incursions did not come as a culture shock to Indians; rather they seem to have located the incident within the horizon of their expectations. The only thing that was new this time was that the newcomers had associated themselves with Islam, a new religion, as an important historical experience and tradition. It is interesting to note that even while carrying out the conquest of India, Mahmud of Ghazni expressed his displeasure against his superiors when he said, 'The creed of Islam was being used as a bulwark for protection of vested interests and time honoured abuses in Islam.'[35]

It is important to keep in mind that the unity of religious institutions and the state was a characteristic of pre-Sultanate state formations in India, but not of the Turkoman polity in Central Asia. It was because of their agnostic ideas that they were more concerned about material progress than religion.[36] Perhaps, this was also one of the factors that enabled them to make progress in terms of science and technology, and gave them leverage over other societies that they came into contact with.[37] Besides this, the frequent interventions in each other's disputes by supplying soldiers, weapons, and other materials to alter the balance of power to their own advantage was an age old practice. This happened on several occasions, as also illustrated by Kalhana. During the Second Battle of Tarain in 1192, when Mahmud of Ghur fought against Prithviraj Chauhan, he was assisted by an Indian ruler, Hamir of Kangra.[38] The Raja of Jammu, Bijay Dev, sent his son Narsing Dev to facilitate the Turkoman army's victory in India.[39] When such was the nature of relations, it is likely that common people were also guided by economic and political expediency. Hence, such collisions cannot be characterized by their casualness or intermittent nature, because they ultimately transformed into a contact which laid the groundwork for the establishment of the Delhi Sultanate and subsequent developments in different regions of India wherever Turkomans went.

The main concern of the Turkomans, like the Kushans and other predecessors, was to lose no time in establishing peaceful relations with the native people on whom they depended for their sustenance, trade, geographical knowledge, and assistance in many other fields, which created a social basis for their political power. The establishment of the Sultanate saw a relationship based on trust and mutual dependence, which led to the growth of both the state and society in the medieval Indian environment. Even though at the political level we have evidence of conflict between the Turkomans and some Rajput chiefs, the contacts at the popular level between the people of the two cultures do not reflect even the slightest symptom of aggressive behaviour.[40] Everything that the Turkomans did on Indian soil as loyal soldiers of their masters had no theological motivation, but was intended to demonstrate that their presence had brought a new and final authority as an alternative to the existing conditions in northern India.[41] It is valuable to find an unbiased assessment of such a phenomenon by a colonial historian like William Erskine, who observes:

> In India the Turks never effected to monopolize all the authority of kingdoms which they obtained. The natives shared in the administration of the country and in the military commands. They found a country already populous and its territories fully occupied by civilized inhabitants as well as by a race of conquerors of their own religion. They had none of the ferocity of Chengiz and were not so insane to have a wish to expel their cultivators from lands, the value of which was solely owing to their labor.[42]

The commencement of the functioning of Central Asian ideas and institutions in early thirteenth century India can be understood in terms of the warrior aristocracy's efforts towards territorialization and administrative coherence. The fundamental element in this whole scenario was the growth of a centralized monarchy revolving around the personality of the Sultan, which was not possible in Central Asia.[43] In times of war, the Turkoman Sultan was expected to be braver and fiercer than any other warrior (this was the Central Asian military ethic), but in times of peace, he sought to temper the violence of his people.[44] The contacts further culminated in the application of *iqta* and enforcement of tribute-paying relations that helped the newly established Sultanate seek the acquiescence of Indians as loyal subjects. *Iqta* was a transferable territorial assignment and was originally evolved by the Abbasid ruler Mutawakkil (AD 847–61) when he handed over Armenia, Azerbaijan, and Faras to his younger brother Mutazz.[45] When a branch of Turkomans ruled over Persia as Seljuk rulers, they further organized the *iqta* system on an institutional basis as a widespread form of beneficium.[46] As an element of Central Asian administrative heritage, it helped the Turkomans in establishing their administrative, institutionalized, political supremacy in northern India. Its application, based on *iqta*, linked together various parts of India. According to Athar Ali, 'It clearly reinforced the concept of India as a country if not as a nation.'[47]

In this manner, the Indo-Central Asian contacts produced a new administrative pattern and territorial organization carefully defining the roles and responsibilities of Central Asian and provincial authorities in India. It also helped the Turkomans tackle the fiscal crisis in northern India more effectively and resolve the problems concerning their lack of legitimacy, both by guaranteeing governability and by resolving the varied contradictions which were likely to surface in a newly acquired political space.[48]

The Turkoman Sultans worked hard at this task and developed a community with a distinct identity as members of Turkoman royalty and nobility.[49] At the coronation ceremonies, each Sultan made his commitment to protect his subjects from external threat and internal violence. Born in a family of the Ilbari Turkoman tribe, Balban was the first Sultan to blend the Turkoman tribal traditions, which were embedded in traditional Central Asian tribal polity, with Indian polity and develop the institution of kingship in medieval India. Sultan Balban attempted to restore the etiquette of the court and the prestige of the crown.[50] He believed in coercing his subjects into submission and even while using force, ceremonies were conducted.[51] This was to signalize the importance of political discovery and to establish dominance. It also was meant to leave lasting impression on the natives to ensure their respect and obedience. Making his nobles kneel or prostrate to ensure their loyalty powerfully enhanced Balban's sense of personal importance. None of the natives had the faintest notion as to what this ritual meant and, hence, their ignorance made it more inspiring. While seeking increased personal prestige by even claiming descent from the mythical Turkish hero Afrasiab, and insisting on the practice of *paibos* (kissing of the monarch's feet) and *sijda* (prostration), Balban was also imitating the rituals of Seljuq and Khawarzam kings of Central Asia and testing how these ceremonies could help him gain legitimacy in the medieval Indian context.[52]

In fact, the process of medieval Indian state formation owes much to Central Asian politics and its origins must be sought partly in response to developments in Central Asia. What facilitated the legitimization of these contacts in various fields can, to a certain extent, be attributed to the nature of Indian and Turkoman typologies because India also had to adopt its political organization according to the exigencies of Central Asian influence. For example, in introducing Persian as the official language, the Delhi Sultanate, the Bahmani Sultanate in the Deccan, and the Shahmiri Sultanate in Kashmir—all underlined the enduring importance of Central Asian culture to the Indian state and highlighted the key nature of India's relationship to Central Asia.

When these developments were taking shape from above, the Indian society was building its bridges in the social, economic, and cultural spheres from below. From very early times, Indian culture acted as an autonomous entity—expanding, contracting, and submitting to outside influences—and under the Turkomans, it was again subjected to a process of reconstruction. Therefore, Indians also saw the onset of the thirteenth century as part of a continuous process that had been transpiring from the early Bronze Age. But this time, the Central Asians, including the Turkomans, felt unquestionably superior with respect to their adherence to Islam, particularly when they encountered the ramifications of Indian polytheism and caste system which had contributed significantly to the stratification of the society. They blended their military, administrative, technological, and cultural heritage with the principles of peaceful co-existence of Indian religious systems. The establishment of *khanqas* and *madrasas* as centres of imparting Persian, the new language, as a source of information and knowledge developed in almost all parts of India, where disciples from various social and religious layers devoted themselves to music and art, placing spirituality at a different level of reality.[53]

In the field of technology, the Turkomans also promoted the importation of varied art forms, decorative elements, craft production, technology, masonry, cloth printing, paper making, calligraphy, gold beating, smithy, and new building styles and techniques from Central Asia to gain popular support in various regions of India.

Zain-ul-Abidin of Kashmir (1420–70) invited skilled craftsmen from many Central Asian cities, including Samarkand, Bokhara, Herat, and Balakh.[54] The calligraphers from Samarkand were given assignments of land in Pargana Phag of Kashmir for teaching the art of calligraphy.[55] Mulla Zada, a disciple of Mulla Qadiri of, Khorasan was invited to give lute recitals.[56] These developments were not confined to Kashmir alone. They were widespread wherever these Central Asian communities went across India. Even in the far off region of the Deccan, the establishment of the Bahmanis and Qutb Shahis (who came directly from the Qara Qoyunlu tribe of Turkmenistan) would not have been possible without the growth of contacts between the two cultures.[57] The Sufi claims to universal brotherhood, egalitarianism, and respect for other religious fraternities were backed by a new pattern of military organization, economic activity, and their residence in the midst of non-Muslim Indian population. This provided a chance for Indians to establish new identities.[58] As a result, people were obliged to repudiate their allegiances and enter into contacts with Central Asians and organize themselves into new social settings. The spinning wheel was introduced in India on a wide scale in the thirteenth century.[59] The multiple spindles, which made its appearance in China around the last quarter of the thirteenth century, were brought into India in the early fourteenth century.[60] Among other technological devices were the Persian wheel, the art of manufacturing paper, the horseshoe, and the horse-stirrup.[61]

Athar Ali appropriately sums up these details as follows:

> It was in these three centuries (thirteenth to fifteenth) that India received the spinning wheel, the pedals of the loom, cloth-printing, paper, magnetic compass, techniques of large scale arcuate construction, lime mortar, pindrum gearing (to complete the apparatus of the Persian wheel), more effective devices for distillation and sericulture. These undoubtedly led to an expansion of craft production, possibly even to greater cloth production per capita, and certainly to more-extensive use of masonry. There is evidence, literary as well as numismatic, that commerce expanded; and

archaeology attests to the fact that the urban decline postulated from the previous period was over and an urban economy of impressive size rapidly developed.[62]

All these tools helped in the growth of contact between the two civilizations. The popularization of these items by Turkoman soldiers, Sufis, artisans, and traders provided them a much wider audience, particularly in a society where other means of vertical and horizontal social mobility were very limited. Technology played a tremendous role in growing the popular receptivity towards Central Asian ideas and institutions, and facilitated the legitimization of their rule. According to Mohammad Habib, 'They [Turks] could do so because public opinion was with them because to an extent, and only to an extent, in pursuit of their careers the selfishness of which no one should deny, they were consciously or subconsciously sub-serving to the public good.'[63]

What was novel about these new relations between the two civilizations was that both of them possessed long historical traditions. While Central Asia regarded itself as the centre of the inhabited world, India saw itself as the cradle of an ancient civilization and a centre of all refinement and culture. As a result of the Turkoman initiative, everything at the popular level got reflected in mutually profitable relationships between the Indians and the Central Asians.

After loosely weaving together a relatively coherent tapestry from these disparate threads of evidence, one may highlight the comparative nature of the two types of Indian and Turkoman social formations. Although some ideas of synonymy are possible, a clear identification can be made in many respects. On the eve of the Turkoman arrival in the post-Gupta period, the Indian society represented a type in which the regional polities were organized on a stable basis, even though the social hierarchy of caste and occupational grading divided people both vertically and horizontally. This stratification at the social ladder helped the political elements in controlling the public without facing a cohesive protest. In comparison, the Turkomans had tribal culture as a unifying force, but they were in a disruptive phase during their long history because of a protracted intra-tribal warfare.

In Central Asian society where sub-cultures were distinct, discrete, and discordant, the rise of shared values was weakened. The question of legitimate political ends and means was not easily resolved in such tribal political cultures. The long-term stability of the regime was uncertain. The critical question in Central Asian society was not the mere presence of ethnic pluralism or actual workings of tribal groups and clans, but the degree to which they were set apart from each other in separate value systems and priorities.

It is an established fact that the plural ethnicity in Central Asia (of which Turkomans were an integral part) implied more intra-group and intra-tribal hostility. The group and the value system were often shaken and violence ruled the streets. One of the classic examples is that of Sultan Sanjar. The last days of Sultan Sanjar saw the consolidation of Qara Khita power in Turkistan and the Guz Turks carried him in a cage and plundered district by district. The solution to such violence was seen in returning to migration, stability, and security by expressing loyalty to join the invaders.

In comparison, the Indian type differed from the Turkoman in the sense that it possessed a carefully persuasive, theocratic ethic (Brahmanism), which was integrally harnessed to the interests of the Indian state. In India, it gave greater stability and strength to the state in evolving political ideology and deriving legitimacy to control the masses. The Turkoman polity in Central Asia, on the other hand, was characterized by ethnic disputes and rivalries, which always erupted and re-erupted to challenge each other's boundaries. According to Frank, 'State power was organized and reorganized by nomadic peoples on the basis of first tribal allegiance, then of political alliances, rivalries and conquests and lastly on shifting and temporary territorial basis.'[64]

In India, the polity was centrally controlled by the king, whose will was implemented by a body of officials including priests, who mediated the will of the king as divine. The bureaucracy constituted the literati in society where position was determined by the amount of land they possessed. The achievement was not possible on the basis of merit, but was the prerogative of the dominant class. Among Turkomans, the society was democratically governed and diffusedly controlled by a body of elders with rotating political roles. All the subsidiary organizations were responsible to this body of elders whose authority was granted by the tribe. George W. O'Bannon rightly remarks: 'The Turkomans had no position in their social structure equivalent to King, Khan, Shah ruler with special powers which would be used politically, militarily in controlling or in directing action of all the Turkoman as a nation.'[65]

Among Turkomans, there were a variety of occupational categories but limited functional differentiation status, which tended towards achievement. This was not the case in India. In India, we had (and still have) the caste system. Therefore, people had limited choice in terms of profession. For example, learning was only confined to the literary elite because caste acted as a restrictive mechanism, whereas among Turkomans, it was open to all. Among them the actual political operation did not necessitate literacy, but it could hardly have functioned without informed citizens. In India, the incorporation of tribes into a varna-oriented society led to social fragmentation.

The Central Asian society was always given to experimentation and innovation. It was brilliant and transient, democratic and violent. This state of affairs prolonged itself indefinitely because Central Asia was actually a congeries of conflicting tribal formations, each packed with its own weaknesses and contradictions. But outside Central Asia, and particularly in India, the Central Asians in general and Turkomans in particular proved themselves a desirable cultural asset, representing skill and strength for shaping the Sultanates which were in various regions of India the ultimate product of the convergence of these contacts. We should remember that when a relationship lasts for such a long time it is bound to encourage a process of acculturation. In India, this process made its appearance in so many forms that one must be selective because the different aspects of polity, society, economy, history, and culture are so deftly interwoven that it becomes difficult to separate one from the other.

Perhaps the most important basis of these contacts was the exchange of people's ideas epitomized by the millennia of contacts, which produced and reproduced the cultures of India and Central Asia periodically, and are now too strong to be broken.

NOTES

1. Even before the beginning of these metal production techniques, references existed on the Indo-Iranian treaties on trading of horses, which were introduced to West Asia. See R. Ghirshman, *Iran: From the Earliest Times to the Islamic Conquest*, London: Penguin, 1951, pp. 62–72. For details see also E. Herzfeld, *Archaeological History of Iran*, London: British Academy, 1935. Also by the same author, *Iran in the Ancient East*, London: Oxford University Press, 1941, pp. 149–209.
2. V.M. Masson and V.I. Sarianidi, eds., *Central Asia: Turkmenistan before the Achaemenids*, London: Thames and Hudson, 1972, pp. 124–8. See also, V.M. Masson, *Turkmenistan in Mirror of World History*, Ministry of Foreign Affairs of Turkmenistan Republic in the frame of International Scientific Conference, St. Petersburg, 2000, p. 7.
3. Studying mentalities in the pre-modern history is indisputably of great relevance. It helps in examining multiple social realities that motivated people of different regions, ethnicities, and religions to contact each other before their rulers patronized or promoted these contacts. This establishes the fact that the history of mentalities grew much before the formal definition of the concept came into being. It needs to be emphasized here that French historians of the Annales School played a very important role not only in studying the history of mentalities but also validating the applicability of this concept as an important methodological tool. M. Vovelle, *Ideologies and Mentalities*, tr. Eamon O'Flaherty, Oxford: Polity Press, 1990, pp. 4–12. See also Elsepth Davies, *The Years of Barbarians*, Edinburgh: Pentland, 1988, pp. 7–13 and 183–91.
4. For details see Marija Gimbutas, *The Early Civilization of Europe*, Indo-European Studies Centre, Los Angeles: University of California Press, 1980. But the migrations of Central Asians to India are continuously spread over the entire pre-modern period

apart from the Persian chronicles of the Sultanate and Mughal periods in Indian history. See also: E.D. Phillips, *The Royal Hordes, Nomadic People of Steppes*, London: Thames and Hudson, 1965; Gavin Hambly, *Central Asia*, Weidenfeld and Nicholson Universal History, vol. 16, London: Weidenfeld and Nicholson, 1969; and also William McNeill, *Rise of West: A History of Human Community*, Chicago: Chicago University Press, 1963.

5. Gimbutas, *The Early Civilization of Europe*, pp. 27–54.
6. Ghirshman, *Iran*, p. 74. See also Andre Gunder Frank, *The Centrality of Central Asia*, Comparative Asian Studies, vol. 8, Amsterdam: V.U. University Press, 1992, p. 9; Y.Y. Kuzmina and K.F. Smirnov, 'The Origin of Indo-Iranians in the Light of Recent Archaeological Data', *Journal of Central Asia*, vol. 1, no. 1, 1978, pp. 68–70. For details of early migrations of Aryans to India, see R.S. Sharma, *Advent of Aryans*, Delhi: Manohar, 1999, pp. 74–96.
7. Ghirshman, *Iran*, pp. 126–47. When the Achaemenians lost Egypt, Palestine, Southern Syria, and some parts of the coasts of Asia Minor, King Seleucus ceded the territory of Arachosia and Gedrousia to King Chandragupta of India in exchange for elephants, which he needed for protecting his Western Frontiers; Ibid., pp. 163, 204, 220–2.
8. Ibid.
9. The Kushana Empire extended to Russian Turkestan, Port of Chinese Turkestan and a large portion of India, Ibid., pp. 223 and 355. Romila Thapar also attributes a Central Asian origin to Kushanas; Romila Thapar, *A History of India*, vol. 1, London: Penguin, 1966, p. 97. However, Kalhana is more specific and traces the origin of the Kushanas to the *Turushkas*. See Kalhana, *Rajatarangini*, tr. M.A. Stein, 3 vols., London, 1900; repr, Delhi: Motilal Banarasidas, 1979, vol. 2, verse 3412, p. 268.
10. Earlier also, the Selucid king Antiochus crossed the Hindu Kush to renew his friendship with the Mauryan king. The Selucids also imported gold from north-west of India, Armenia, Bactria, and Caucasus and in return exported iron, copper, and lead. Ghirshman, *Iran*, pp. 126–47 and 223.
11. Thapar, *A History of India*. See also A.L. Basham, ed., *Cultural History of India*, Oxford: Clarendon, 1975; repr., Delhi: Oxford University Press, 1998, pp. 11–59, 124–40 and 245–93.
12. Frank, *The Centrality of Central Asia*, pp. 12–13. See also Denis Sinor, *Inner Asia, History–Civilization–Languages: A Syllabus*, Uralic and Altaic Series, vol. 96, Bloomington: Indiana University and The Hague: Mouton, 1969, p. 171.
13. No Doubt, the reasons for the transformation of Indo-Central Asian contact into the collision at times must have been complex. Their

nature can be reconstructed from the sources which are scattered in various regions. The early days of the settlement of Central Asians in India (even on the periphery of India) would helve been hard and they could not have survived without the local support in many respects. But at the same time, there must have been many reasons or the conflicts as well.

14. G. Watson, 'Interpretations of Central Asian Influence of Mughal India: The Historical Debate', *South Asia*, vol. 18, no. 2, 1995, pp. 1–22.
15. William McNeill, *Rise of West*, pp. 316–91; See also Thomas J. Barfield, *The Perilous Frontier: Nomadic Empires and China*, Cambridge, Mass.: Basil Blackwell, 1989, pp. 6–7.
16. Aziz Ahmad, *Studies in Islamic Culture in Indian Environment*, Oxford: Clarendon, 1969, pp. 23–52. See also Yusuf Husain, *Indo-Muslim Polity (Turko-Afghan Period)*, Simla: Indian Institute of Advanced Study, 1971, pp. 1–47 and 169–214.
17. Fernand Braudel, *On History*, tr. Sarah Matthews, London: Weidenfeld and Nicolson, 1980, p. 52.
18. Central Asia is a huge landmass bounded to the west by Caspian Sea, to the south by the Kopet Dagh mountainous regions of Iran and the Hindu Kush mountain ranges in Afghanistan, to the east by Pamir's and Tian Shan mountains, and to the north by the Kazak Steppe roughly from Lake Balkhash on the east to the northern edges of Aral and Caspian seas. The topographical specificity is located in its Kyzylkum and Karakum deserts and the two main rivers of Central Asia, the Amu Darya (Oxus) and the Syr Darya (Jaxartes). Central Asia's unique attributers result from its geographical position, which allows it to harmoniously integrate the varied influences of the Western and Eastern world. George W. O'Bannon, *The Turkoman Carpet*, London: Duckworth, 1974, pp. 13–33.
19. Ahmad, *Studies in Islamic Culture*, pp. 32–56.
20. K.M. Ashraf, *Life and Conditions of the People of Hindustan*, 2nd edn., Delhi: Munshiram Manoharlal, 1969, p. 5.
21. M. Athar Ali, 'Encounter and Efflorescence: Genesis of Medieval Civilisation', Presidential Address, *Indian History Congress Proceedings*, Golden Jubilee Session, Gorakhpur, Delhi, 1989, p. 14.
22. Marc Gaborieau, Muzaffar Alam, Francoise 'Nalini' Delvoye, eds., *The Making of Indo-Persian Culture: Indian and French Studies*, New Delhi: Manohar and Centre de Sciences Humaines, 2000, pp. 1–14 and 54–171.
23. For details see Lawrence Krader, *Peoples of Central Asia*, Bloomington: Indiana University Press, 1971. Also L.D. Phillips, *The Royal Hordes: Nomad People of the Steppes,* London: Thames

and Hudson, 1965. The other ethnic groups referred to by our sources are Uzbeks, Kazakhs, Tajiks, Iranians, and Mongols. O'Bannon, *The Turkoman Carpet*, pp. 13–33. See also Kalhana, *Rajatarangini*, p. 311; R.L. Hangloo, 'Sufism in Medieval Deccan: Politics and Worship', Presidential Address (Medieval Section), Proceedings of Andhra Pradesh History Congress, 24th Annual Session, Rajahmundry, Andhra Pradesh, January 2000, pp. 49–57.

24. V.V. Barthold, *Four Studies on History of Central Asia*, tr. V. and T. Minorsky, vol. 3, Leiden: Brill, 1958, p. 90, and F.H. Skrine and Edward D. Ros, eds., *The Heart of Asia*, London: Methuen, 1888, pp. 267–75.
25. It is generally believed that the Turkomans extended their influence all over the world. Many of their tribes served the Khalifa of Baghdad and many of them earned the distinction of being the best soldiers in Asiatic armies. Many of them rose to important positions. Subaktagin was also a Turkish slave whose son Mahmud not only extended his domain up to the Oxus and the Caspian, but also carried his victorious armies into central India. William Eriskine, *History of India*, quoted in Stanley Lane-poole, *Mediaeval India Under Mohammedan Rule, 712–1764*, London: Haskell House, 1903; repr., Delhi: Low Price, 1994, pp. 14–18. H.G. Knee remarks, 'Few races of men at any period of world, have acted a more distinguished part than the Turks, who in one form or the other for centuries ruled a great part of the old world and who, even at present day influence, directly or indirectly, the government, manners, and the limits of Hungary and Poland to the farthest bounds of the empire of Hindustan.' H.G. Knee, *The Turks in India*, London: W.H. Allen and Co., 1879, p. 9.
26. Kalhana, *Rajatarangini*, vol. l, verse 179, p. 131.
27. Ibid., verses 152–5, p. 206.
28. Ibid., p. 272.
29. Ibid., p. 311.
30. Ibid.
31. Ibid., verse 1149, p. 357.
32. For details see William Moorcroft, *Tour Diary*, MS, EURD-265 available in Jammu University Library, Jammu; T.D. Forsyth, *A Report of a Mission to Yarkund in 1873, under Command of Sir T.D. Forsyth*, Calcutta: Foreign Department, 1875; Robert Shaw, *Visit to Higher Tartary, Yarkand, and Kashgar (Formerly Chinese Territory) and Return Journey over the Karakoram Pass*, London: John Murray, 1871; Mir Izzatullah Safar-Nama (AD 1812–13), unpublished MS, Research Department Library, Kashmir University, Srinagar. Besides these, there is bulk of evidence on Indo-Central Asian relations and Silk Route trade between these two regions in

English, Persian, and Urdu in various archives and repositories in India and abroad.

33. Augusto Azzaroli, *An Early History of Horsemanship*, Leiden: Brill, 1985, p. 66.
34. Hassan Nizami, *Taj-ul-Masir*, in *The History of India, as Told by its Own Historians*, tr. Elliot & Dowson, vol. 2, pp. 204–43. For details see also S.D. Dwivedi, *Relation of Rajputs with Delhi Sultans,* AD *1206–1526*, Agra: Sriram Mehta and Co., 1978, pp. 22–57.
35. Mohammad Habib, *Sultan Mahmud of Ghaznin*, 1951; repr., Delhi: S. Chand, 1967, p. 2.
36. Frank, *The Centrality of Central Asia*, pp. 9–20.
37. Ibid., pp. 12–13.
38. Minhaj-i-Siraj, *Tabaqat-i-Nasiri*, ed. Nasu Lees, Khadim Hussain and Abdul Hai, 2 vols., Calcutta: Bibliotheca Indica, 1864; repr., Delhi: Low Price Publication, 1981, vol. 1, pp. 466–7.
39. Ibid.
40. A.B.M. Habibullah, *The Foundation of Muslim Rule in India: A History of the Establishment and Progress of the Turkish Sultanate of Delhi, 1206–1290 A.D.*, 2nd revd. edn., Allahabad: Central Book Depot, 1961, pp. 1–72.
41. Mohammad Habib, *Sultan Mahmud of Ghaznin*, pp. 2–7. See also M. Nazim, *The Life and Times of Sultan Mahmud of Ghazna*, Delhi: Munshiram Manoharlal, 1971, pp. 12–26.
42. Erskine, *History of India*, cited in Knee, *Turks in India*, p. 9.
43. K.M. Ashraf, *Life and Conditions*, pp. 52–65.
44. Ibid.
45. A.K.S. Lambton, 'Reflection in Iqta', in *Arabic and Islamic Studies in Honour of Hamilton A.R. Gibb*, ed. George Makdisi, Leiden: Brill, 1965, pp. 358–76.
46. Bert G. Fragner, 'Social and Internal Economic Affairs', in *The Cambridge History of Iran*, vol. 6, ed. Laurence Lockhart and Peter Jackson, Cambridge: Cambridge University Press, 1986, pp. 501–2. See also M.A. Shaban, 'The Origins of Iqta', in Shaban, *Islamic History: A New Interpretation (*AD *75–1055)*, Cambridge: Cambridge University Press, 1976, pp. 71–88.
47. Athar Ali, 'Encounter and Efflorescence', p. 14.
48. Irfan Habib, 'Agrarian Economy', in *The Cambridge Economic History of India*, ed. Tapan Raychaudhuri and Irfan Habib, 2 vols., Cambridge: Cambridge University Press, 1982, vol. 1 (1200–1750), pp. 68–75.
49. Some of these Turkoman officials were: Malik Tja-uddin Sanjar, Kazlakh Khan, Kabir Khan Ayaz, Malik Nasir Aldin al Tamar-al-Bahia, Malik-Saif-uddin, Aibeg Uchch, Yughantat Khaitai Turk, Malik Nusrat Al-din, Tayisi-ul-Maizvi. Malik Izz-al-din, Tughan

Khan Tughril, Malik Tamar Khan, Malik Iindu Khan, Muayyid Aldin, Karkash Khan, Iktiyar al-din Ali Tegin, Malik Babar al-din, Sungar-al-Rumi, Malik Saif-ud-din, Arkali Dad Beg, Malik Bahar-ud-din Nausrat Khan, Malik Nusar -al-din Shakan, Malik Kesli Khan, Saif-al-din, Ali Beg al Sultani, Malik-al-Hajjab, Alkhanal-Muazzarn al Khaqan, Azim Ulag Khan (Balban), Baha al-Haqq, Wal-al-din, and many others who held distinct positions under Turkoman Sultans of Delhi. Siraj, *Tabaqat*, vol. 2, pp. 1–89.

50. Husain, *Indo-Muslim Polity*, pp. 61–5.
51. Ibid. See also Zia ud-din Barani, *Tarikh-i-Firuzshahi*, ed. Syed Ahmad Khan, W.N. Less and Kabiruddin, Calcutta: Bibliotheca Indica, 1862, pp. 34–7.
52. Ibid.
53. Hangloo, *Presidential Address*, pp. 49–57.
54. Mirza Haider Dughlat, *Tarikh-i-Rashidi*, tr. N. Elias and E. Denison Ross, London: Sampson, Low, Marston, 1895, p. 434.
55. Sayyid Ali, *Tarikh-i-Kashmir*, Persian MS, folio 16a, Research Department Library, Srinagar, Jammu and Kashmir.
56. Pandit Srivara, *Jain Rajatarangini*, tr. J.C. Dutt, Calcutta: I.C. Bose, 1898; repr., Delhi: Low Price, 1990, vol. 1, pp. 31–2. See also R.L. Hangloo, 'Kashmir under Sultan Zain-ul-Abidin', *NEHU, Journal of Humanities and Social Sciences*, vol. 1, 1998, pp. 21–30.
57. Hangloo, *Presidential Address*, pp. 4–7.
58. S.A.A. Rizvi, *History of Sufism in India*, 2 vols., Delhi: Munshiram Manoharlal, 1978, vol. 1, pp. 131, 135, 136, 151, 169 and 191. For details, see also K.A. Nizami, *Some Aspects of Religion and Politics in India during the Thirteenth Century*, Delhi: Idarah-i Adabiyat, 1961; repr., Delhi: Oxford University Press, 2002.
59. Irfan Habib, 'Technology and Social Change', *Presidential Address, Indian History Congress*, Varanasi, 1969, pp. 139–61. See also *American Historical Review*, vol. 65, no. 3, April 1960, p. 517.
60. Khwaja Abdul Malik Isami, *Futuh-us-Salatin* (Persian), ed. A. Mahdi Husain, Delhi: Educational Press, 1938, p. 134.
61. Amir Hassan, *Fawaidu-al Fawad*, ed. Latif Malik, Lahore: Amir Ali Sijzi Dehlvi, 1966, pp. 334–5. See also Irfan Habib, 'Technology and Social Change', pp. 139–61.
62. Athar Ali, 'Encounter and Efflorescence', p. 16.
63. Mohammad Habib, *Sultan Mahmud of Ghaznin*, p. 94.
64. Frank, *The Centrality of Central Asia*, p. 14.
65. O'Bannon, *The Turkoman Carpet*, pp. 15–16.

CHAPTER 3

Tools of Seeking Legitimacy in Medieval India: A Case Study of the Delhi Sultanate

> The state is invisible, it must be personified before it can be seen, symbolized before it can be loved, imagined before it can be conceived.[1]
>
> —MICHAEL WALZER

CEREMONIES AND symbolism have always been an integral part of Indian polity. To understand the nature of medieval Indian polity, it is necessary to examine the role of ceremonials and symbolism and how these elements presented the ways in which the notions of legitimacy and power were transmitted by the sultans of Delhi as a means of ordering and sustaining their power and dominance. Taking into account the fact that the relationship between power and splendour is much more complex and broad than the simple formulation presented in this chapter, I attempt to understand the subject of ceremonials and symbolism with its various complexities. Some examples have been chosen from the Delhi Sultanate to indicate that the ceremonies and symbolism, though ephemeral, were central to the legitimacy of medieval Indian polity.

In endowing the world around them with their own symbolically constructed versions of reality, the sultans of Delhi promoted and patronized a host of ceremonies and symbols as one of the most powerful mechanisms to structure people's dependence and to reinforce their authority from time to time. The pomp and ceremony connected with the coronation of the sultans, their assumption of royal titles, reading of *khutba*, issuing of *sikka* (coins), *farmans*, and conducting of royal amusements and other ceremonies involved enormous human activity and provided materials for the sultans to construct the social basis of their power.[2]

On 24 June 1206, when Qutb-ud-din Aibek (1206–10) was enthroned by the Turkish nobles and a *khutba* was read in his name in all mosques of Lahore, Ghiyasud-din Mahmud of Gazni sent him the royal insignia and conferred on him the title of 'Sultan' with a royal *chatr* (parasol) and *durbash* (mace) as symbols of royalty to rule over Hindustan.[3] In the political context, the ceremonial seems to have furnished the means by which people made sense of political processes which were presented to them in a symbolic form.[4] Hassan Nizami, the contemporary chronicler of Aibek writes: 'The public prayers, *khutba* and *sikka* (coinage) of *dinnars* and *dirhams* throughout the whole country received honour and embellishment for his (Qutb-ud-din's) name and royal titles.'[5] The *chatr* was adorned with jewels and accompanied the sultan to the court and in procession. The *aftabtir* (parasol), which had an oval shape and was covered with brocade and studded with precious stones, served to protect the sultan from sun rays. However, its symbolic function was to shore up the sultan's authority and bolster his status. It was an emblem of awe-inspiring rulership and an abstract idea denoting sovereign power. Besides, such ensigns provided unifying symbols for Turkish nobles who recognised the sultan as their superior and offered their allegiance to him. Creating a royal symbol or identifying with it was a potent means of gaining power, for the hallmark of power was construction of reality.[6] Clive S.Kessler remarks: 'The symbolic is not a residual dimension of purportedly real politics, still less is it an insubstantial screen upon which real issues are caste in pale and passive form. The symbolic is real politics articulated in a special and often most powerful way.'[7] Therefore, the Sultanate of Delhi was defined by the *chatr* as much as the *chatr* was by the Sultanate. In fact, if the position and power of Aibek has to be seen in association with the status of established kingly institutions of his time, the thrust of political behaviour was always directed by him towards stability and order in the kingdom as well as towards dignity of his office and authority. The nature of relative success or failure after his death is related to those problems which produced a variety of patron-client relations universal to medieval Indian polity.

In medieval Indian polity, royalty was always associated with such considerations as wealth, birth, power, wisdom, religion, and the decorum of the court. The richness of all these objects signified and symbolized the greatness of power, and carved out a new basis for political allegiance. Initially, the Turks in India lacked a formal social organization and a material base. They were also perceived as outsiders. Therefore, they needed a mode of defining a new collectivity which provided them a political identity and a means to reunite others on their side, particularly when medieval Indian political environment was complex and faction-ridden. Irfan Habib writes, 'The unity of Turkish *Amirs* was, however, subject to continuous internal disruption.'[8] With the gradual expansion of the Sultanate of Delhi, the sultans succeeding Aibek created a web of ceremonies to facilitate the mediation of their power and make the subjected world appear as the actual social reality at the popular level.

In 1229, when the ambassador of Caliph al-Mustansir arrived in Delhi to bestow the investiture on Sultan Iltutmish (1210–36), he was awarded a warm welcome. There was a great pomp and splendour all around. The day of the presentation of robes of honour to Iltutmish celebrated the recognition received by newly founded Sultanate from the legal sovereign of the Islamic world. The entire city of Delhi was decorated with arches. Drums were beaten to demonstrate the felicity and thanksgiving. Coins were issued with al-Mustansir's name inscribed on them along with that of Iltutmish, while the copper coins bore only the name of the Caliph as Srishalipah.[9] The validity of the sultan's government depended on an oath of allegiance to the Caliph. In turn, the sultan was the member of *Ahlal-hallwal-aqd* and was the constituted authority to nominate a Caliph. Al-Ghazali writes:

An evil doing and barbarous Sultan, so long as he is supported by military force, so that he can only with difficulty be deposed and that the attempt to depose him would cause unendurable civil strife, most of necessity he left in possession and obedience must be rendered to him exactly as obedience must be rendered to *Amirs*. We consider that the Caliph is contractually assumed by that person of Abbasid house who is charged with it and that the function of government in the various lands is carried out by means of Sultan who owes allegiance to Caliph. Government in these days is a consequence solely of the military power and whoever he may be to whom the military power gives his allegiance that person is Caliph. And whoever exercises independent authority so long as he shows allegiance to Caliph in matters of his prerogatives of *Khutba and Sikka*—the same is Sultan whose command and judgments are valid in several parts of earth.[10]

Such ceremonies acquired munificence through people's participation which helped the sultans define the nature of medieval Indian political universe the way they wanted to. The ceremonies were conducted on the occasion of victory, marriage of a member of the royal family, birth of a prince or princess, visits of foreign envoys, and coronation. At every occasion, the royal processions were held with horses, elephants, guards, and retainers in rich and glittering costumes and the nobles passed through the capital in full splendour. All this was held amidst public audience and *baiat-i-am* (general oath) was part of the process of the ceremonial. These were followed by all kinds of rejoicings and amusements such as banquets and *qasida* recitations.

The power of these ceremonies did not alone stem from the social matrix but also from their psychological underpinnings. All such ceremonies stressed on a direct contact between the sultans and their subjects. Even as mere spectators, people's participation in these ceremonies involved psychological stimuli. The ceremonies structured people's sense of reality and their understanding of the world around them. Through these collective representations, the Turkish sultans interpreted medieval Indian social order and their place in it. When Sultan Iltutmish was introduced to the public as *Zil Allah fil Almin* (shadow of God), and also as 'The Mighty Sultan Sun of Empire, Faith Conquest-laden

Iltutmish, Commander of Faithful, *Nasir-Amir-al-Muminin*', no rationalization of secular power prevailed in such a ceremony; instead, the Sultan was portrayed as divine and supernatural.[11] Such titles were deliberately assumed to shore up the sultan's power as supreme and independent of every human authority. These titles created a new self of the sultan for the subjects and the sultan began to be treated differently.[12]

While defining Balban's conception of kingship, Ishwar Topa says:

> Kingship ought to be considered sacred as well as a trust as it was a divine vice-regency. To Balban it did not signify a man-made institution of political control and guidance. It had the manifestation of the divine will that caused its existence.
>
> While sermonizing his son Shahzada Muhammad Shah, on politics Balban brought forth in colourful setting the idea of the pre-eminence of kingly power emanating directly from the divine source. He made the Shahzada realize the importance of the superiority of royalty over human beings because of its close semblance to the divine traits. Kingship could not be classed with other human institutions. Balban believed that it was the will of God that the heart of a king was made not only superior to and different from the heart of the people, but there could be, at the same time, no comparison to the king's heart which was to be looked upon as the abode of God in contradiction to the absence of divine refraction in the people's heart. So long as God cared to bestow favour on king's heart, the importance for the general welfare of the people would be realized by the ruler, as the initiative in the improvement of the affairs of the people depended on the royal head and heart. In case the king's heart was denied this divine favour, he would be incapacitated to discharge such a public duty. In other words, the presence of the divine guidance and benevolence would be an influential and decisive factor in the rightful discharge of royal duties.[13]

To understand the force and impact of such symbolically nourished conceptions in the political order of the Delhi Sultanate, it is important to consider how Sultan Balban manipulated the ceremonial and the symbolic to establish the basis of his political power and monarchical authority. Balban ruled for forty years: first as the *Naib-i-Mamlikat* of Delhi (1246–65) and later as its Sultan (1266–87).[14] When the envoys of Halaqu visited Delhi, Balban was the *Naib-i-Mamlikat*.

He arranged a colourful ceremonial by involving people of different communities.[15] The splendour and grandeur that he organized not only impressed the emissary, but also acted as a means of communication with the public because in these ceremonies, the people's participation involved the individual sense of self and furnished the means by which people made sense of the sultan's political strength that was presented to them through the ceremonial and the symbolic. For reasons of legitimacy, Balban did not hesitate to claim descent from the mythical Iranian hero Afrasiab.[16] Probably, the Sultan knew that in the day-to-day business of politics, the myths would set the terms for popular respect to his rule. Lance Bennert observes: 'Myths condition the public to the powerful symbols used by politicians. Myths underwrite the status quo in times of stability and they chart the course of change in times of stress.'[17]

In fact, it was the contemporary political compulsions which forced Balban to turn to Persian monarchical traditions. He introduced the custom of *paibos* (kissing the sultan's feet) and *zaminbos* (lying prostrate on the ground before the sultan).[18] He also mutated the Seljuq and Khawarzam kings of Persia to restore the etiquette of the court and the prestige of the crown. He believed in the enforcement of submission and disguised coercion in the cloak of religion and the ceremonial. As a result, Balban's sense of his own importance was powerfully enhanced when he initiated the regalia of Seljuq and Khawarzam kings.[19] Such ritual acts defined the Sultan's status and his prerogatives, which appeared to him as essential in the construction of a social hierarchy within the structure of political power. People had to prostate themselves before the Sultan of Delhi when he was present and to stand up even when his name was mentioned as a mark of solemn reverence. When at a distance from Delhi, they bowed towards the seat of the Sultanate. K.M. Ashraf writes:

> The Monarch of Delhi scrupulously copied his Sasanian predecessors in Persia whose love of luxury and ostentation was phenomenal. It was all the more necessary in a foreign country where state had no better sanction than the awe and fear that it could inspire in the hearts of people

by gorgeous displays of its pomp and power and through the glorious surroundings of the *Sultan*. There are a number of examples on record of terror which the presence and appearance of the monarch inspired 'among his enemies'.[20]

It was believed that if the personality of the monarch did not succeed in inspiring awe and fear, he was fit to lead just a *tuman*, i.e. *dah hazar* (ten thousand) troops or at best to govern a minor province rather than to rule over a kingdom.[21]Therefore, the added emphasis on ceremonial and court etiquette by Balban does reflect his desire to keep up with the style of the Persian monarchs and also to exalt himself in the minds of his own subjects. This entire scenario came to be known as Balban's theory of kingship.[22] In the words of Topa:

> As a staunch and ardent believer in the institution of kingship, Balban maintained that the royal dignity, awe, and prestige could only become real and effective if the ruler enforced the court decorum as observed by the famous Naushervan. To him royal words, deeds, activities and movements served to bear a semblance to royal dignity. If kingship failed to create a sense of admiration and respect for royal dignity and lacked the power to instil dread and fear into the heart of the people for the court and state processions, its prestige and grandeur would be lowered.[23]

We should not hesitate in regarding all these efforts as the result of the Sultan's design. There is no doubt about the fact that when the whole style was in place, the Sultan used it for the purpose of both personal and official aggrandizement. Sultan Balban treated kingship as an embodiment of authority and always emphasized: 'It is the superhuman awe and dignified position which can ensure people's obedience.[24] To him, the head of a Sultan alone was the repository of God's beneficence and, in that, he had no equal in mankind.

While evolving the conceptual image of the Sultan and his obligations, Balban's doctrines like pre-Sultanate polity attached great importance to the role of political authority in upholding the divine order of society. The main difference, however, was rooted in the division between secular and sacred authority. In pre-Sultanate polity, the concept of the king had a necessary function, which was carried out according to moral statecraft, and which also opened the way for evolving the secular authority that was not subjected to religious authority.[25] On the other hand, in the Sultanate under Balban, there was no such neat division because everything was governed by an all-pervasive religion in which Balban's political ideas were rooted.[26] The symbolic linkages of the sultan's authority with divinity established an impression as if the sultan had all the authority of God behind his actions. The sultan, as the head of the Sultanate, became the representative of God, to whom alone all power belonged. Laws of the Sultanate were to be the manifestation of higher laws and the concept of authority was, thus, absolutist, according to which only the powerful could act with confidence because they embodied the divine will.[27] However, by symbolically identifying himself with the divine, Sultan Balban asserted his importance in a more effective and socially acceptable manner than if he were to boast of his virtues more directly. By establishing his self-image in part through his symbolic and ceremonial identification with different processes, in which rituals played a significant role, the relationship between the Sultan and the subjects was objectified. Crowds of people would come from large distances to see the Sultan's pomp and majesty.[28]

The introduction of the Persian festival of *Nauroz* by Sultan Balban was one of the potent political rituals to raise the prestige of the royalty in the public eye.[29] The celebration of the festival not only produced a cognitive effect on the popular perception of the political reality, but also involved popular emotion, and people derived a great deal of satisfaction from their participation in the festival, because the success of Balban's political processes also depended on the degree of popular enthusiasm generated by *Nauroz*. The festival also gave regularity to state ceremony. For the Sultan, the power of ceremonies and rituals was based on symbolism and its social context. Since the power of the Sultanate was derived from such rituals, their celebration, in turn, depended upon a range of groups and communities that were involved in them.

Though some ceremonies were not frequent, there was always a possibility that people would have forgotten the message, as the *umarah* (nobles) forgot their ordering, but the popular sentiment was rekindled by conducting these ceremonies. Therefore, conducting such a spectacle in which all the themes of royal propaganda were presented became a political necessity, because nothing was better calculated to rouse the loyalty of the people than these ceremonies and symbols.[30] The success of the state's ceremonial was also linked to the amount of enthusiasm it generated in the public. The ceremonies would have ended up merely as a bureaucratic affair if people had not turned up in great numbers to witness the ceremonies and carry them, through the word of mouth, to the rest of the public, with all the exaggeration at their command.

Interestingly, after Balban's death, the incumbent nobility did not even spare the funeral ceremonies which became a grandiose spectacle. 'The *maliks* in grief at Balban's death tore their garments and threw dust on their heads as they followed bare feet [*sic*] the king's bier to the burial ground at *Darul Aman*. For forty days they mourned his death, slept on the bare floor.'[31] Such an impassioned cry at the funeral marked the continuity of royal dignity. These ceremonies also often asserted the group's or the dynasty's superiority. Since Balban had been an important symbol of Turkish organizational unity in India, and his death could threaten that unity, the solution was to keep the symbolism connected with Balban alive even after his death.

Besides, such prolonged mourning was directed to arouse public emotion in support of the legitimacy of the nobles who were associated with him and wanted to generate popular enthusiasm for the Sultanate. Interestingly, the funeral ceremonies and the coronation in medieval times always drew large crowds. The special quality of coronation and also of issuing of coins was that they united symbolic representation with actual exercise of power, which no other ceremony did. The coronation and receiving of the royal insignia were a singular event. Hence, the public spontaneity on such occasions was a key source in reinforcing the state's power and dominance. Machiavelli rightly remarks, 'Men in general make judgments more by appearances than by reality, for sight alone belongs to everyone, but understanding to few.'[32]

Among the Khalji Sultans, even though Jalaluddin (1290–6) 'devoted himself assiduously to business of kingdom' without much pomp and splendour, the conception of power in medieval Indian society was in great part based on the understanding passed on through ceremonies and symbolism because it was established that they were the valued norms of conduct and criteria of success in getting public acquiescence to their rule.[33] According to Topa, 'As a ruler Jalaluddin took the greatest care and interest in the general discharge of governmental duties and must have succeeded in bringing the people nearer to the government by raising their status or position in life. The public was no more considered as a chattel to be driven by the dictates of officials. The people were given scope for their development and were made to sense and feel their own individuality.'[34]

However, politics devoid of ceremonies did not suffice to make him a good ruler. Despite Jalaluddin's efforts to affect this kind of harmony between the people and the state, there was a continuous interaction between the popular expectations and the Sultan's ways of dealing with the actual contours of polity in which ceremonies and symbolism had their own role to play.

Jalaluddin held his first public durbar at Khilugari, and then came to the city of Delhi and visited the Kaushak Lal (red palace) of Balban.[35] He took the throne of his predecessors and immediately organized only a simple thanksgiving ceremony during which he wept profusely.[36] Perhaps, the Sultan thought that he was best assured of his nobles' loyalty if he remained simple, modest, and sentimental in style in the midst of his itinerant court. But he did not know that under such simplicity, the patriarchal ideal receded in popular perception and the conviction became widespread that political dignity, awe, severity, and magnificence were necessary constituents of the ruler's daily setting.

From then on, desperate nobles surrounded him charged with ambition, downplaying his glorification of modesty and intriguing to take over his power.[37] According to Zia-ud-din Barani '...the nobles and great men spoke of him with disparagement, saying that he knew not how to rule and had none of the awe and majesty of the kings.'[38] This attitude towards Jalaluddin's policies was led by Ahmad Chap, the leader of the nobility at the court. The representatives of the Balbanite school of political thought in the court of Jalaluddin were still obdurate in the exposition of their ideas to such an extent that to them, kingship signified oppression and cruelty. They conveyed the view that it should be understood as nothing more or nothing less than absolutism. The idea was harboured by the representatives of this school of politics that Jalaluddin would be a great failure if he were to stick to his concept of morality in politics.

Given the licentious nature of his authority, Jalaluddin Khalji thought to conduct the court's affairs with the hope that he would be able to consolidate his rule and, thus, counter the rising forces of resistance. When the rebellious forces supported by Malik Chhaju were defeated by Jalaluddin's army near Badaun, the nobles did not expect their Sultan to exercise leniency towards the rebels. When they observed this attitude of the Sultan,

> . . . they whispered to each other that the Sultan did not know how to rule, for instead of slaying the rebels he had made them his companions. Malik Ahmad Chap, deputy lord chamberlain, a personal attendant and counsellor of Sultan told him that a king should reign and observe the rules of the government or else be content to relinquish the throne.[39]

Jalaluddin, however, adopted the same attitude repeatedly. As a result, when the symbolic and the ceremonial element associated with the propagation of political power and authority was undermined by refractory socialization, the potential for change was ever present in which, ultimately, the sword became the decisive symbol for the assumption of political power.

In order to play the role expected of a Sultan in the Delhi Sultanate, one had to possess various qualities, among which legitimacy was the most important. In comparison to Jalaluddin, when Alauddin Khalji (1296–1316) came from Kara to Delhi, he distributed gold to secure followers and seek public acquiescence.[40] With the shadow of a criminal political background, he took his seat upon the throne in *Daulat Khana-i-Jalus* amidst great ceremonies and then proceeded to Kaushak Lal. The gathering was full of *iqtadars*, nobles and men of lofty status.[41] With great pomp and celebration, public festivities followed in which Sultan Alauddin distributed to officers 'purses and bags filled with *tankas* and *jitals*.'[42] Mere heredity was not enough to appoint a sultan; he assumed Sultanate in reality when his coronation was over. From that day onwards, the titles could be assumed and regnal years could be counted. He used ceremonies to make peace and sue for war, particularly when laws of succession were inexact and ties of blood did not designate one person. Yusuf Hussain says: 'The gifts and honours that he bestowed (on such ceremonial occasions) so deluded the people that no one ever mentioned the horrible crime which the Sultan had committed.'[43]At every stage from Kara to Delhi, five mounds of gold stars were placed in *manjaniq* (catapult) and distributed among spectators in front of the royal tent. This distribution of wealth provided the way for the people to understand such an abstract political entity as sovereignty and also compulsive means of identifying with them.[44] Such ceremonies stemmed from the psychological underpinnings associated with this distribution of wealth, which were evident in the way they generated popular receptivity towards the Sultan. When Alauddin entered Delhi, he was accompanied by 56,000 horsemen and 60,000 foot soldiers, and at every stop en route, he was waved at by the officers and nobles of the late Sultan Jalaluddin.[45] Ashraf remarks that the exalted nature of the office of the Sultan, surrounded as it was by a halo of divinity, compelled the monarch to a standard of benevolence and generosity far above other people. In this respect, a key and a hallowed tradition of magnanimity, chivalry, forgiveness, generosity, benevolence, and of other noble virtues was built around the person of Sultan, which made his rule attractive. Both the Persian and Indian traditions were rich in this direction.[46]

Barani states that when Alauddin became the sultan, he came to the conclusion that polity and government is one thing, and rules and decrees are another. Royal commands belong to the king and the legal decrees rest upon the judgements of *qazis* (jurists) and *muftis* (penal authority). He also realized that allegiance to the sultan does not stem from culture-free judgements alone, but also from symbolically nourished perceptions of the Sultanate. While debating political necessities and legal decrees with one of the *qazis*, when the Sultan was told that his expenditure on the *harem* was unlawful, he got infuriated and the *qazi* replied that if, however, the Sultan sought his advice in political matter, he would say that whatever money his Majesty spent on his *harem* no doubt tended to raise his dignity in the eyes of men, and the exaltation of a king's dignity is essential to good policy.[47] People conceived of authority in terms of an individual rather than of groups. For instance, when Alauddin came to see the functioning of the government, he got frustrated by going from office to office and, therefore, transformed the administrative apparatus and ordered to thoroughly restrict the revenue administration.[48]

In this manner, the Sultan structured the understanding of medieval Indian polity and the attitude of the political elite who populated it. This helped him to create a political entity that encompassed a large number of cultural groups such as Rajputs, Telugus, Marathas, and various Central Asian communities, each with a separate regional, linguistic, religious, and social organization. People began to imagine that their society represented both the best and the most natural order, and took part in various ceremonies and rituals (both as participants and spectators) which expressed and renewed this view.

In order to escape the humiliation of appearing before Sultan Alauddin Khalji personally, Sital Deo, the Raja of Siwana in Marwar (in Rajasthan) had his image made in gold and sent it with a hundred elephants and many other gifts to the Sultan with a great ceremonial procession in the durbar.[49] Holding public durbars, beating of drums, reading of dispatches from the pulpit were a frequent phenomenon on all such occasions. Booths were also erected for the distribution of food and drinks. When Malik Kafur returned from the conquest of southern Mathura (Madura), the Sultan held a public durbar in front of the Golden Palace and all the nobles and chiefs stood on the right and left according to their rank. When the durbar was held in Chabutra Subbani after crushing the Mongol rebellion led by Ali Beg and Tartakat Amroha, a large crowd gathered there and because of so many people, the price of one pitcher of water jumped from twenty *jitals* to half a *tanka*.[50]

On all such occasions, the common public displays with their standardized presentations not only helped to relate local people to the Delhi Sultanate, but also provided the symbolic means for them to identify with the Sultanate. One of the most potent and widely found mechanisms for tying the locals to the Sultanate was sometimes the simultaneity of symbolic action, as evidenced in the celebration of the durbar by Alauddin at Siri and his attack on Kili.[51] By engaging people in such standardized and often emotionally charged social actions, rituals make the symbols silent and promote an attachment to them.

During the Tughlaq period (1321–1412) Muhammad bin Tughlaq (1325–51) used to present robes of honour twice a year, with a lot of ceremonies and symbolic action. Every year, whenever he went to the palace for the first time in the month of August, his visit was celebrated with great gaiety, gifts, and entertainment.[52] Even though he was a free thinker, because he was under the influence of *Sad* (the Iranian logician) and Ubaid (the great literary figure), he knew that politics could not exist without the ceremonial and could not merely be based on rational principles devoid of ceremonial and symbolic connotations.[53] The city of Delhi was decorated before the entrance of his royal retinue, cupolas were erected, streets were embellished with coloured and picturesque pieces of cloth, and drums were beaten in honour of the emperor. As soon as the royal parasol entered the city, gold was showered in the lanes and streets along with handfuls of gold and silver *tankas*.[54] Ibn Batutah states:

> It is the custom of the ruler (i.e., Sultan Muhammad bin Tughlaq) of India to send to every *amir* in command of city and to the principal officers of his troops two robes of honour every year, a winter robe and a summer robe. When the robes arrive the *amir* and the troops go out to receive them, and on reaching the person who has brought them they alight from their horses and each one takes his robe, lays it on his shoulder, and does homage in the direction of Sultan.[55]

Presenting of robes was not only limited to official ceremonies, but Muhammad bin Tughlaq sought to use them in larger regions in which the Delhi Sultanate was located. Giving these robes reinforced obligations and allegiance between the giver and receiver. In *Rehla* of Ibn Batutah, there are frequent references to the robes of honour given by Mohammad bin Tughlaq. According to Stewart Gordon:

> Such visible gradation of robes of honour opened the possibility of disparities between rank and robe. A ruler could subvert the expectations of nobility. The Sultan, for example, could signal to the whole court a rapidly rising favourite by the grant of a robe above the recipient's current rank. Displeasure might mean a meagre, less adorned robe. Throughout the favour of ruler could cross-cut the nobility's expectations of robing the ceremony and subvert bureaucratic rankings and postings.'[56]

It also bound together local scattered groups and made them see their nobles as an expansion of common political force through symbols and ceremonies conducted during such occasions. The Sultan's ceremonial tastes and the vast entourage was a great drain of public money. Hussain argues:

> To the most lavish generosity he (Sultan Muhammad Tughlaq) united revolting and indiscriminate cruelty, to scrupulous observance of the ritual and ceremonials prescribed by Islamic law an utter disregard of that law in all public affairs, to debasing and superstitious veneration for

all whose descent or piety commanded respect, and ferocity which when roused respected neither the blood of prophet nor personal sanctity.[57]

Muhammad bin Tughlaq also conceived the notion of *swargdawari* (heaven's gate) according to which no king could legitimately exercise his authority unless he was commissioned by God's vice-regent on earth, the Caliph and commander of the faithful, and set himself diligently to inquire who the Caliph was and where he was found.[58] When he ascertained from travellers that there still existed a Caliph in Egypt, a puppet of the house of Abbas, who claimed that dignity, he sent a petition along with very costly gifts. After three years, when two messengers of Ghiyas-ud-din Mahmud, the descendent of Caliph al-Mustansir, arrived in Delhi to finalize the details of their master's visit, they were given a warm welcome. The Sultan gave five thousand *tankas* to them and also thirty thousand *tankas* for Ghiyas-ud-din himself.[59]

When, ultimately, Ghiyas ud-din arrived, the leading ecclesiastics and theologians were sent as far as Sirsa (in present day Haryana) to meet him. The Sultan also went to Masudabad in Bahadurgarh (in Haryana) to meet him. After the ceremonial exchange of gifts, he held the royal umbrella over the heads of both Ghiyas-ud-din and Caliph al-Mustansir. The Caliph received extraordinary privileges at the court of the Sultan and this profusion of the Sultan's liberality to him is not to be reconciled with sanity at a time when many people were suffering to barely sustain themselves. The vessels in his palace were of gold and silver, and on the first occasion, Caliph al-Mustansir was gifted 400,000 *tankas*. He was also supplied with male and female servants and slaves. He was also allowed a daily sum of 300 *tankas*, though much of the food consumed by him and his household came from the royal kitchen. He received in free the whole of Sultan Alauddin Khalji's city Siri. He was also appointed to govern the eastern district of the province of Delhi. As if it was not enough, he was also offered thirty mules with trappings of gold, and whenever he visited the court, he was entitled to receive the carpet on which the Sultan sat. Even after his death, charitable institutions were established. Such practices were adopted by nobles as well as those who acquired large incomes.[60]

The organization of royal amusement ceremonies such as *shikar* (royal hunt) was another important means of defining the state's power. Shams Siraj Afif informs us that when Sultan Firuz Shah Tughlaq (1351–88) used to go out for a chase, a big procession was formed. Forty to fifty special standards and two specially designed emblems adorned with peacock feathers accompanied him. The emblems were carried in front of the Sultan on both sides. Just before them were four trained wild animals and birds of prey to the right and left of the Sultan respectively. A vast number of other animals, namely cheetahs, panthers, lynxes, hounds, eagles, and falcons with their keepers on horseback, followed the Sultan.[61] 10,000 falconers were also maintained during Muhammad Tughlaq's time, who rode on horseback and carried birds trained for hawking, and 300 beaters went in front and put up the game.

Besides these, 3,000 dealers in articles required for hawking accompanied him when he was on a hunting expedition.[62] Ibn Batutah also informs us that a number of nobles used to go with the Sultan to chase with their tent and canopies and a big crowd of porters and attendants. It lasted for seventeen to eighteen days at a stretch.[63]

Such meticulously organized processions described by Afif and Ibn Batutah show us how widespread the state's influence was through such ceremonies. The royal caravans and the cavalcades passed through at night with hundreds of men and animals to magnify the splendour of royal retinue through medieval rural India. Nobles carrying the regalia following the Sultan attracted crowds of astonished peasants who were not only material creatures but were also part of the process of symbol production. Incidentally, the vast population in rural areas was ruled by traditional power holders who were never encountered directly by large public, except in highly symbolic representations when, for instance, they accompanied the sultan during his hunting expeditions.

It was through these symbols that people used to give meaning to their lives and a holistic understanding of political allegiances and political action hinged on this fact. Since the sultans of Delhi and the nobles lived in a society that extended well beyond their direct observation, the royal ceremonies and symbols such as these always helped them relate themselves to a larger political universe or entity. Without tracing much historical record from medieval literature, it is difficult to visualize the reality of the dynamics of power politics and the forces that were transformed and disguised as tools of legitimation. However, on the basis of whatever evidence I have gone through, I would like to submit that apart from their other relevance, the royal ceremonies and symbols also provided a camouflage to the sultans for their political ambition.

NOTES

1. Michael Walzer, 'On the Role of Symbolism in Political Thought', *Political Science Quarterly*, no. 82, June 1967, p. 194.
2. Different ceremonies and symbols assume significance in different contexts. They help to establish order out of chaos at societal level. See for details D.N. Mann, 'Symbolism in Ritual Context', in *Handbook of Social and Cultural Anthropology*, ed. John J. Honigmann, Chicago: Rand McNally, 1973, pp. 579–612.
3. Minhaj-i-Siraj, *Tabaqat-i-Nasiri*, tr. H.M. Elliot and John Dowson under the title, *The History of India as Told by its Own Historians*, in 8 vols, London: Trübner, 1867–77, vol. 2, pp. 300–1 (henceforth Elliot and Dowson). Ishwar Topa says: 'It becomes clear on the basis of historical data that Qutbshahi suzerainty was not recognised on all hands, though he was proclaimed as a king. His political status was halfway home between kingship and dictatorship. This is attested by the political happening after his death. The colossal failure of the supporters of his son Aram Shah is a signal proof of a partial recognition of Qutbuddin's kingship.' See Ishwar Topa, *Politics in Pre-Mughal Times*, Delhi: Idara-i Adabiyat-i Delli, 1938; repr., 1976, p. 53.
4. For details, see Dan Sperber, *Rethinking Symbolism*, tr. Alice L. Morton, Cambridge Studies in Anthropology, Cambridge: Cambridge University Press, 1975; and Marshall Sahlins, *Historical Metaphors and Mythical Realities: Structure in the Early History of*

the Sandwich Island Kingdoms, Ann Arbor: University of Michigan Press, 1981. See also David Kertzer, *Ritual, Politics, and Power*, New Haven: Yale University Press, 1988, pp. 5–14. Also B.M. Singer, 'Emblems of Identity: A Semiotic Exploration' in *On Symbols in Anthropology: Essays in Honor of Henry Hoijer, 1980*, ed. Jacques Maquet, Malibu: Undena, 1982, pp. 73–132.

5. Hassan Nizami, *Taj-ul-Maasir*, in Elliot and Dawson, vol. 2, pp. 222 and 236.
6. See Clive S. Kessler, *Islam and Politics in Malay State*, Ithaca: Cornell University Press, 1978, pp. 244–5.
7. See David Cannadine and Simon Price, eds., *The Rituals of Royalty: Power and Ceremonial in Traditional Societies*, Cambridge: Cambridge University Press, 1987; and H.L. Nieburg, *Culture Storm: Politics and Ritual Order*, New York: St. Martin's, 1973, p. 54.
8. Irfan Habib, 'Formation of Sultanate Ruling Class of the Thirteenth Century', in *Medieval India I: Researches in the History of India, 1200–1750*, ed. Habib, Delhi: Oxford University Press, 1992.
9. Abu Hamid Al-Ghazali, *Ihya-ulum-ul Din*, vol. 2, p. 124. Extract translated in *Islamic Society and the West*, ed. H.A.R. Gibb and H. Bowen, 1950; repr., London: Oxford University Press, 1960, p. 31.
10. Ibid., p. 31.
11. Minhaj-i-Siraj, *Tabaqat-i-Nasiri*, ed. Nasu Lees, Khadim Hussain and Abdul Hai, Calcutta: Bibliotheca Indica, 1864, pp. 654–5.
12. K.M. Ashraf, *Life and Conditions of the People of Hindustan*, 2nd edn., Delhi: Munshiram Manoharlal, 1969, pp. 65–70.
13. Topa, *Politics in Pre-Mughal Times*, pp. 67–8.
14. Even as *Naib-i-Mamlikat*, Balban used to have the insignia of royalty. Zia-ud-din Barani, *Tarikh-i-Firuz Shahi*, ed. Syed Ahmad Khan, W.N. Less and Kabiruddin, Calcutta: Bibliotheca Indica, 1862, p. 23; also Amir Khusrau, *Qiran-us-Sadain*, ed. Muhammed Faizullah and Mirza Sher Ali Beg, Lucknow: Newal Kishor, 1845, p. 18.
15. Minhaj, *Tabaqat*, pp. 317–19. See also Yusuf Husain, *Indo-Muslim Polity (Turko-Afghan Period)*, Shimla: Indian Institute of Advanced Study, 1971, p. 84.
16. Barani, *Firuz Shahi*, 1862, p. 102; E.G. Browne, tr., *Chahar Maqala: ('Four Discourses') of Nizami-i-Arudi of Samarqand, Followed by an Abridged Translation of Mirza Muhammad's Notes to the Persian Text*, London: Luzac, 1921, p. 22. See also Minhaj, *Tabaqat*, pp. 900–10.
17. Lance W. Bennett, 'Myth, Ritual and Political Control', *Journal of Communication*, vol. 30, no. 4, 1980, p. 168.
18. Minhaj, *Tabaqat*, pp. 317–19; see also Barani, *Firuz Shahi*, pp. 30–4.

19. Ashraf, *Life and Conditions*, pp. 30–5.
20. Ibid.
21. Ibid., p. 31. The public audience of Sultan Balban and some envoys and Hindu vassals who were conducted to the throne for the first time for presentation trembled and fainted in the presence of the Sultan. The reports of these pageants had a salutary moral effect on discontented elements in the kingdom. Ibn Battuta, *Kitab-ur-Rahla of Ibn Battuta*, vol. 2, Cairo, 1870, p. 70. See also Ashraf, *Life and Conditions*, pp. 65–6.
22. Husain, *Indo-Muslim Polity*, pp. 83–106.
23. Topa, *Politics in Pre-Mughal Times*, pp. 64–5.
24. Barani, *Firuz Shahi*, 1862, p. 34.
25. Husain, *Indo-Muslim Polity*, p. 119.
26. B.A. Saletore, *Ancient Indian Political Thought and Institutions*, Bombay: Asia Publishing, 1963, chapter 2.
27. K.A. Nizami, *Some Aspects of Religion and Politics in 13th Century India*, Aligarh: Aligarh Muslim University, 1961; repr., Delhi: Idarah-i-Adabiyat-i-Delli, 1978, pp. 104–5.
28. Ibid.
29. Barani, *Firuz Shahi* (Elliot and Dowson), vol. 3, pp. 100–1.
30. Minhaj, *Tabaqat*, (Bib Indica), pp. 317–19.
31. Husain, *Indo-Muslim Polity*, pp. 91–9.
32. Machiavelli (quoted in) Edward Muir, *Civic Ritual in Renaissance Venice*, Princeton: Princeton University Press, 1998, pp. 74–5.
33. Barani, *Firuz Shahi*, 1862, pp. 137–9.
34. Topa, *Politics in Pre-Mughal Times*, p. 119.
35. Barani, *Firuzshahi*, 1862, pp. 136–41.
36. Ibid.
37. Ibid. see also Topa, *Politics in Pre-Mughal Times*, pp. 103–4.
38. Barani, *Firuz Shahi*, 1862, pp. 141–2.
39. Ibid.
40. Ibid., pp. 160–1. See also Topa, *Politics in Pre-Mughal Times*, pp. 130–3.
41. Barani, *Firuz Shahi*, 1862, p. 161.
42. Ibid.
43. Husain, *Indo-Muslim Polity*, pp. 119–40.
44. Ibid.
45. Ibid., p. 158. See also Ashraf, *Life and Conditions*, p. 39.
46. Ashraf, *Life and Conditions*, pp. 38–9.
47. Barani, *Firuz Shahi*, 1862, pp. 186–7.
48. Ashraf, *Life and Conditions*, p. 141.
49. Wolseley Haig, ed. *The Cambridge History of India*, vol. 3, Cambridge: Cambridge University Press, 1987, p. 114.
50. Barani, *Firuz Shahi*, 1862, p. 161.

51. Ibid., p. 166.
52. Ibid.
53. Ibid.
54. Ibid., 1862, p. 428.
55. Ibn Battuta, *Safar Nama*, tr. H.A.R. Gibb, *The Travels of Ibn Battuta, A.D. 1325–1354*, Cambridge: Hakluyt Society, University Press, 1958, p. 731.
56. Stewart Gordon, 'Introduction: Ibn Batuta and a Region of Robing', *Robes of Honour: Khil'at in Pre-Colonial and Colonial India*, Delhi: Oxford University Press, 2003, p. 12.
57. Husain, *Indo-Muslim Polity*, p. 136.
58. Ibid. See also Haig, ed., *Cambridge History of India*, p. 158.
59. Ibid. For details see Mahdi Husain, *Tughlaq Dynasty*; repr., Delhi: S. Chand, 1976.
60. Shams Siraj Afif, *Tarikh-i-Firuzshahi*, ed. Vilayat Husain, Calcutta: Bibliotheca Indica, 1888–91, pp. 178–9.
61. Ibid. See also Ashraf, *Life and Conditions*, p. 65.
62. Ashraf, *Life and Conditions*, p. 226, note 4.
63. Ibid.

CHAPTER 4

Medieval Indian Town as a Clue to State's Perception of Territoriality

> The first man who, having enclosed a piece of ground, bethought himself of saying 'This is mine', and found people simple enough to believe him, was the real founder of civil society. From how many crimes, wars and murders, from how many horrors and misfortunes, might not any one have saved mankind, by pulling up the stakes and filling up the ditches and crying to his fellows, 'Beware of listening to this impostor; you are undone if you once forget that the fruits of the earth belong to us all and the earth itself to nobody.'[1]
>
> —JEAN JACQUES ROUSSEAU

THE CONCEPT OF territoriality is as old and ubiquitous as society itself because space has always been perceived with varied intensions at different levels from very early times. This variation in territorial perception stems from the very definition of territoriality. Some people define territoriality in terms of frequent and regular use of an area, while others regard the strict overlapping and exclusive use of place as an important element of territoriality. At the core of territoriality is home, but the perceptions about the organization of space vary in scale from small objects, homes, villages, towns, cities to larger geographical areas, the personalization of which manifests in occupation, control, protection, defence, conditioning, organization, and reorganization by individuals, groups, and institutions. When we look at these perceptions of territoriality, it appears that, at each level, the organization of space defines the relationship between people and things in specific contexts of a set of practices. Therefore, what territoriality means to people depends on how they occupy it or how they interact within or through a space.

In medieval Indian society, among other agencies, the state was always concerned with the territoriality of human activity because the state perceived territoriality not only to control people and material resources, but also to construct the popular assumptions about its political power. In order to construct these assumptions, the meanings were never inherent in the spatial order, but were always invented or introduced by the medieval Indian state through various agencies which manufactured the state's claims to legitimacy by organization and reorganization of space to correspond to the interests of the state. As a result, the medieval Indian state emerged as the main actor in defining the location of cities and towns and the nature of social, economic, and political life in them. But the analysis of this territorial perception of the medieval Indian state as a reflection of the social category presents a number of problems, some of which are: Why and how does the state encode meaning into its territorial perception?How does the state's territorial perception relate itself to social relations and structures? When and how does the state's perception of territoriality come to have a meaning and how is this meaning maintained through a socio-spatial perception?

All these problems point to the fact that any discussion of territoriality in relation to the medieval Indian state would be incomplete without some indication of how the organization of space was linked to the ordering of the medieval Indian social experience, where the ideological and the material are joined together in the notion of a boundary constituted through the ways in which people perceived, controlled, built, and classified their social and natural worlds.

Generally, how people assigned themselves the privileges of both access and use of a space, and the way they demarcated and defended it, characterized their spatial perception. This whole issue is complex because neither all territorial perceptions are identical, nor are the meanings given to these varied perceptions of territoriality fixed and immutable; they are, instead, differently invoked in different contexts. Therefore, the meanings attached to territoriality are always expressed by virtue of their relationship with the total medieval Indian spatial order.[2]

Andrew Sayer argues, 'Space, particularly in the sense of territory, does not just exist outside or prior to society, but something produced by society.'[3]However, the purpose of this chapter is not to build a broad topical base on the concept of territoriality in medieval India in general, but to put together various pieces of information to understand how the medieval Indian state used cities and towns to express its territorial perception, both implicit and explicit, to achieve its political goals.

The territorial perception of the medieval Indian state was based on articulating political relations across different territorial scales and, in this process, the topographical model of medieval Indian towns/cities provided a space in which the structure of the medieval Indian urban society and the preponderance of the state in the economic and social life of the cities created a configuration of political actions through which the medieval Indian state spread its tentacles.

From the very beginning, when the medieval Indian State wanted to furnish itself with the material and ideological means for its existence and for the existence of various social actors, through whom it exercised its political power and authority, cities and towns turned out to be the most convenient cogs for the establishment and penetration of its authority. In this regard, an appropriate characterization of the medieval Indian city is provided by K.M. Ashraf. He says:

> An average city of contemporary Hindustan may be described somewhat as follows. It was situated on the bank of river or on the converging points of many trade routes, usually on a high level than the surrounding country, for reasons of defence and security. A high massive wall ran round the city, intercepted by gates which were heavily guarded day and night under the direct supervision of a special officer known as 'kotwal'. On entering the city enclosure, the principal mosque or a temple usually struck the visitor

by its unusual height and on conspicuous sight; the principal mosque was within the measurable distance of every part of the city and was big enough to accommodate a very large gathering of men on Fridays and on other occasions for public prayers. Big reservoirs were laid within and very nearer the city for supply of water especially in case of siege or scarcity of rain. These aqueducts were particularly important for hilly fortresses. Two main roads running at right angles intersected in the middle and were connected with the main gates of the outer wall. On the both sides of these main roads where the four wings of the city bazaar with rows of shops facing each other. These wings of bazaar were occupied by special classes of tradesmen and guilds of craftsmen. For their own amusement and comfort, monarchs sometimes built bazaars inside and outside of their palaces. Bridges sometimes added to the charms of a city.[4]

This characterisation of the medieval Indian city points to some specificities which reflect the personalization and control of access to space that was concerned with establishing distinctiveness of the overall environment that also helped small craftsmen to enlarge their opportunities.[5] The regulation of the internal environment and the protection from external threats by the state not only illustrates the medieval Indian state as a physical entity but also as a bounded container for a particular portion of the earth and as the chief custodian of overall social order. Be it the medieval cities of Delhi, Agra, Lahore, or medieval Indian towns like Patna, Khairabad, Daryabad, Lucknow, Samana, Sehwan, Kabul, Kandahar, Thatta, Bhakkar, Multan, Peshawar, Sirhind, Mathura, Dholpur, Gwalior, Burhanpur, Ajmer, Meertha, Sidhpur, Patan, Naharwala, Ahmadabad, Benaras, Monghyar, Bhaghalpur, Qasimbazar Hugli, Balasore, Bahraich, Ujjan, Dhar, Moradabad, Bareilly, Gulbarga, Golconda, Daulatabad, and other urban areas, the medieval Indian state did identify meaningful boundaries in the spatial and social environment while visualizing the territoriality in the physicality of these cities and towns. Physical walls and boundaries of these cities and towns were always vivid symbols of political and economic factors and had close relationship with the communities living there.[6]

The objective world was replaced by similar, subjectively perceived images and the organization of various cities and towns was also based on their images. The actions of various individuals pursuing their individually and collectively defined interests were at once shaped by the state in the patronization and promotion of these cities. This was how the medieval Indian state reproduced the basic principles of organization of urban society. As a result, structural relations were also routinely socially produced and reproduced in the course of everyday life. Of particular importance was the routine acceptance of the legitimacy of the Karkhandars, Kotwals, Amirs, Wazirs, Diwans, by merchants, artisans, and people working in various medieval Indian cities as a normal feature of such society, for in this way was grounded the reproduction of social relations within the specific space of medieval Indian cities. The attachment of people of various professions was grounded in routine—not only for working in a particular place but also for learning and living there.

This also reflected the people's reliance on these cities as a means of introduction to new sources of employment, should the traditional relations disappear. Here, we cannot ignore the useful information provided by Mohammad Habib on this aspect which reads:

> By the end of the (thirteenth) century all kinds of trained city artisans could be found in enormous number and their ranks were swelled by even a larger number of unskilled *hammals*, *paiks* and the like. As a result unemployment became acute and unemployment led to distress and distress to rebellion. The government on the one hand tried to find remedies for unemployment, such as useless public works like enormous columns near Qutubminar or when unable to do it met rebellion and discontent with sword. This spectra of unemployment is one of the chief features of regime of Khaljis (1290–1320) and the Tughlaqs (1320–1357).[7]

Here, it becomes clear that it was the promotion of the city that helped the medieval Indian state to lay claims to authority by containing the people's aspirations through intervention in the space but, at times, when the space did not correspond to the state's needs, it constrained the will of the subjects and gave rise to coercion. The establishment of a relationship of these medieval cities and towns with the elements of spatial structuring was conceptualized on the basis of distance and directional referents. The process that transformed Quila Rai Pithora (Prithiviraj Chauhan's Delhi) to the capital city of Shahjahanabad (Shah Jahan's Delhi) or Agra, and the Pargana headquarters from a small commercial town to the imperial city of Patna or any other medieval metropolis, at the hands of various rulers, represents all these features. The medieval Indian state took upon itself the power to direct locational choices of the cities, bestowed politico-administrative status on them and, thereby, developed an atmosphere to counter the potential threats to its legitimacy from surrounding areas. The case of Agra is an important and fascinating example in this context.

Nimatullah writes:

> It had for a long time occurred to the Sultan (Sikandar Lodhi) to found a town on the bank of Jammuna, which was to be the residence of the Sultan and the headquarters of the army and to serve to keep the rebels of that quarter in awe, and deprive them of further opportunity of growing refractory, for frequently the jagirdars and government servants and the peasantry in general in Sarkar Bayana had complained of violence to which they were subject. With this view he commissioned in year A.H. 911 (i.e. A.D. 1505) some judicious and intelligent men to explore the banks of the river, and report upon any locality which they might consider the most eligible. Accordingly, the exploring party left Delhi in boats and, as they proceeded, examined carefully both sides of the river i.e. Jammuna until they arrived at the spot where Agra now stands and having approved of it communicated their selection to the Sultan. Upon this he left Delhi and marched to Mathura, where he took boat, amusing himself by the way with various kinds sport. When he approached the site indicated, he observed two elevated spots which seemed suitable for building and inquired of Mihtar Mulla Khan, who was called 'Naik' and commanded the royal barrage, which of those two mounds appeared to him the most suitable.' He replied, "That which is Agra or in advance, is preferable one". The Sultan smiled and said, "The name of the city then shall be called Agra." He then repeated the ...fatiha.... and in an auspicious movement issued orders for founding the city, when the portion of Mauza Pashi and Moza poya pargana Duli Sarkar Bayani were occupied for the purpose; and the pargana of Agra was hence forward added to the fifty two parganas which comprised the Sarkar of Bayana. From that period this city continued to advance in population and became the seat of the government of Sultan of Hind.[8]

Ibrahim Lodhi, Babur, Humayun, and Sher Shah also spared no efforts in building this city and connected it with rest of India with a good network of roads. However, it was finally during the reign of Akbar that a systematic layout of Agra was executed to correspond to the interest of the state.[9]

The state's perception of organizing the spatial landscape of cities like Delhi, Agra, and Lahore had a lot to do with how different people could be constituted differently in them. The plan and layout of homes and their density in most medieval Indian cities gave favourable treatment to some while constraining the social existence of others. There is plenty of evidence to argue that these medieval cities were divided into separate quarters for various social classes. The residences of the poor in the city of Agra have been defined by Palesart as 'home of stark want and dwelling places of bitter woe'.[10]In medieval Indian cities, the groups rendering menial services were usually settled close to city walls, and when the cities expanded they were even pushed outside the wall. Abul Fazl says, 'He (Kotwal) should allot separate quarters to butchers, hunters of animals, washers of dead and sweepers.'[11] The localities of the ordinary people were generally dirty with no proper arrangements for water, unorganized into narrow and small lanes. According to K.M. Ashraf:

> The city was divided into separate quarters for various social groups. In keeping with the ideas of the day, some classes of people, for instance, scavengers, leather dressers and the poorest beggars and wretches were segregated from rest of the population, and were made to live on the outskirts of the towns. The rest of the population divided itself into religious, racial, and even occupational groups. Muslims and Hindus had separate quarters. Nobles and common people lived in two distinct parts of the city.[12]

This evidence points to the socio-spatial engineering through which social relations were composed and contextualized by the medieval Indian state. It is true that this social segregation would have perhaps reduced stressful social contacts, but the very physical structuring of the space and the opportunities associated with it influenced social behaviour which had a greater political significance and social consequences, because spatially structured dominance and subordination were among the essential instruments of the medieval Indian state for maintenance of social order. The medieval Indian state felt that there was an unending cycle of inter-relationships between politics and space on one hand, and people occupying that space on the other. To understand the laws of medieval political India, the state needed to know the laws of physical India, the laws that governed men and unfortunately subordinated women. These laws should not be seen in isolation, but as ancillary to the higher ends of religion and morality together with space. This also helped to generate a form of social differentiation and different access to power. Such a pattern of spatial organization represented and reproduced social relations—the relations of likeness that grew between social distinctions and boundaries that formed the basic link between the state's perception of space and the social and physical life of the city in medieval India. Therefore, the expression of the state's spatial perception has also to be sought in the processes permeating the medieval Indian state and the medieval city life, the former expressing its way through the latter.[13]

The medieval official world of kotwals, *iqtadars*, mansabdars, *nadims*, *wazirs*, *amirs*, sarjandars, *dabirs*, *ulema*, and other officials was located in cities to reflect the presence of the government, with a purpose to legitimize the order of the state before the society as if it was rationally given. They also prescribed measures geared towards the protection of such rationality. Interestingly, the dominant rational model was the medieval Indian state's existence. Therefore, the whole social, physical, and natural environment was rethought in a way that the state's spatial perception rested on the wilful consent of these individuals, and a society of such individuals became the objective of the medieval Indian state itself.

The official world of the medieval Indian state was particularly a powerful social entity. Even though the state at times had opportunities for some nobles, it does not seem to have affected their social position at large. The expectations of the medieval Indian state varied over time and space. As social changes took place, the pressures for the state's institutional change also led to the pressure for spatial change. These pressures were opposed by groups which benefited from the status quo and would risk losing power if a change occurred. The hierarchically established interdependence and solidarity of these officials living in the cities enabled them to ensure the protection and perpetuation of such a state at various levels, but all of them had their basis in the space.

In popular perception, the cities were the rich people's domain. The term 'shahar' (city), its amenities, its association with markets, merchants, administrators, religious and political elite, and their activities drew their identity from city life. These cities were well demarcated for residential and commercial purposes. The residences of the rich in Agra have been described as built entirely of bricks or stone and spacious, enclosed with a high wall for reasons of privilege and security. Ashraf writes:

> The royal residences occupied a conspicuous site, an elevated spot if possible, it was generally built by the side of a river so that the beauty of the building was enhanced by the stream which reflected it by day and threw its shadows by night. It is difficult to convey in words what one feels on a visit to the royal buildings of Agra and Delhi or Lahore and Mandu. Beautiful gardens and other open spaces surrounded the palace. The mansions of nobility were big buildings with spacious apartments. There were drawing rooms, baths sometimes, water tanks, a spacious courtyard and even a library.[14]

These spaces were indicative of the roles that their occupants played within the established socio-spatial hierarchy and also defined their jurisdictional responsibilities so that the state's authority could be effectively exercised. It was through the state's spatial intervention that the dominant ones demonstrated their personal superiority and the subjected ones bent, accommodated, assimilated, and finally took cognizance of the ways and actions which created the overall social and political patterns.

Although the construction of *baradarees*, forts, roads, temples, mosques tombs, bazaars, *sarais*, *karkhanas*, *madrasas*, and separate residential complexes for the royalty and the nobility anticipated the basis for social interaction within them, the dominant groups, by separating their quarters, protected themselves from what they perceived to be negative influences or associations. They interacted among themselves through increased propinquity, friendships, and marriages, which led to the sharing of common space, reinforcing social togetherness. This is how the expression of the state's spatial perception in the physical landscaping of medieval Indian cities influenced the access to various opportunities. Moreover, the creation of such a self-segregated community that pointedly excluded and distanced people of lower social standing created an atmosphere that was conducive to the perpetuation of social dominance.[15]

Space was delimited or bounded by the state that had effective control over it and provided both security and opportunity for those who lived within its limits. On the one hand, it reflected an inward-looking ideal with isolated space, self-sufficiency, and emphasis on security; on the other hand, there was also an outward perspective with the participation of various communities that came from outside in these cities for trade, pilgrimage, or employment. How space was used and the landscape perceived also has powerful symbolic links to the people's spatial identity. Hamida Khatun Naqvi remarks:

> On the surface the setting up of a military post, than as with an imperial deputy, appears to be a simple matter. Even when a new town for the purpose was to be founded the procedure was equally uncomplicated. Forty Nimazis, (i.e. worshippers) a central mosque and central bazaar was all that, according to Muslim legalists, was needed to find a town. Given this nucleus for a town, it would entice villagers from its vicinity—people with or without skill moved to town to provide its core inhabitants with water, housing, personal services and other goods and services.[16]

By meticulously rearing social relations through layouts of cities and towns, the state could open up a whole range of opportunities by substantially transforming the prospects of the urban elite whose existence was linked to that of the medieval Indian state. In such a situation, space assumed a real, social form that developed to promote a quasi-hegemonic lifestyle and caused ample class schisms in the medieval Indian societal format.[17]

The other focal point of medieval Indian cities was the market network through which the exchange of various goods took place and the cities were able to dominate the areas around them. The growth of commerce also led to the development of political activities in the cities. As a result, cities became the centres of political control that attempted to steer the medieval Indian economy in a direction beneficial to their territory. As central points of material life, they also aided the medieval state's centralization process. The various markets in medieval Indian cities promoted avenues of occupational and social mobility, and gave people shared experiences and social expectations that both explained and justified the vicissitudes of life and the functioning of the state. Given the opportunities and the important symbolic qualities of medieval cities, there was a significant stimulus to consumption and to the acquisition of possessions. Just as the city was central to the notions of security and ownership, so one could see this spilled over into the state's functioning.[18]

The development of market in these cities also led to the growth of industrial production, expansion of social differentiation and exploitation, and creation of wage-earning occupations. The existence of various industries in medieval Indian cities is testimony to this fact. Sujan Rai says, 'Its (Agra's) excellent artisans of every art and work men of every profession are skilled in their respective trade, gold and silver embroidery on turbans and other kinds of cloth is very nicely done [*sic*].'[19] This is also acknowledged by Emperor Jahangir (1556–1628). He says, 'Inhabitants of Agra exert themselves in great acquirement of crafts.'[20] Gradually, these occupational groups came to recognize that they acquired their social positions by dint of their stay in towns and cities and they served the legitimacy of the state to promote an economy suitable to their needs.

The contingency and open-endedness was nowhere more apparent than in the execution of the state's territorial perception of the cities as centres of social production and social activity. Through the promotion of cities, the state sought to modify the local socio-economic environment in ways that made the cities more attractive for local and non-local merchants to invest in and created employment opportunities. Therefore, the dynamics of the socio-economic system can only be fully comprehended in the context of the territorial, for the possibility and the limitations of human actions were specifically constructed in circumstances peculiar to the space. As the network of medieval Indian cities grew into a system of spatially different units of organization, it took the form of an extraordinarily varied mosaic of socio-spatial relationships. The medieval Indian economy that incorporated this mosaic provided widened conceptions of historical social service which, according to Harbans Mukhia, originated in friction at all the multifarious joints in society, and each social stratum participated in it, however differential its contribution.[21]

The establishment of commercial centres in cities helped the state maintain its links with the outside world. This was of vital importance on two accounts. It was in the interest of the state to make the city an important commercial centre to strengthen its financial foundations. It also became—intentionally as well as unintentionally—a means of organizing and structuring the territories which would ultimately perpetuate the hegemony and authority of the state at various levels.

The spatial structure of the medieval Indian state was usually hierarchical with nested levels of authority, such as division of the country into regions, and regions into other big or small units like iqtas, sarkars, parganas, and subas. In each of these units, the state's interventions involved the erection of boundaries that did not exist before. As a result, the space became more confined and controllable.

The perception of the state produced a typology where it was defined in terms of the internal and the external. The former was concerned with the state's relations with the society—its social and economic activities that existed within its territory. The latter had to do with the state's relations with the outside world. The two relations of the external and the internal were treated separately by the state and its links with outer world were maintained through arts, architecture, craftsmanship, and through commercial life housed in cities. Interestingly, it was the same state that operated in both spheres looking inwards and outwards.

The other noteworthy feature of medieval Indian cities was that as commercial centres, they were not situated equally across the space, but were in particular locations. The prevalent mix of these was more or less effective in bending particular people's consciousness in certain direction rather than others. The more distinctive the mix, the greater was the likelihood that the people producing—and being produced by—the local mix of the medieval cities' institutions generated strong bonds as well as acute divisions. In certain cities, the mix of some institutions was so distinct that it produced a local economy and culture potent enough to bring a dignified reputation to the locality.

Additionally, with the economic growth of cities, the spatial requirements of social formation at the same time also changed the various locations, for local social structures became a source of new pressures on the character of the state, affecting the roles it played. Sometimes, the state's spatial perception underwent changes with the growth of cities because the cities were established under one set of spatiality and tended to remain in force even after their physical conditions had changed. The rationale for a particular set of boundaries and distribution of responsibilities vanished with the expansion and improvement of cities, but sometimes the boundaries and responsibilities survived intact, even if rendered inappropriate by their changed circumstances.

The spatial perception of the medieval Indian state can be examined at many levels in the growth of the cities, but at each level, the dominant element was the self-interest of the state. The state always intruded into many aspects of social and economic life. Therefore, the detail of each intrusion reflects the aims and beliefs of the relevant government in a particular place, at a particular time. The extent of each intrusion can generally be measured by taking into cognizance the spatial layouts of the cities.[22]

It did not matter to the state whether people's values in these cities were shaped by a special environment. To help the people apply those values and to understand the relations between those values and everyday life, the medieval Indian state did not assume that the administrative and economic aspects were the only bases for linking people with territory. Religion and culture were equally operative in perceiving the space at various levels in the growth of medieval cities. The construction of domed mosques and other religious establishments silently brought religious and cosmological elements into the city's life. For the public, religious values were carried out directly into the social and spatial design of their dwellings. Through temples, mosques, or *khanqas*, a new conception of the universe was grown parallel to various economic and social changes. Religious and cosmological concepts always influenced the nature of medieval cities and its inhabitants.

Thus, medieval Indian cities were not independent collectives, but essential units in the functioning of a larger society in which the state's spatial perception found expression through a spatial intervention. The state's relationship with the cities stood as a key component in the process of its existence.

NOTES

1. Jean Jacques Rousseau, *Discourse on the Origin and Foundation of Inequality among Mankind*, New York: P.F. Collier, 1976, pp. 211–21. Proto-hominids (precursors to *Homo sapiens*) are said to have protected and defended their territories from intruders, even though they were not so well marked. See Irwin Altman and Martin Chemers, *Culture and Environment*, Cambridge: Cambridge University Press, 1984, pp. 120–50. For details see also C.F. Hockett

and R. Ascher, 'The Human Revolution', *Current Anthropology*, no. 5, 1965, pp. 165–8; I. Mamalbery, *Human Territories*, Amsterdam: John Benjamins, 1977, pp. 47–54. Whether or not one wishes to argue for presence or absence of space from a particular period of time, the fact remains that spatial behaviour has always been widespread not only among humans but even among animals. C.R. Carpenter, 'Territoriality: A Review of Concept and Problems', in *Behavior and Evolution*, ed. Anne Roe and George G. Simpson, New Haven: Yale University Press, 1958, pp. 224–50.

2. Vijay Lakshmi Labh, *Researches on the Economics of Delhi Sultanate: Collection of Some Challenging Historical concepts in Re-Interpretations*, Delhi: Abhijeet Publications, 2015, p. 28.
3. Andrew Sayer, 'The Difference that Space Makes', in *Social Relations and Spatial Structures*, ed. Derek Gregory and John Urry, London: Macmillan, 1985, p. 58.
4. K.M. Ashraf, *Life and Conditions of the People of Hindustan*, 2nd edn., Delhi: Munshiram Manoharlal, 1969, pp. 199–200.
5. Adam Smith also acknowledges the existence of such a phenomenon that certain kinds of small industries could not be operated anywhere but in great cities. He gives an example of a porter who cannot find work in a village or even in a small market town. Only in a relatively populous city can a worker specialize to such an extent that he can devote all his time to carrying bags for other people. Adam Smith, *An Inquiry into the Nature and Causes of the Wealth of Nations*, London: Strahan and Cadell, 1776; repr., New York: Scholars' Press, 1980, p. 26.
6. Alexander I. Tchitcherov, *India: Changing Economic Structure in the Sixteenth to Eighteenth Centuries: Outline History of Crafts and Trade*, Delhi: Manohar, 1998, pp. 109–10.
7. Mohammad Habib, *Politics and Society during the Early Medieval Period*, vol. 1 of *Collected Works of Professor Mohammad Habib*, ed. K.A. Nizami, 2 vols., Delhi: People's Publishing House, 1974, pp. 79–80.
8. Khawaja Nimatullah Harawi, *Makhzan-i-Afghana* (also known as *Tarikh-i-Khanjahan Lodi*), in *A History of India, as Told by Its Own Historians: The Muhammadan Period*, ed. and tr. H.M. Elliot and John Dowson, vol. 5, London: Trübner, 1867–77, pp. 98–9.
9. Ishwar Prakash Gupta, *Urban Glimpses of Mughal India: Agra, the Imperial Capital, 16th & 17th Centuries*, Delhi: Discovery, 1986, pp. 18–32.
10. W.H. Moreland and Pieter Geyl, eds. and trs., *Jahangir's India: The Remonstrantie of Francisco Palesart*, Cambridge: W. Heffer, 1925, p. 60.
11. Abul Fazl, *Ain-i-Akbari*, tr. and ed. Henry Blochmann and H.S.

Jarrett, 3 vols., 2nd edn., Calcutta: The Asiatic Society, 1927, vol. 2, p. 45.

12. Ashraf, *Life and Conditions*, p. 200.
13. Hermann Kulke, ed., *The State in India, 1000–1700: Themes in Indian History*, New York and Delhi: Oxford University Press, 1995, pp. 134–5.
14. Ashraf, *Life and Conditions*, p. 201.
15. Ibid.
16. Hameeda Khatoon Naqvi, *Urbanisation and Urban Centres under the Great Mughals, 1556–1707*, Simla: Indian Institute of Advanced Study, 1971, p. 5.
17. Gupta, *Urban Glimpses*, pp. 45–64.
18. Muhammad Umar, *Urban Culture in Northern India during the Eighteenth Century*, New Delhi: Munshiram Manoharlal, 2001, pp. 28–9.
19. Sujan Rai Bandari, *Khulasat-ul-Tawarikh*, tr. J.N. Sarkar, under the title *India of Aurangzib*, Calcutta: M.C. Sarkar & Sons, 1912, p. 23.
20. Nooruddin Jahangir, *Tuzuk-i-Jahangiri*, tr. Alexander Rogers, ed. Henry Beveridge, 2 vols., London: Royal Asiatic Society, 1909, vol. 1, p. 7.
21. Harbans Mukhia, 'Peasant Production in Medieval India', in *Feudalism and Non-European Societies*, ed. Harbans Mukhia and Terry J. Byres, London: Frank Cass, 1985, p. 232.
22. R.C. Majumdar, ed., *The History and Culture of the Indian People: The Delhi Sultanate*, 4th edn., 11 vols., Bombay: Bharatiya Vidya Bhavan, 1990, vol. 6, pp. 640–1.

CHAPTER 5

Assimilation during the Mughal Rule (1526–1740)

> As we enter this arena, a fascinating paradox stares at us: in some important ways the court and its culture stood in splendid isolation from the rest of society, though supported by it, somewhat like a film of oil on water; and in some very profound ways, the two merged with each other and became inseparable.[1]
>
> —HARBANS MUKHIA

THE MUGHAL RULE from Babur to Aurangzeb is a very important period in Indian history. It was during this period that many regional polities got incorporated into the colossal Mughal Empire. It also saw the growth of well-structured civil and military administrative institutions. Economic prosperity grew significantly. Art forms such as music, dance, painting, and sculpture flourished with the participation of all religious communities. However, the opposing forces of religious liberalism and orthodoxy continued to contend for supremacy. An important feature of the Mughal state was to hold a balance between them with appropriate policies and administrative measures. Whether it was Akbar's resistance to Muslim orthodoxy or Aurangzeb's tilt towards it, it must be noted that religion was an important reference point in Mughal polity.[2] Naturally, the see-saw between the two contending forces has left a deep imprint on popular Indian culture.

After the battle of Panipat in 1526, Babur assumed supreme authority and assigned the administration of his dominions in India to Mughal nobles, but they did not show much interest in Indian affairs except war and plunder.[3] Babur himself did not seem to like India very much. He wrote:

> Hindustan is a country of few claims. Its people have no good looks; of social intercourse, paying and receiving visits, there is none of genius and capacity, none of manners, none in handicraft work there is not form or symmetry, method or quality; there are no good horses, no good dogs, no grapes, no musk-melons or first rate fruits, no ice or cold water, no good bread or cooked food in their bazaars, no hot baths, no colleges, no candles, torches or candle sticks.[4]

The only Indian fruit that received some appreciation from Babur was the mango.

Against this background, it is legitimate to ask how a successful but reluctant warrior tried to establish a powerful empire that lasted more than two centuries. For one, the explanation lies in his great ambition and long cherished dream of a large empire. He wrote in his memoirs: 'As it was always in my heart to possess Hindustan and as those several countries had once been held by the Turks. I pictured them all my own and resolved to get them into my own hands peacefully or by force.'[5] In order to get his hands on Hindustan, Babur had to fight the Rajputs and the Afghans. While fighting the Rajputs, he portrayed himself as a Ghazi (Islamic soldier) and the war against them as a *jihad* (holy war). While fighting the Afghans, he posed as a champion of pure Islam by renouncing wine, his favourite drink, and by adopting other similar measures. To get the support of Muslim tradesmen, he remitted *tamgah* (transit dues) on their merchandise. Thus, Babur subordinated his personal preferences to the pursuit of his ambition of possessing vast territories. As most of his time was spent in waging wars, he did not pay much attention to policies of governance vis-à-vis his vast non-Muslim population.[6]

In recent times, Babur's name has figured prominently in connection with the controversy about a mosque in Ayodhya. It was called the Babri Masjid, on the basis of the following statement in *Babur Nama*: 'By the command of Emperor Babur, whose justice is an edifice reaching up to the very height of the heavens, the good hearted Mir Baqi built this alighting palace of angels. May this goodness last forever.'[7] The year of the construction of mosque becomes manifest in the saying, 'May this goodness last forever', for the Persian words carried numerical connotations. Although Babur mentions in his memoirs that he visited Ayodhya in 1528 and stayed there for a few days to settle the affairs of Oudh (Ayodhya), he does not mention anywhere the existence of a Ram Temple at Ayodhya or its demolition or the building of a mosque in its place. But can one conclude from this that no such event is connected with Babur's reign? Moreover, Babur's use of the Islamic notion of *jihad* for mobilizing his forces against the Rajputs in India had no theological intentions but purely political ones.[8]

Several historians and archaeologists have locked horns on the issue of the Babri Masjid. Some archaeologists suggest the possibility of a Buddhist place of worship under and around the Masjid, while others argue in favour of further excavations at the site to get at the truth of whether a temple existed at the site. But how to find the truth and sublimate the unpleasant memory of the mosque's demolition in the larger interests of national integration and political peace in the present circumstances? The following questions have to be addressed for the purpose. Leaving aside the controversial issues of Rama's birthplace, the existence of a Rama temple or a Buddhist vihara, let us ask: Why did Babur 'command' or permit Mir Baqi to construct a mosque at a holy pilgrim centre of the Hindus just two years after the victory at Panipat? Was he acting as a self-declared Ghazi or *jihadi* or as a deft practitioner of statecraft? Was he not trying to send a loud message to the large body of his Hindu subjects? Considering the ethos of the times, is it proper or possible to separate political decisions from their religious overtones and assert that the decision was purely political?

When it comes to Humayun, the second Mughal ruler, we do not have much information about his attitude towards his non-Muslim subjects. For one thing, he had to concentrate first on defending his throne from Afghan attacks and later in wresting back power from the Sur Sultans. For this purpose, he had to depend on the help of the Persians and the Rajputs. Harbans Mukhia says, 'Comparing Babur's and Abul Fazl's versions of battle of Kanuwa between Babur and Rana Sangram Singh makes an interesting exercise. If on the eve of battle and afterwards, Babur turns a fantastic Muslim in his narration, Abul Fazal, even as he remains very hostile to Rana, avoids any term suggestive of religious dogma.[9] After regaining the throne, Humayun did not have much time to make policies in his name.

A word about the Sur Sultans, particularly Sher Shah, needs to be mentioned here. K.R. Qanungo remarks: 'Sher Shah followed a policy of religious toleration towards Hindus.'[10] Even though he demolished Hindu temples at Jodhpur, he is considered tolerant towards Hindus, because he provided them with many jobs in civil and military administration. Ishwari Prasad states that Sher Shah's policy of religious toleration laid the foundation for Akbar's greatness.[11]

Akbar succeeded Humayun when he was in his teens and his trusted noble, Bairam Khan, managed the affairs of the state. As soon as he came of age, he removed Bairam Khan, for they developed differences of opinion. Akbar seems to have entertained the idea of building a strong and stable Mughal Empire. Therefore, he decided early in his rule that it was essential to win the confidence of all sections of the multi-religious and multi-cultural society of India. To establish a centralized rule and control the far flung empire, an institutional apparatus had to be set up.[12] This required the sprucing of the mansabdari system; and to maintain the hierarchy of mansabdars, an efficient agrarian base was needed. Akbar also realized that a strong army and a sound agrarian base were only half the task accomplished, and that a stable empire of his dreams could be built only on the foundation of goodwill of the people and not on coercion. He, therefore, worked consciously to gain wide public support to legitimize his rule. These attempts led him to distance himself from the Muslim orthodoxy. He perceived that the reason that a strong Muslim state could not be set up in Hindustan was that the orthodox *ulema* always put up obstacles in a bid to perpetuate their dominance, thereby alienating people of other religious groups. All these considerations were playing in his mind when he formulated his ideology of tolerance and liberalism. He was cognizant of the fact that it was not possible to lay a strong foundation for the Mughal Empire without the participation of non-Muslims, the majority of his people, in the processes of the state's functioning. Thus, it can be said that Akbar's liberalism towards non-Muslims stemmed from his political ambitions. The other important aspect which Akbar realized was the necessity of Indianizing the Mughals and acculturating or assimilating them in the Indian environment in which he was brought up.

It is interesting to note that Muslim historians like I.H. Qureshi, S.M. Ikram, S.M. Jaffar, and Aziz Ahmad describe Akbar as unorthodox and un-Islamic and condemn his ideology. Such criticism is not fair to his flair and vision. Akbar's pro-Hindu policies and his appeasement tactics had a much larger aim; he wanted all his subjects to be content and loyal as the recipients of equal justice. It was purely political expediency that was at the root of his liberalism. Otherwise, he had no grudge against the *ulema* on religious grounds. It was only that they were a powerful entity and had to be tackled as they stood in the path of his grand imperial design.

Within a few years of his accession, Akbar enacted a number of laws which reflected his policy of liberalism. In 1562, a *farman* was issued abolishing the custom of enslaving prisoners of war and allowing construction of new Hindu temples at Brindavan and Benares, and Jain temples at Satrujaya and Ujjain.[13] Old temples were also renovated at Kangra, Thaneswar, and Batala. He also gave permission to build churches at Agra, Lahore, and Cambay.[14] In 1563, he abolished the tax on Hindu pilgrims visiting their sacred places. In 1564, *jaziya*, the tax on non-Muslims, was abolished. A bureau for translating Hindu religious books into Persian was established. Akbar realized that the Rajputs were a powerful race and sought to obtain their cooperation by entering into matrimonial relations with them by offering them positions of power and prestige in his administration. In 1562, he married Jodhabai, the daughter of Raja Bhara Mal of Jaipur. In 1570, he married the princesses of Bikaner and Jaisalmer. He also awarded high offices to Hindus in his administration. *Ain-i-Akbari* mentions that among the 137 mansabdars of 1,000 rank under Akbar, fourteen were Hindus. Raja Bihar Mal and Raja Todar Mal were appointed finance ministers in 1572, Birbal was made a court noble, and Raja Man Singh and Raja Bhagwandas were taken in as commanders of the armed forces.[15]

Many steps taken by Akbar in furtherance of his policy of tolerance also reflect the spirit of Indianization of the Mughals, which Akbar consciously encouraged. Abdul Qadir Badauni tells us that to fulfil the wishes of his Hindu wives, Akbar did not hesitate to permit the keeping of pigs in the vicinity of the palace, because it was considered an act of worship to see the pigs every morning.[16]According to Hindu belief, pigs are one of the ten forms in which God incarnates himself. Akbar also allowed his Hindu queens to practise their religion freely and never interfered with their rituals like chanting Vedic hymns or making offerings to fire. Akbar introduced the practice of *jharokha darshan* or the viewing of the emperor every morning by the common people.[17]This was a Hindu practice and invited the ire of the *ulema* who considered it un-Islamic. Modern-day communal Muslim historians concurred with this line of argument and equated the practice to idol worship, which is thoroughly un-Islamic. Akbar also indulged in the un-Islamic practice of *tuladaan* (weighing himself) in gold and silver, which were later distributed among the poor.[18] Abul Fazl writes that Akbar had even started using the *tika* (vermillion mark) on his forehead, a Hindu custom as well as performing *suryanamaskar* (Sun worship).[19] Badauni tells us that Akbar celebrated Diwali, Dussehra, Rakshabandhan, Holi, and Shivratri with pomp and gaiety.[20] In fact, on Shivratri, he used to listen to lectures of *jogis*. Akbar prohibited cow slaughter and ordered abstinence from meat-eating for a hundred days in a year. All these measures not only brought Akbar closer to the Hindu population, but also secured the trust and loyalty of the powerful Rajputs.

Rana Pratap of Chittorgarh was the only Rajput ruler who refused to accept Mughal supremacy and continued his war-like activities against the Empire till his death in Haldighat in a fierce battle. The folk songs and ballads of Rajasthan have hailed the Rana as a staunch Hindu and an uncompromising opponent of alien Mughal/Muslim rule, although one of his principal commanders was a Muslim. There is also the view that the Rana was no more than an insolent Rajput with a swollen ego and deep hostility towards other Rajput tribes who had made peace with the Mughals. This view is, very likely, highly biased and does not find much support from history. Rana Pratap was, like Akbar, a ruler who dreamt of a strong empire for himself and his people. All his actions, be they an attack on fellow Rajput tribes or striking peace with the Mughals, are attempts to safeguard his interests. The time has come to take a balanced view of the events and the memories of the past. While Rana Pratap was, undoubtedly, a brave ruler with an independent mind and dogged determination, he could not understand the realities of political power in the country and, accordingly, chose the path of martyrdom. It will not be correct to describe his fight in terms of Hindu versus Muslim or Indian versus foreign. For, by then, Akbar the Mughal had not only self-consciously become Indian, but had also patronized several Hindu ways of life, albeit only for political purpose. This is how the historical memory of Rana's glorious resistance to Mughal expansion is sublimated.

It was not as if Akbar had nothing to do with other religions. He held discussions with Christian priests and his quest for religious enlightenment led him to propound a set of religious principles, hailed as *Din-i-Ilahi*. It is another matter that it had few takers, perhaps no more than 120 people. Akbar is also known to have participated in a number of feasts held by Muslims and Parsis. Muharram, mainly observed by Shia Muslims, was commemorated for a period of forty days. Islamic festivals such as Eid-ul-Fitr,

Eid-ul-Zuha, Shab-e-Baraat, and the Parsi festival of *Nauroz*, were also celebrated by the Emperor. It is also recorded that certain measures of Akbar were not in conformity with orthodox Islam.[21] People were allowed to wear flashy dresses while offering prayers, observing *roza* and performing Haj. I.A. Khan refers to Akbar's reply to a query sent by Murad from the Deccan, instructing him to admonish any person performing *namaz* and guide them to the path of reason.[22] There is also a report that new mosques were not to be built, nor could old ones be repaired. Such information certainly cast a shadow on the hitherto accepted image of Akbar. However, any view which brands Akbar as un-Islamic needs to be subjected to a thorough probe as Akbar's policies were purely motivated by political considerations. Along the way, these policies might have left behind a few disgruntled *ulema* who later labelled Akbar as un-Islamic.

Jahangir ascended the throne in 1605 and inherited an empire which was based on the firm foundation of a strong institutional apparatus. He did not, however, show much interest in reinforcing the existing institutions, particularly the liberal attitude towards religions other than Islam. Badauni records that it was during Jahangir's reign that the orthodox *ulema*, who had been sidelined during Akbar's rule, staged a comeback.[23] It is not clear, however, how and why a king of Hindu-Muslim parentage, brought up in the liberal atmosphere of his parents' court and palace, could let this happen. The contention of some historians that Jahangir was opposed to the liberal ideas of his father and, therefore, did away with some of those policies is not, however, acceptable. Beni Prasadsays, 'There is not the slightest reason to suggest that Salim was an ardent Mussalman or that he was by temperament or reputation fitted to champion the cause of orthodoxy against Akbar.'[24] Jahangir was miffed with the support given to his son Prince Khusrau by the Sikhs. Any emperor would have reacted in a similar manner to a group who gave support to a rebel. As a retaliatory step, the fifth Sikh Guru, Arjan Dev, was brought to the court and put to death by Jahangir. This was the genesis of the Sikh-Mughal antagonism that culminated in the collapse of the Mughal Empire. These events must have provided opportunities for the *ulema* to revive their influence in the court. Initially, Jahangir was not averse to giving land grants to non-Muslims. t When he started awarding *altuntamgah* jagirs to the *ulema*, he neglected the Sikhs and only patronized the Muslim orthodoxy to provide strength to the Empire. As a result, the Sikhs revolted against him and lent their support to his son Khusrau to revolt against Jahangir. This created lot of instability in the Empire. The economic difficulties (described later) accentuated this tilt. Thus, Akbar's policies of liberalism in matters of religion slowly began to lose steam.

Meanwhile, institutions like mansabdari, jagirdari, and zamindari had started weakening during the rule of Jahangir, mainly due to the Emperor's neglect. In fact, the first example of sub-letting of jagirs is reported from this period.[25] Under Shah Jahan, who came to the throne in 1628, the situation worsened. Even the *madad-i-maash* grants, which could neither be transferred nor sold, were inherited by the family members of the grantees.[26] The massive funds required for buttressing Shah Jahan's extraordinary projects in the fields of art and architecture only compounded the imminent crisis. There was heavy extraction of rural surplus and this led to the impoverishment of the peasantry. The crisis in the system of revenue assignments began to have its impact on the economy and the treasury. While the bureaucracy—the key support to the Mughal administration—continued to expand, the agrarian base which accommodated all these classes of elites kept becoming weak and sick. The state never bothered to give incentives to the peasants who were left at the mercy of avaricious jagirdars. The *khalisa* lands had decreased tremendously and the *hasil* (total revenue collected) rarely ever corresponded to the *jama* (total estimated revenue). Ultimately, the incompatibility between the resources needed to maintain a large administrative and bureaucratic apparatus on the one hand, and decreasing amounts of revenue generated by the support system on the other, caused a major agrarian crisis. This was a major reason for the downfall of the Mughal Empire in the early eighteenth century. [27]

Shah Jahan's period is notable for the large scale interaction of ordinary people like artisans and stone workers with Persian architects and other Muslim supervisors at the sites of his great projects like the Taj Mahal in Agra, and the Jama Masjid and the Red Fort in Shahjahanabad (Delhi). Hindu motifs came to be incorporated in the works, not deliberately, but because of the routine process of the workers displaying what they knew best. These trends of syntheses which originated in Akbar's time and continued during Jahangir's period reached their apogee under Shah Jahan's patronage. However, there is nothing significant to report on the religious policy and inter-community relations.

Aurangzeb assumed emperorship in 1658 after killing his brothers in bitter fights and imprisoning his father. This is completely unlike the manner in which his two predecessors came to power. Furthermore, he inherited an empire plagued by an economic crisis and badly depleted coffers. Akbar S. Ahmad is of the opinion that this period was also witness to a cultural-religious revivalist movement, where ethnicity, rather than pedigree, played a dominant role. Major examples are the Jat, Maratha, and Sikh uprisings against Muslim domination.[28] Along with this, threats from across the sea were emerging in the form of European trading companies which were establishing their factories in various parts of India.[29] To Aurangzeb, who—like his illustrious forefathers—nurtured the desire to expand his empire, all these events were enough cause for anxiety. He naturally viewed all the developments as obstacles to his designs. Therefore, while analysing Aurangzeb and his policies, it is important to keep in mind the circumstantial framework in which these policies were made. However, most historiographies dealing with Aurangzeb tend to brand him as an orthodox fanatic with an anti-Hindu frame of mind. In doing so, they rely on a critique of his religious policy.

Jadunath Sarkar points out that under Aurangzeb, schools of Hindu learning were broken down, Hindu places of worship were demolished, and Hindu fairs and festivals were forbidden. The Hindu population was subjected to special fiscal burdens and the service of the state was closed to them.[30] Sriram Sharma, who studied various aspects of the religious policies of Mughal emperors, reached a conclusion which is no different from Sarkar's. Sharma is of the view that Aurangzeb was a zealot who wanted to create *Darul Islam* in India.[31] To support this argument, he cites how Aurangzeb systematically destroyed temples in Gujarat, Bengal, Orissa, Kashi, and Mathura. However, it is not correct to characterize Aurangzeb's campaigns against the Sikhs, Jats, Satnamis, Rajputs, and Marathas as the products of an anti-Hindu frame of mind; political expediency would be a more plausible motive. These groups that threatened the process of imperial consolidation merely happened to be non-Muslim. According to Dr B.N. Pande, the freedom fighter and historian, the Vishwanath Temple of Kashi was ordered by Aurangzeb to be demolished in response to the complaint of a Hindu Maharani of Cutch who was molested and humiliated by *pandas* (priests) during her visit to the temple. This incident is reported to have happened when the Emperor Aurangzeb was camping in the vicinity of Kashi along with the Maharaja of Cutch and his entourage. Why did the Emperor not stop with punishing the offending *pandas* when the Maharani prayed to him? Why did the Emperor not allow the temple management to follow their own purificatory rites to undo the desecration? Why was a mosque simultaneously ordered to be built close by, using the remains of the temple? These questions have to be answered satisfactorily if Aurangzeb is to be cleared of religious bias and his action to be described as a sheer act of judicial punishment, and the answers have to be reconciled with his generosity to other Hindu temples, till our voyage of sublimation of historical memories is fruitful.[32]

Aurangzeb, though infamous for his suspicious nature, interfered with the process of succession in Rajput kingdoms that accepted his suzerainty. Ajit Singh of Mewar is a classic example. When Aurangzeb withheld his consent to the successor of Ajit Singh and wanted to bring the area under his direct control, it was not appreciated by the Rajputs, who saw this as a breach of trust they had reposed in the Mughal Emperor. The growing strength of Shivaji, who attacked the southern parts of the Empire, plundered Surat, and spared neither Hindus nor Muslims, was a matter of grave concern for Aurangzeb. Similar uprisings, though on a smaller scale, were occurring among the Sikhs in Punjab, and the Jats and Satnamis in the vicinity of Delhi. Aurangzeb was expected to retaliate in a manner befitting an emperor. His attack on the Sikhs, and their subsequent persecution, was motivated by his desire to curb their opposition to his rule rather than their religions identity. It had nothing to do with fanaticism or being anti-Hindu. Mathura and its adjacent regions were scenes of Jat and Satnami uprisings. The destruction of the temple at Kashi and Mathura was supposed to be a lesson to insurrectionary movements in these areas. It was a form of punishment meted out to these groups as these temples were religious centres and symbols around which they mobilized their strength and asserted their common socio-religious identity despite their internal divisions based on castes and tribes.

Aurangzeb re-imposed *jaziya* in his twenty-second regnal year. Again, this was guided by fiscal motives as it yielded Rs.500,000 for the state as additional revenue, a welcome addition to the crisis-ridden treasury.[33] Had Aurangzeb been a fanatic Muslim ruler, he would have re-imposed *jaziya* in the very first year as the emperor and harassed the Hindus from the beginning. Of course, he attached no importance to the adverse sentiments generated by this discriminating tax. With regard to the participation of Hindus in the administration of the Empire, the available records show that there were 240 Hindu mansabdars in Aurangzeb's service in spite of his policy of reducing the number of Hindu officials in his administration.[34]

Aurangzeb is credited with the grant of land to a temple at Gaya and grants to priests of a temple along the Brahamputra River in Assam.[35] Satish Chandra's analysis of grants to Hindu temples in the state of Marwar illustrates the point that Aurangzeb was not fanatically anti-Hindu. He cites an official document in Persian which says that a *faqir* named Ganesh Bharati, living in Kharantiya (Pargana Siwana), should not be disturbed so that he might feel reassured and pray for the Sultanate.[36] A certain grant of land to *jogis* in December 1688 by Aurangzeb, addressed to Dharmarth, was exempted by the Emperor to pay *hasilat*.[37] It can be seen that Aurangzeb's policies never had a theological basis but were guided by the need of the hour.[38]

In the last years of Aurangzeb's rule, a crisis in the assignment system had developed which ultimately led to the collapse of the Mughal Empire. During his southern campaigns, there was an influx of Deccani officers from the Deccan and Maratha kingdoms into the Mughal army. This led to an increase in the number of mansabdars, but the land to be allotted as jagir was not sufficient. The existing jagirdars were not very prompt in sending the state's share to the treasury and were busy exploiting the overburdened peasantry with high rates of revenue. The pressure thus exerted on the economy broke the back of the empire. Its collapse was guaranteed as the economy had plunged to depths from where no ruler, however capable, could have rescued it. It had nothing to do with Aurangzeb's religious conservatism which was, in the main, a natural reaction to seditious forces uniting on the basis of their ethnicity. The forces resisting the Mughal rule made Hindu religion their label for legitimizing their struggle. Therefore, at the popular level, the feeling that the subjects of the empire opposed the dominant political power for religious reasons and the latter, in turn, opposed the subjects for theological reasons, became deeply entrenched in the Indian mind. Such notions were further given legitimacy by colonial historiography which was interested in portraying the colonial rule as superior to that of the Mughals. Describing the Mughal rule as anti-Hindu became an essential step for legitimizing the British rule and covering up its own oppressive character.

A word about Shivaji and the Marathas who emerged as a significant political force during Aurangzeb's rule is necessary here. As Hindus with Muslim opponents, the exploits of the Marathas have given rise to a powerful legend that Shivaji led a Hindu counter-attack against Muslim domination. However, research hasshown that Shivaji, the son of a Maratha fief-holder of Bijapur Sultanate, was an ambitious leader, desirous of carving out a large domain for himself, and ready to use his religion as a tool for mobilizing his forces. It was in pursuit of this desire that he came into conflict, first with Bijapur and then with the Mughal Empire. At one point of time, he was willing to accept the suzerainty of the emperor, but when he was dissatisfied with the reception given to him at the Delhi Durbar, he became an inveterate foe and went on to set up his own kingdom. The Hindu religious rites of coronation and the sanction provided by the Pandits of Benaras for Shivaji's lineage have, no doubt, provided the flavour of a defiant king in opposition to a Muslim emperor. Shivaji's famous letter to Aurangzeb urging religious tolerance, his own liberal policy towards his Muslim subjects, and the presence of Muslims in high positions in his armed forces provided a perfect foil to Aurangzeb.

According to Percival Spear, Shivaji welded the 'caste-conscious Brahmin and independent sudra into a harmonious whole' and made 'the defence of cow and country, of religion and the homeland' his 'war cry'.[39] These facts must be taken into account in evaluating the historical memory regarding Shivaji.

However, it must be noticed that way in which the successors of Shivaji behaved has removed all the gloss from the Maratha claims to Hindu patriotism and benign governance. Khafi Khan, the court historian of Aurangzeb, had noted the moderation and restraint shown by Shivaji's troops against the foes and civilians, respectively. After the demise of Shivaji, the Maratha troops became ruthless and rapacious raiders, and were dreaded by other Hindus and Muslims alike. Shivaji's distinction between Swarajya areas (homelands) and Mughalai areas (foreign lands), the latter being treated as a legitimate target of raids in his guerrilla warfare, was abused without restraint. Levies like *chauth* (one-fourth) and *sar-deshmukhi* (one-tenth) were collected periodically from these lands, ostensibly as quid pro quo for protection. The violence accompanying these collections and their capricious timings made the Marathas hated throughout the country. All pretensions to consolidate and continue the heritage of Shivaji were rudely ended by the break-up of his empire, soon after his death in 1680, into several parts headed by semi-independent overlords like Gaikwad, Scindia and Holkar, the internal dissensions in the families of Peshwas, the hereditary ministers, and transformation of the troops into raiders.

Aurangzeb died in 1707, after campaigning in the Deccan for twenty-six years. Golconda, the last of the Deccan Muslim kingdoms, fell in 1687. This did not, however, give him the satisfaction of a final victory, as the Marathas continued to harass his armies. Aurangzeb had to persist in his campaign despite being an octogenarian. It was left to his son, Bahadur Shah I—whose reign lasted only five years—to make a settlement with the Marathas, 'tranquilise' the Rajputs, and take the last Sikh Guru into his service.[40] Then followed a succession of imbecile rulers propped up by a band of kingmakers and overly dependent on the military support of Maratha potentates like Scindia. The Mughal throne managed to remain an imposing institution till the blitz of Nadir Shah in 1738–9. It finally passed out of history with the capture and exile of Bahadur Shah Zafar by the British after they crushed the uprising of 1857, which has since come to be hailed as the First War of Independence. Several historians attribute the decline of the Mughal Empire to the policies of Aurangzeb and his never-ending wars. Satish Chandra, however, puts the blame on the 'jagirdari crisis' and the consequent deterioration of the economy, which had already begun during Jahangir's time, for the rapid decline after Aurangzeb. Of course, the three successors of Akbar had neither the vision nor the ability to stem the rot in time.

One interesting aspect of 1857 is that the disaffected soldiers of the British Indian Army and other fighters, Hindu and Muslims alike, chose the last Mughal emperor as their rallying point, although he had neither power, nor funds, nor the attributes of leadership. This happened despite the bitterness created by some of Aurangzeb's measures and the ineffectiveness of the Mughal emperors in times of crisis such as the raids of Nadir Shah and Ahmad Shah Durrani. How can one explain his phenomenon? According to Spear, we have to go back to Akbar for a plausible answer. Akbar 'set out to establish a cult of the monarch, to present him as a semi-divine personage, whom it was religious duty to obey and sacrilege to oppose. In doing this he used fragments of Persian tradition and ideas current at the time. Hence the aura, hence the religious prostrations.'[41] (For example, *sijda*, a complete prostration to the monarch or divinity, or *sashtanga namaskar*.) Furthermore, 'Akbar succeeded in regrowing the divinity that doth hedge a king. He provided India with the first Muslim dynasty to receive the free allegiance of Hindus as well as Muslims and whose claim to rule was accepted for reasons other than the possessing of superior force.'[42] If the above interpretation is correct, Akbar can be hailed as an assimilator par excellence.

The trends of assimilation and syncretism were noticeable in other areas, too. Sculpture and architecture have been mentioned earlier in the context of Shah Jahan's great projects. Miniature paintings of the Kangra and Persian schools incorporated Persian and Indian ideas and images. Mention must be made in this context of Mansur's masterpieces of flora and fauna which are illustrated in *Babur Nama*, which was translated during Akbar's time. Jahangir who, it is said, would have been happier as a head of a natural history museum, took Mansur with him on his hunting tours and other excursions so that the latter could paint the birds and animals seen by them. Mansur's innovation was to paint individual species of flowers as opposed to the earlier practice of making general floral designs on the margins. Another development was carpet weaving which Akbar introduced by persuading Persian carpet-weavers to migrate to India and set up looms near Agra and Lahore. The Sufis, who became influential, particularly after Akbar's patronage of Khawaja

Moinuddin Chishti, also enlarged their activities for cultural harmony. The Hindu counterpart of Sufism is the Bhakti movement. Dnyaneshwar and Tukaram in Maharashtra, and Chaitanya in Bengal are some of the propagators of the Bhakti philosophy. Brindavan, the fabled city of Lord Krishna, regained its importance. The religious ferment and the exchange of ideas initiated by Akbar also affected the royal family. When Akbar participated in Hindu rituals and festivities, it made the Hindu population more receptive towards him. His practice of *Tuladan*, *Jharokadarshan* and participation in Diwali, Dussehra, Rakshabandan, Holi and Shivratri indicates that he promoted harmony and liberalism in Indian society.[43] Dara Shikoh, the Crown prince, took so much interest in the Vedas that one is tempted to speculate on the shape of India had he succeeded his father, Shah Jahan. The teachings of Guru Nanak (1469–1539) led to the founding of a new sect called Sikhs, whose numbers and importance grew rapidly during the Mughal period. Sikhism, having borrowed liberally from Hinduism and Islam, stood out as a major effort at syncretism. These religious movements led to the increasing use of local languages that common people spoke. Tulsidas of Benares (1534–1623) produced his monumental work, *Ramcharitmanas*, in Hindi. The musical innovations of Tansen, the court musician of Akbar, were another instance of syncretic culture. The admixture of Persian, the language of the court, and Hindi, the language of the streets, resulted in the birth of Urdu and the popularization of new modes of entertainment like Qawwali. Kathak, a new dance form, also evolved.

Before concluding this chapter, brief notice must also be taken of contrary trends. The orthodox Sunnis deeply resented the syncretic trends initiated by Akbar and waited for a suitable opportunity to mount a counter-attack. The accession of Aurangzeb, a staunch Sunni, to the throne provided this opportunity. He allowed himself to be persuaded to stop certain practices which were declared patently un-Islamic. The seeds of the *Tablighi* movement were, thus, sown in the final years of the Mughal rule. Shaikh Ahmad Sirhindi, who despaired at the growing syncretism, preached: 'When the Commander of the Faithful in India (the emperor) failed to command and the temporal power collapsed, he (the Indian Muslim) could fall back on the sovereignty of God and the congregation.'[44] In other words, if there is no Muslim state in India, the Indian Muslim may take solace in his own community. Another theologian, Shah Waliullah, also propagated the same idea. Thus, the struggle between the forces of syncretism and those of separate identities continued, while India entered the eighteenth century. A new political force, the British, appeared on the scene and gave its own twists and turns to the struggle for power in the centuries that followed.

NOTES

1. Harbans Mukhia, *The Mughals of India*, London: Blackwell, 2004, p. 156.
2. Salma Ahmed Farooqui, *Islam and the Mughal State*, New Delhi: Sundeep Prakashan, 2005, pp. 36–96.
3. Stanley Lane-Poole, *Mediaeval India Under Mohammedan Rule, 712–1764*, London: Haskell House, 1903; repr., Delhi: Low Price, 1994, pp. 202–3.
4. Zahir-ud-din Muhammad Babur Padshah Ghazi, *Babur Nama*, tr. A.S. Beveridge, London: Luzac, 1922, repr., Delhi: Low Price, 1989, pp. 518–19.
5. Ibid., p. 380.
6. Lane-Poole, *Mediaeval India*, pp. 200–14.
7. Ibid., p. 602.
8. Ishwari Prasad, *History of Medieval India from 647 A.D. to the Mughal Conquest*, 2nd edn., Allahabad: The Indian Press, 1931, pp. 40–2.
9. Mukhia, *The Mughals of India*, pp. 69–70.
10. K.R. Qanungo, *Life and Times of Sher Shah*, Calcutta: Orient Longman, 1965.
11. Prasad, *History of Medieval India*, pp. 34–54.
12. J.N. Sarkar, *Mughal Polity*, Delhi: Idarah-i Adabiyat-i Delli, 1984, p. 394. See also Farooqui, *Islam and the Mughal State*, pp. 38–40.
13. Sarkar, *Mughal Polity*, p. 394.
14. Ibid.

15. Ruby Lal, *Domesticity and Power in the Early Mughal World*, New York: Cambridge University Press, 2005, pp. 167–75.
16. A.Q. Badauni, *Muntakhab-ut-Tawarikh*, ed. George S.A. Ranking, W.H. Lowe and Sir Wolseley Haig, 3 vols., Calcutta: Bibliotheca Indica, 1925; repr., Delhi: Low Price, 1986, pp. 54–6, 141–54, 172–87 and 205–12.
17. Mukhia, *The Mughals of India*, p. 162.
18. Abul Fazl, *Ain-i-Akbari*, tr. and ed. Henry Blochmann and H.S. Jarrett, 3 vols., 2nd edn., Calcutta: The Asiatic Society, 1927, vol. 1, p. 109.
19. Abul Fazl, *Ain*, vol. 3, pp. 103–4.
20. Ibid., p. 210.
21. Badauni, *Muntakhab*, p. 336.
22. Iqtidar Alam Khan, 'Akbar's Personality Traits and World Outlook: A Critical Reappraisal', *Social Scientist*, vol. 20, no. 9, September–October 1992, pp. 26–7.
23. Badauni, *Muntakhab*, vol. 2, p. 375.
24. William Forster, *The Embassy of Sir Thomas Roe to the Court of the Great Mogul, 1615–1619*, London: Hakluyt Society, 1899, pp. 110–1. See also Beni Prasad, *History of Jahangir*, Allahabad: Indian Press, 1930, p. 35.
25. Irfan Habib, *The Agrarian System of Mughal India, 1556–1707*, Bombay: Asia Publishing House, 1963; repr., Delhi: Oxford University Press, 2013, p. 309.
26. Ibid.
27. Abdul Hamid Lahori, *Padshahnama*, ed. Moulvi Kabiruddin and Moulvi Abdurahim, Calcutta: Bibliotheca Indica, 1878, vol. 2, pp. 365–6 and 506–7. See also W.H. Moreland, *The Agrarian System of Moslem India*, 2nd edn., Delhi: Oriental, 1968, pp. 238–54.
28. Akbar S. Ahmed, *Discovering Islam: Making Sense of Muslim History and Society*, London: Routledge, 1988, pp. 77–8.
29. Ibid.
30. J.N. Sarkar, *A Short History of Aurangzib*, Delhi: Orient Blackswan, 1979, p. 392.
31. S.R. Sharma, *The Religious Policy of the Mughal Emperors*, London: Asia Publishing House, 1940; repr., Delhi: Munshiram Manoharlal, 1972, pp. 160–7.
32. Farooqui, *Islam and the Mughal State*, pp. 58–71.
33. Zahiruddin Faruki, *Aurangzeb and His Times*, Delhi: Idarah-i Adabiyat-i Delli, 1972, pp. 153–254.
34. S.R. Sharma, *Religious Policy*, pp. 160–7.
35. Ibid., p. 178. See also I.H. Qureshi, *The Administration of the Mughal Empire*, Delhi: Oriental, 1979, pp. 41–2.

36. Satish Chandra, 'Some Religious Grants of Aurangzeb to "Maths" in the State of Marwar', *Proceedings of the Indian History Congress*, Jabalpur, vol. 32, 1970, pp. 405–8.
37. Ibid., p. 407.
38. B.N. Goswami and J.S. Grewal, *The Mughals and Jogis of Jakhbar*, Simla: Indian Institute of Advanced Study, 1967, pp. 5–40.
39. Percival Spear, *A History of India*, London: Penguin, 1990, vol. 2, p. 59.
40. Ibid., p. 56.
41. Ibid., p. 37.
42. Ibid.
43. Farooqui, *Islam and the Mughal State*, pp. 97–9.
44. Ibid.

CHAPTER 6

Sufism in Medieval Deccan: Politics and Worship

> The rulers of the world are the 'chosen' of god, the almighty under no conditions showing disrespect to them for disobeying their orders is proper or permitted in *shariat*. It is for this reason that god had committed to their care so many prayers and religious services, e.g. Friday prayers, Eid prayers, control of public treasury. Opposing their commandments, openly or secretly, is not permitted. O careless fellow! thou (whom the sultan gives) villages, rewards and territories, etc. (why) do you not help the king in (getting over) the difficulties that come in his way, and why do you not meet his enemies with anger? If thou does not do all this, it is unlawful for thee to eat or accept all these means of livelihood ... tomorrow on the Day of Judgment you shall be severely punished for this. The prophet has said: 'Whoever obeys the sultan, obeys God and whoever obeys and attains salvation.'[1]
>
> —SUFI SAINT SAYYID JALAL-UD-DIN BUKHARI

SINCE TIME IMMEMORIAL, there have been inextricable connections between religious and political institutions in India. Religion was always considered the supreme force that held society together and dictated people's duties and obligations. Polity was also an absolute necessity and the rulers were thought of as divine figures from ancient times. In medieval times, kingship in India was always treated as sacred. The Indian king was eighth of the sacred objects. According to Narda:

> Whatever a King does is right, that is a settled rule because the world is entrusted to him on account of his majesty and his duty towards living creatures. As a husband, though feeble, must constantly be worshipped

by his wives, in the same way the ruler, though worthless must constantly be, worshipped by his subjects.[2]

This phenomenon of interrelations and secular power are of almost infinite variety. The problem of understanding these relationships in the medieval Indian context lies not only in the complexity of traditional Hindu beliefs but also in the complications added by waves of non-Indian, non-Hindu immigrants, such as Arabs, Persians, Turks, Mughals, and others who brought with them their distinctive ideas of power, politics, religion, and culture to India and settled here.

The Muslim influences not only added grandeur and cultural excellence but also certain doctrinal views, especially with respect to acceptance of political authority and one's place in overall medieval Indian society. In Hindu culture, the concept of the king as having a necessary function which must be carried out according to normal statecraft opened the way for the building of a secular authority that is not the prisoner of priests and religious leaders. In Islam, of course, there has been no such neat division because everything is governed by an all-pervasive religion in which every act seeks to implement the words of the Prophet as recorded in the Koran.[3]

The religious institutions of both the Hindus and Muslims communicated their messages in terms of symbols, perceptions and rituals to reinforce the worshipper's sense of other-worldliness. For these religious elements and institutions, the medieval society represented just such an agglomeration of isolated individuals, incapable of ruling themselves and liable to adopt the most extreme ideologies. Therefore, sharp ideologization of Islam by Sufi ideologues made Sufism easily a potent force to secure legitimation of Muslim rule in India by subjecting people with false hope of other-worldly attractions. The preaching of Sufis in *khanqas* provides many such examples which indicates the conditioning of behaviour by Sufi ideology. While explaining the meaning of *zahud* (giving up of interest in worldly goods and attractions) Abul Mawahib Shazili says, 'If you do not renounce the better goods of this vile world surely you are far from the beneficence of the glorious life to come.'[4] Not only did these institutions convey their messages to those initiatives into their fold but they also increased the potency of their belief system as an agent of social control at popular level. Such is the case with Sufism in the Deccan. The state has been the political expression and instrument of Islamic orthodoxy which the Muslim *ulema* interpreted as the form of a transcendent Unitarian orthodoxy. When the rulers ignored it with secular ordinances, laws and decrees, the people also escaped it by resorting either to custom and convention or mystical Sufism. Sufism also emerged as an individual quest for spirituality among holy men. It gradually evolved into a social organization acquiring disciples and took up the missionary work, spread to various parts of the world and facilitated the spread of Islam and consolidation of Muslim rule.[5]

From the late tenth and early eleventh century AD, Sufism evolved into an institution and took upon itself the missionary activity and task of defining and redefining state–societal relations to facilitate the legitimization of conquerors of infidel lands in the name of Islam, and Sufis came to be considered the defenders of faith.[6] The region of the Deccan could not escape their attention. The migration of Sufis from Central Asia, and also from various other parts of India into the Deccan, led to the establishment of various Sufi orders which organized their relations as saints and disciples (*pirs* and *murids*), and in the process related their presence to larger issues of regions—political stability, instability and social control. The various Sufi *silsilas* (orders) which entered the Deccan were *Chistitya*, *Qadiriya* and *Shattari* orders. In northern India, some of the Sufis and their orders kept themselves away from political establishments but in the Deccan, from the very beginning, the Sufis worked under the patronage of Bahmani rulers. The *khanqas* became political centres and the Sufis functioned in connivance with the sultans and nobility.[7] Therefore, the investigation of this theme in this chapter is not entirely arbitrary. While many aspects of this phenomenon have been investigated, many others have remained unexplored. Interestingly, the hagiographical literature left behind by the Sufis and their disciples constitutes a very valuable source for understanding their role and popular culture in the Deccan.[8]

The subject of Sufism which remains the domain of few specialists is very well known in India. The patient and meticulous research conducted in this field by Khaliq Ahamd Nizami and Sayyid Athar Abbas Rizvi characterizes Sufis on the basis of their spiritual and worldly roles.[9] They establish the fact that the relationship between the Sufis and the medieval Indian state was very close. There were areas of communication and cooperation between the two. But what precisely this communication at cooperation consisted of has been defined with lesser clarity in the context of medieval Deccan. Though little exploited, Deccani Sufi literature has immense potential to shed light on this relationship between worship and politics and the way Sufism was used to control the social and political life at the popular level.[10]

The Arab traders had been visiting various coastal towns in south India much before the birth of Islam.[11] The origin of Muslim settlements in the south dates back to the Caliphate of Abdul Malik bin Marwan (AD 692–705).[12] These settlements grew more and more with the coming of the Persians. The armies of Ala-ud-din Khalji and Muhammad-bin-Tughlaq, inter alia, were accompanied by various Sufi saints who facilitated the spread of Islam in the Deccan. When Ala-ud-din Khalji's general Malik Kafur was pursuing Raja Bir Dhul at Kandur, he met some Muslim soldiers of the Hindu raja and spared their lives only because of their faith.[13]

Khalid Ahmad Nizami rightly says:

> Long before the Khalji armies marched into Deccan the Sufi saints had settled in various parts of south and their ways and their concern for the welfare of people had made them a welcome group in large society. Their efforts, however, could not crystallize in the form of some movement. It was with the exerts demanded by Mohammad bin Tughlaq, the organized *silsalas* reached south and the settlement of small Muslim cultural groups in various towns the Sufi movement assumed a new dimension. All the

traditions of Muslim mysticism as they had developed in north India were transplanted in south. Soon the *mudakhirs* (preachers) of Delhi could be seen delivering sermons in various towns and *qawalls* (musicians) could be found reciting the verses of Amir Khusro and Amir Hassan in the courts and in the streets. The exiled Sufis tried to recreate the atmosphere of Delhi *khanqas* in the newly setup hospices. No doubt, the woof and warp of the Sufi movements in the Deccan had come from Delhi but in no time the movement developed its indigenous characteristics.[14]

On the eve of the establishment of the Bahmani Sultanate, the various Sufis of the *Chisti silsila* were sparsely settled in different parts of the Deccan which loosely constituted the territory of the Bahmani state. The *Chisti silsila*'s reputation for egalitarianism, universal brotherhood, piety, honesty, etc. was widely acknowledged in the whole of India.[15] In the Deccan also, their presence and work obliterated the impression of indifference that some of the Muslims accompanying the army of the Delhi Sultanate had left behind earlier. Some Muslims, who joined the armies of Delhi sultans invading the south, tried to convert people forcibly. For example, Sarmast, Mabari Khandyat, Sheikh ali Pahhalwan, Sheikh Shahid, Jumana, Karim al-din, Sayyid Hussamal-din and Tigh Barhana were all killed in different parts of the Deccan along with their associates for having indulged in forcible conversions. Unfortunately, R.M. Eaton has conferred on them the status of 'warrior Sufis' while their antecedents as Sufis are doubtful. Eaton seems to have been quite keen to revive the much-hated colonial historiographical stereotypical notion of the Hindu–Muslim divide which serves imperial interests in South Asia even today. Treating the warriors (some of whose real existence has not been established conclusively) as Sufis or vice versa is not only historically unintelligible in the medieval Indian context but also a wild distortion of historical reality. The promotion of Hindu cultural and religious phenomenon at the hands of Vijayanagara rulers should not be necessarily taken to mean what Eaton calls 'anti-Muslim bull-work', but a usual politico-ideological infrastructure for the political exigencies of the state. Interestingly, the Muslim Turks were employed by Vijayanagara and Hoyasala rulers for their loyalty and valour.[16]

The growth of the Sufi movement and the increasing Muslim presence formed a crucial turning point in shaping the future course of polity and society in the Deccan.[17] Besides this, the onset of the fourteenth century saw the collapse of the Kakatiya rule (1158–1326) and the incorporation of other smaller polities into the new emerging states of the Vijayanagara (1336–1565) and Bahmani kingdoms (1347–1489).[18] This development in the Deccan was being aided by political conquest and growth of new land-based relations in which the growth of secular landed elements played a significant role.[19] The growth of trade and urban production also formed the important elements of this process. All these forces brought about the rise of a new political elite and gave people a role at the centre stage. At this juncture, the Bahmani sultans demanded the cooperation of Sufis in the implementation of their policies because they were guided by the conviction that the 'state and religion are twins'.[20] The Bahmani sultans were also conscious of the fact that the efforts to look after and give direction to orthodox Islamic attitudes like some of the earlier Muslim soldiers (*ghazis*) alone could not help them in consolidating their position. Therefore, as the rulers of non-Muslim subjects, they had to think and act differently. They encouraged Sufis to take up various assignments in the functioning of the state.[21]

This process provided space to Sufis to combine their religious roles with the politics of the time. Their claims to egalitarian society, universal brotherhood and assertion respecting the new religious fraternity were backed by new patterns of military organization, economic activity and their residences in the midst of non-Muslim population. This served to establish a new community, which had lost its organic character by shattering their earlier identities.[22] Earlier, the region's population looked back to their lineage, mythical cults, tribes, clans, Shaiva, Vaishnava, Veera Shaiva and non-Veera Shaiva structures/markers as the basis of their identity because the overarching Hindu identity was totally absent.[23] The genesis of the process of incorporation of varied smaller identities into a broader one goes back to the thirteenth century when Muslim presence in the Deccan was assuming prominence. However, it was in the fifteenth century that the term 'Hindu' occurred for the first time and crystallized in the course of time.

At the popular level, the people reacted to these changes by organizing themselves into communities based on religious affinity. At times, it resulted in conflict and confrontation and encouraged people to undertake actions which were liable to interfere with their own interests. As a result, they were obliged to repudiate their allegiances. Besides, the availability of meagre resources, the efficient political factionalism, the non-local and non-Hindu nature of the Bahmanis, the problem for them (Bahmani sultans) was how to install their new administrative missionary, to keep peace, to collect taxes, to ensure effective governance and to maintain societal stability. They felt that in this process, if the members of the medieval Deccani society were to fulfill their social and political obligations, they should have a morally acceptable explanation of the society's specific system of institutional arrangements. It was not merely a question of commands and obedience, but an understanding that portrayed these practices as natural or moral for common interests. In the Deccan, Sufism also spread like diffused power in a more spontaneous and unconscious way at the popular level.[24]

Initially, this problem was further compounded by the cultural distances between the ruling elements and their subjects. The resolution of all these problems was quite necessary, particularly when some erstwhile elements of the Deccan's ruling class perceived the Bahmani rule as illegitimate and considered it an imposition on them (the Deccani nobility) because they were completely excluded from sharing powerful positions. Therefore, all sections of the society were not equally attractive to the Bahmani rule from the point of commanding authentic support of society.[25] It is quite probable that among the excluded groups of nobility and Sufis under the Bahmanis, one also finds some unpopular ones whose isolation and distraction was often presented by the rulers as a political necessity that justified the Bahmani rule.[26] Apart from this, the inheritance of power and exercising of authority by the Bahmanis depended not only on how well they performed but also how effectively they used the state's coercive apparatus.

Amidst these developments when the Bahmani rulers took over, they neither suddenly disrupted the dominance of socio-cultural life nor were they new in the enforcement of submission of society. But what was new was the convenient aid of Sufis which they obtained for legitimating their rule.[27] Nizami writes:

> The kingdoms that rose up in various parts of India following the disintegration of Sultanate of Delhi sought the help of saints and divines in consolidation of their power. The founders of these dynasties offered endowments in the form of villages, stipends, buildings, etc., to saints and they in their turn gave moral support to them and whipped up public opinion in their favour. The Bahmani rulers also enlisted from the very beginning of their rule in Deccan the goodwill and cooperation of the saints and *mashaikh* who apart from many other contributions in the cultural sphere carried the roots of the Bahmani power deeper in public confidence. In many moments of crises connected with accessions, campaigns and factional political elements in history of the Bahmani dynasty, the saints exerted their influence in favour of the one or the other political claimant and their support or opposition went a long way in determining the course of political events.[28]

Whatever differences existed among their respective systems of preaching, the various Sufi *silsilas* were united in using religious discourses through their preachings in *khanqas*, *madrasas* and *maktabs*, as a subtle mechanism of defining the nature of relations between the people and the state. Although there were ubiquitous disparities between the people's aspirations and their achievements, the Sufis retained the ideal standards and in turn buttressed them through their teachings which were supported by this and the other-worldly sanctions which formed the important element of Sufi ideology.[29]

In medieval Deccan, the phenomenon of Sufism did not limit itself to individual cases, but it generally concerned various factions and groups of people who perceived the same religious goals. In this respect, one can speak of the conditioning of believers to pursue the principles which ordinary experience prohibited them from attaining. Sufism thus found a place in medieval Deccani society and polity through its specialized techniques like *sama*, *urs*, *ecstasy*, etc., which the dominant in Deccani society were aware of, whereas those who were oppressed were ignorant of its ways and goals.[30] These specialized techniques were not demonstrated unexpectedly; they coincided with events which were well defined in time, such as the period of initiation, the period of rights for obtaining rain, deliverance from disease, and so on.[31]

The belief in Sufi ideology greatly influenced people at the popular level and oriented their material and spiritual life. Surely, such methods of practising spirituality and manipulating divinity required very unusual techniques. They defined the human being not only as a single, indissoluble entity but also emphasized that he enjoys a certain plasticity which defined him more in terms of becoming than being. Sufis defined human life as a storehouse of miseries from which man could get salvation only by renouncing worldly pleasures.[32]

It would be wrong to consider these Sufis in the Deccan only as contemplators whose ecstasies placed them in a separate realm. In fact, the Sufis in the Deccan, unlike *Chistia silsila* in north India, did not live in isolation nor did they strip themselves from their social and political loyalties. Instead, they used their mystical identity to realize more fully their political aspirations in the Deccan.[33] Even though Muslim presence assumed prominence in south India much before the thirteenth century, undifferentiated concept of religious and secular authority in the medieval Deccani political context grew only after the arrival of Sufis which coincided with the establishment of the Bahmani kingdom in the Deccan.[34] Therefore, with the establishment of the Bahmani state, Sufis appeared as a result of a very well-defined strategy on the path of different Sufi *silsilas*. The Sufis assumed the protection and endowment of worship, the organization of *khanqas*, mosques, and *madrasas*. To facilitate the legitimization of Bahmani rule, they also adopted Arab, Turkish, Persian, and Deccani ideas and impressions alongside their Islamic identity.[35]

Since the Bahmani state in the Deccan was the first to benefit from these Sufis, it took care to patronize and promote their settlements in the region on permanent basis and even invited them from outside the region. Ifthikar Ahmad Ghauri writes:

> The Bahmani sultans, in order to maintain their authority over the vast population of Hindus, wanted more and more Muslims, as their number was as yet quite insufficient to occupy all the key posts of state. That is why Alauddin Hassan Bahman Shah Bahmani (AD 1347–58) had successfully seduced some of the Turkish and Afghan nobles from allegiance of Tughlaq sultans. The domicile of these chiefs and their descendants in the Deccan and also their marriages with Hindu women had made them Deccanis to the core. They had settled in Deccan with no intension of leaving it and considered this region their home.... When the Bahmani sultans failed to seduce a large no of Muslims from their loyalty of Delhi sultanate in order to fill the higher posts of state they hit upon a new idea. Tajudin Feroz Shah Bahmani (AD 1397–1422) sent a large number of ships every year to Iran inviting soldiers of repute, artisans, men of letters, etc., to settle in the Deccan and enjoy royal favours. This policy was continued by his successors with varying successes. It appeared to Sultan Shahabudin Ahmad (AD 1422–36) that if he could persuade any leading mystic to come to his country his interminable disciples and followers might follow him, probably this was one of the motives, which urged him to invite Shah Naimatullah from Kirman to settle in his kingdom.[36]

Initially, efforts were made to woo those Sufis and the *ulema* who could help in developing the Persian language, which also proved of immense assistance in building the state's administrative machinery. A few among those who received the state's patronage in this direction included Isami, the author of *Futuh-us-Salatin*; Sheikh Mohammad Ibn Ain-din; Ganj-ul-alim Lutfullah Sabzwari; Mufti Ahmad Harrawi; Mir Mohammad Badakhshani; Shareef Samarqandi; Saif-ud-din Gori; Qazi Mohammad Siraj; Mohammad Minhaj Ullaha; Syed Mohammad Al Hussain Gais-ud-daraz; Hakeem

Husssain Gilani; Abad al Rahman Mulla Isaq Sirhandi; Hakeem al-Tabrezi; Sadr-ul-Shareef Samarqandi; Riyaz-al-din; Fazlullah Anjum; Khalilullah, and many more.[37] They were accompanied by a large number of their disciples which included the *ulema*, *umara*, and people skilled in various professions. They opened up *madrasas*, *maktabs*, and *khanqas* in various parts of the Deccan.[38] Some of these were located at Elchipur, Gulbarga, Daulatabad, Khuldabad, Aurangabad, Warrangal, Ferozabad, Naldureg, and many others places in the region.[39]

The opening of these centres served to popularize the Persian language, which influenced other languages in the course of time. The development of this language at the hands of Sufis in and outside *khanqas* allowed them to share information over space and through time, independent of an oral context. Despite the fact that only a tiny percentage of population was literate, literacy in Persian and later in Rekhta (Deccani Urdu) nonetheless effected radical transformation,[40] since those few who learned to read and write Persian and Rekhta took the medieval Deccani state's responsibility for programming the activity of medieval society within and outside the region.[41]

The growth of Persian language and the establishment of the Bahmani state in the Deccan was not a mere coincidence; actually, access to a large body of information strengthened the focal position of those working in the state's missionary. It increased their powers of organizational control and also facilitated its widespread use in the exchange of ideas.[42] However, what one needs to keep in view is the fact that the Persianization of culture and promotion of Persian language always lay behind the administrative preference of the medieval Deccan. Therefore, the Bahmani state carried Persianization far enough to propose it as an official language of the state.[43] It is true that initially the local Deccani officials would have drawn little guidance from the vague proclamations of their administrative superiors (who were from among the non-Deccani stock), but they had the expediencies of their own careers to consider and, therefore, they did well to cultivate their associations with Persian-knowing *ulema* and Sufis by assuming compliance in the collection of tax and other revenues, and the provision of recruits for civil and military services by mediating the affectivity of royal proclamations at the popular level.[44] The medieval Deccani state also provided scholarships to those scholars who facilitated the teaching and learning of Persian. Adari, a Persian migrant, composed the history of Bahmani rulers in verse and Daud Bidri wrote *Bahman-Nama* on the lines of Firdausi's *Shah Nama* to legitimate the rule of his patrons.[45] Sayyid Mohammad-al Hussain Gesu Daraz also wrote more than 125 books on varied subjects. Shah Miranji Sams-ul-Ushsaq, his son Shah Burhan-ud-din Janam, Sheikh Mohammad Khoush Dahen, Kamal-ud-din Biabani and others did not produce their works in Persian but in Rekhta. As a recognized medium of Sufi literature, this clearly indicates an attempt by Sufis to reach out to a much wider audience and some degree of indigenization.[46] Anniemarie Schimel remarks, 'Sufis wanted to explain the mysteries of divine love and divine grace to people who flocked around them and who understood neither Arabic, the language of Quran and the law divine, nor Persian, the language of poetry and historiography.'[47] Thus, the mystical leaders had to resort to the vernacular, even if they sometimes thought it necessary to start their book with an excuse for using the popular idiom; they composed little songs for their followers, songs which incorporated their teachings and which might also be used in musical ensembles. Then followed the composition of short treatises in the vernacular, mostly rhymed so that they were easy to memorize and, eventually, large books like *Mathnavis* and other prose works. Thus, literature produced by these Sufis had many advantages for the state apart from developing a trained manpower to run the state machinery. The development of Rekhta enabled them to work as appropriate intermediaries between this and the other world, and opened the paths of communication between the people and the world beyond their reach. They realized that it was also necessary to introduce people to finer practices of *tasawuf* (Sufi practice) and *sama* (ecstasy), the experience of which people had not attained until then. The true power of Sufis rested on these practices.[48]

At the popular level, the Sufi preaching emphasized the attitude of *sulhi kul* (peace with all creeds and cults) and social harmony with non-Muslims; appealed to non-Muslims to be receptive to Sufi ideology even if they did not formally accept Islam, to abstain from sin and to remain detached from the material realities of the world, to remain content and to treat poverty as an essential condition of their life.[49] All these ideas and teachings of Sufism point to the evolution of an ideological infrastructure of the medieval state. Through such teachings, Sufism served to justify the punishments inflicted on people by the state, formed the basis for justification of repression in the name of spirituality, morals, other-worldlines, and also contained the decisive tendencies at societal level.[50] It served as a social framework for appropriation of various struggles going on within the medieval Deccani society.[51]

The Sufi ideology affected man's vision of his own position in the centre of the universe. From this point of view, man failed to constitute a closed system in opposition to the outside world in order to better secure his own substance and limitations; on the contrary, he was made to enter into the surrounding environment that in turn penetrated him. Between the two realities, there existed a constant communication in which man found himself always permanently listening, so to speak, to the pulse of the world.[52] In practical terms, all people at the popular level were profoundly religious. As soon as they were able to penetrate superficial beliefs and from the moment they pierced the shell of superfluous elements of religion of a given people, they appeared with absolute faith in the efficacy of their approach to spirituality. It is certain that nowhere in the medieval Deccani society did common man feel a philosophical or religious doubt. His 'faith' and thought showed absolute certainty in the success of his understandings.[53] The belief in Mastania and Gaso Daraz offer best examples of this type in Andhra Pradesh.[54] Basically, people felt assured that in acting in a certain way, be it a Sufi *sama* or faith in *jatara* rituals in honour of village goddesses, they were conforming to the order of things in the universe. People respected the hierarchical nature of society, the characterization of which corresponded to those ideals preached and defined by Sufis, for Sufis believed that this attitude of people placed them closer to God.[55]

Through such mechanisms, Sufism also encouraged pacifism and undermined the power of resistance to dominate political structures. The Sufi preaching worked in two ways—one abstract and other concrete—distinctly yet complementarily employing the two indissoluble aspects of dominance and subjection, and filled the functions of defining social relations which were also rooted in the production process.

The outcome of this close relationship of the medieval state with the Sufis was also the occupation of better lands near both populated and unpopulated areas.[56] The direct exploitation of these lands by the Sufis and their servants made their states more productive. In this way, the Sufis derived their material strength from organizations and the ascetic life, and extended their patrimony.[57] By putting into practice the letter and spirit of the rule, the Sufis obtained a large amount of surplus production which also facilitated the growth of trade, and this, in turn, further helped the state's territorial expansion.

The other consequence of the undue material prosperity of the Sufis was an increasing deviation from their original principles which gradually led to the transformation in the quality of their religious roles and, eventually, they became landed estate owners and indulged in the exploitation of people. Nizami writes:

> Thus throughout the history of Bahmanis one finds the saints and *mashaikh* deeply involved in the politics of time.... The early tradition of keeping away from politics and eschewing the company of rulers had given great moral and spiritual vitality to the mystic movement in India. But when the saints of the Deccan began to work for public welfare under the patronage of Bahmani rulers, their freedom of action was curtailed and the *khanqas* became appendages of the court, subsisting on the state finances and functioning in connect with the policies of the rulers of the

day, with big jagirdars to administer it, it became impossible for saints keep succession to spiritual *gadi* open for men of talent.[58]

These estates of the Sufis were not carved out of reclaimed wasteland but were located in previously inhabited areas where reclamation of the wasteland had already taken place.[59] Unfortunately, these estates of the Sufis where not even associated with innovation in agriculture and rural industry. These estates also helped them to establish relations of domination and subordination. One thing that needs to be overlooked in such holdings is the nature of expending of labour from these estates which was of unpaid, voluntary and free nature.[60] But the charitable character tended to obscure the exploitative characters of such social relations. The financial benefits derived thus, in turn, legitimated the political roles of Sufis and they departed further and further from real roles. The pious devotion was considered to be the cause for efficiency of production; because the Sufis never intended to be active participants in the production process, they clothed the unpaid and voluntary labour on these holding in their worship.[61]

Hence, the inequality and exploitation mechanisms were relegated to a subsidiary role; unpaid labour from these estates did not appear a factor. Though these estates were exempt from tax and state interference, they nevertheless facilitated the hierarchy internal to the Sufi establishment which had much in common with the secular aristocracy.[62] The dominant groups in medieval Deccani society seem to have taken advantage of the Sufi establishments and treated them as an ally in their midst to justify the people's subjection and the exploitation of their resources. One finds that in medieval Deccani society, many fertile tracts of land were held by priests in temple establishments which stood as dwelling places of God and the priests. Therefore, the medieval economy functioned in such a way that local communities and individuals were subjected to temple priests and Sufis in *khanqas* to whom they were obliged to give a major proportion of their produce and labour. These conditions ultimately gave birth to growing agrarian turmoil and disruption which became the principal characteristics of medieval Deccani polity and economy.

In such circumstances, for the dominant class, both in secular and religious institutions, it would have been impossible to continuously impose adequately its culture on subordinated people. It also worked in reverse terms of consciousness at the popular level. Although there was no coherent class consciousness at the popular level, even with definite consciousness, the peasants in the secular domain were controlled by landed aristocracy and its monopoly of other means of production like craft, technology, irrigation, etc.[63] Therefore, Sufism helped the dominant in emphasizing their convenience at the expense of the religio-ethical context. As Nizami writes, 'The acquisition of land its resources entitled them [Sufis] to personal domination and power which they used to exert in different ways and in different conditions, ranging from usurpation and eviction of peasants in order to transform their settlements for maintenance and control of peasant population in these areas.'[64] The formation of such holdings strengthened old landed elements whether or not it took the jurisdictional form through which the relationships of dependence became institutionalized. Hence, the Sufi power was not used for tax administration but for controlling the public, where spirituality allowed the Sufis to exercise unrestricted freedom that generated the state's control and expansion in these areas.[65]

The Sufis in medieval Deccan evolved a value system through their methods of worship, which was directed to justify and perpetuate the established political order to the detriment of the masses. That is how they encouraged a false awareness of historical processes and their place in the scheme of things, alongside their spiritual path.

NOTES

1. Khaliq Ahmad Nizami, *Some Aspects of Religion and Politics in India during Thirteenth Century*, Bombay: Asia, 1961, pp. 250–2.

2. John W. Spellman, *Political Theory of Ancient India*, Bombay: Oxford University Press, 1980, pp. 33–40. This close association of religion and a political element in which the authority of kings and priests was united was the most important characteristic of Indian polity from very early times. For details see B.A. Saletore, *Ancient Indian Political Thought and Institutions*, Bombay: Asia Publishing House, 1963, Chapter 2. For the medieval period, this aspect has been comprehensively dealt with by K.A. Nizami, *Akbar and Religion*, Delhi: Idarah-i-Adabiyat-i-Delli, 1989.
3. L.W. Pye, *Asian Power and Politics: The Cultural Dimensions of Authority*, London: Belknap, 1985, pp. 155–6. See also Peter Hardy, 'Islam and Muslims in South Asia', in *The Crescent in the East*, ed. Raphael Israeli, London: Curzon, 1982, pp. 36–7.
4. Nizami, *Some Aspects of Religion and Politics*, pp. 232–7.
5. Ira M. Lapidus, 'State and Religion in Islamic Societies', *Past and Present*, no. 151, May 1996, pp. 13–14; P.J. Vatikiotis, *Islam and the State*, London: Croom Helm, 1987, pp. 30–3. For details see Syeed Ameer Ali, *The Spirit of Islam*, London: W.H. Allen, 1931, pp. 6–45.
6. Lapidus, 'State and Religion', pp. 13–14; Nizami, *Aspects of Religion and Politics*, pp. 174–229.
7. Ali Musawi al-Qadiri, 'Mishat-i-Nabuwat' (Persian manuscript), *Tazkira*, no. 21, Asafiya Library, Hyderabad; K.A. Nizami, 'Sufi Movement in Deccan', in *History of Medical Deccan (1295–1724)*, ed. K.K. Sherwani and P.M. Joshi, Hyderabad: Government of Andhra Pradesh, 1974, p. 173–99. See also R.M. Eaton, *Sufis of Bijapur*, Princeton: Princeton University Press, 1978, pp. 19–75; Saiyed Ali Tabatabai, *Burhan-i-Maasir* (Persian), ed. Majlis Khatutat Farsi Hyderabad: Deccan, 1936, p. 12.
8. The works which provide us with very clear insight into various aspects of Sufism and society in medieval Deccan are those of Gesu Daraz and his son. Their works were very popular among Sufi circles and also among the masses. The two important works which Gesu Darz's son Syed Akber Hussain wrote are *Kitab-i-Aqaid* and *Tabsirat-al-Istilahat-al-Sufiyah*. Some of their works have been edited by Ashiq Hussain in Hyderabad 1366 AH. The other works include *Irshad-nama* and *Kalimat-al-Haqiaya* by Burhan-ud-din-Janam. For details, see Nasir-al-din Hashami, *Dakan mein Urdu*, 6th edn., Lucknow: Kitab Mahal, 1963, pp. 185–269; Muhi-ud-din Zore, *Deccan Adab-ki-Tarikh* (1350–1750) (Urdu), Karachi: Karachi Urdu Academy, 1960, pp. 32–59. See also Jamil Jalibi, *Tarikh-i-Adab-k-Urdu*, vol. I, *Agaz se 1750 tak* (Urdu), Lahore: Majlis Taraki Urdu Adab, 1975, pp. 181–337.

9. Nizami, *Aspects of Religion and Politics*, pp. 179–260; S.A.A. Rizvi, *A History of Sufism in India*, 2 vols., Delhi: Munshiram Manoharlal, 1978, vol. 1, pp. 241–322.
10. Eaton, *Sufis of Bijapur*, pp. 135–74. The comprehensive treatment of this aspect has been provided by S. Suleiman Siddiqi in his work on *Bahmani-Sufis*, Delhi: Idarah-i Adabiyat-i Delli, 1989.
11. Mahmud Khan Mahmud: *Tarikh-i-Junubi Hind* (Urdu), *Bangalore:* Government Press, 1967, p. 53.
12. Ibid.
13. Amir Khusro, 'Khazain-Al-Futuh', MS, British Museum, 1838, ff. 73b–74a, English translation by Elliot and Dowson, *History of India as Told by Its Own Historians*, London: Trübner, 8 vols., 1871, vol. III, p. 90. The translation of this passage is wrongly carried out in the fourteenth century. Ibn Battuta, *Rehla*, tr. Agha Mahdi Hussain, Baroda: Oriental Institute, 1953, pp. 180–93. Muslims had been employed by Hindu rajas of the south. Taqi-ud-din Abdur Rahman was the minister of Raja Sunder Pandey of Babar. Lula, a Muslim, was the commander of Raja Bas Doe's fleet of ships. Raja Ballal Dev of Dwarsamudra had 20,000 Muslim soldiers in his army. Therefore, it is no surprise to find Muslim presence in Vijayanagara, ibid. p. 228; Elliot and Dowson, *History of India as Told by Its Own Historians*, vol. II, p. 32; J.D.M. Derrett, *The Hoysalas*, Oxford: Oxford University Press, 1957, pp. 71, 112, 153. See also Maulvi Abdul Gafur Khan Rampuri and Moulvi Mir Kazim Ali Khan, eds., *Tarikh-i-Deccan* (Urdu), *Hyderabad*: Azam Steam Press, 1941, vol. III, p. 560; and Agha Mehdi Hussain, *Tughlaq Dynasty*, Calcutta: Thacker Spink, 1963, pp. 145–62.
14. Nizami, 'Sufism Movement in Deccan', p. 195.
15. Ibid.
16. There is plentiful evidence available on this aspect. Battuta, *Rehla*, pp. 180, 185, 188, 193. Elliot and Dowson, *History of India as Told by Its Own Historians*, vol. 11, p. 32; Mahmud Abdul Aziz, 'The Deccan in Fifteenth Century', *Journal of Asiatic Society of Bengal*, vol. 21, 1959, p. 569; V.V. Mirashi, *Chinchani Plates of the Arab Feudatory Ship*, Calcutta: J.N. Banerjee, 1959, pp. 96–109: Derrett, *The Hoysalas*, pp. 71, 112, 153; Rampuri and Khan, *Tarikh-i-Deccan*, p. 560; Agha Mahdi Husain, *Tughluq Dynasty*, Calcutta: Thacker Spink, 1933; revd. edn., New Delhi: S. Chand, 1976, pp. 145, 150, 150, 162; Burton Stein, *Vijayanagara: The New Cambridge History of India*, 2 vols., Cambridge: Cambridge University Press, 1993, p. 29; see also Eaton, *Sufis of Bijapur*, pp. 22–34.
17. V. Yesoda Devi. 'Social and Economic Structure in Andhra Desh in Reddi Age', *S.V. University Oriental Journal*, vol. I, Tirupati, 1972 pp. 51–2.

18. The smaller political groups in the Deccan were those of the Kotas, Telugu Cholas, the Eastern Chalukyas, and the Kayasthas. Ibid.
19. Burton Stein, *Peasant State and Society in Medieval South India*, Delhi: Oxford University Press, 1985, p. 372.
20. Iftikhar Ahmad Ghauri, 'Muslims in the Deccan in Middle Ages: An Historical Survey', *Islamic Culture*, July 1975, vol. 19, no. 3. pp. 150–64.
21. M.S. Sarma, *History of Reddi Kingdom*, Waltair (Vishakapanam): Andhra University, 1948, p. 278.
22. V. Yesoda Devi. 'Social and Economic Structure in Andhra Desh in Reddi Age', *S.V. University Oriental Journal*, vol. I, 1972, pp. 51, 52, 67.
23. Amir Khusro, 'Khazain-Al-Futuh', MS, British Museum, 1838, ff. 73b–74a, English translation by Elliot and Dowson, *History of India as Told by Its Own Historians*, London: Trubner & Co., 8 vols., 1871, vol. III, p. 90.
24. Rizvi, *A History of Sufism*, pp. 241–322.
25. Aziz Ahmad, 'The Sufi and the Sultan in pre-Mughal India', Iranian Studies, vol. 27, no. 1–4, 1955, pp. 142–53.
26. Ghauri, 'Muslims in the Deccan', pp. 155–6; Nizami, 'Sufi Movement', pp. 182–6; Syed Ata Hussain, *Maktubat* (Persian), Hyderabad: Anisul Ushshaq Press, 1901, p. 86.
27. Abdul Qasim Hindu Shah Ferishta, *Tarikh-i-Ferishta*, tr. John Briggs, *History of the Rise of Muhammadan Power in India*, 3 vols., Lucknow: Nawal Kishore, 1864–5. See also Saiyid Ali Tabattabai, 'Burhān-i Ma'āsir', in *The History of the Bahmani Dynasty*, ed. J.S. King, London: Luzac, 1900, p. 57; Nizami, 'Sufi Movement', p. 182. Alaud-din Hassan Bahman Shah (1347–58) had great respect for Sheikh Burhan-uddin Gharib, Sheikh Ain-ud-din Bijapuri, and Sheikh Siraj-ud-din Junaidi. He even invited the Sufi saints to his camp during the campaign and gave them presents. H.K. Sherwani, *Bahmanis of Deccan*, New Delhi: Munshiram Manoharlal, 1953, p. 56. See also Ferishta, *Tarikh-i-Ferishta*, vol. I, pp. 277–89.
28. Ali bin Taifur Bustami, 'Tuhfatulk Gharib and Anwarul Tahqiq', unpublished Persian MS, Hyderabad: Salarjung Museum Library.
29. The concept of ecstasy, *sama* and *Chillah-i-Makus* was known to the Hindu priests but when the Sufis brought it into practice, both the efforts converged. Nizami, *Aspects of Religion and Politics*, pp. 178–9.
30. Eaton, *Sufis of Bijapur*, pp. 244–64.
31. Nizami, *Aspects of Religion and Politics*, pp. 230–9.
32. Ibid.

33. Mohammad Salim, 'The Attitude of Chisti Saints towards Political Power', *Proceedings of Pakistan Historical Conference*, Lahore, 1952, p. 235.
34. Ghauri, 'Muslims in the Deccan', pp. 150–64.
35. Sherwani, *Bahmanis of Deccan*, pp. 17–18. See Mohammad Abdul Aziz, 'The Deccan in Fifteenth Century', *Journal of Asiatic Society of Bengal*, vol. XXI, 1925, pp. 569–71. See for details, Abdul Jabar Malkapuri, *Tazkira-i-Aulaiya-i-Deccan* (Urdu), 2 vols., Hyderabad: Hassan, 1912, pp. 460–670; Eaton, *Sufis of Bijapur*, pp. 22–7.
36. Ghauri, 'Muslims in the Deccan', pp. 151–6.
37. Ibid. See also Nizami, 'Sufi Movement', pp. 173–83. Among all these, the most prominent Chisti saint was Syed-al-Hussain Gesu Daraz (AD 1321–1422) who played an important role in popularizing and indigenizing the *Chishti silsila* in the Deccan. He studied Hindu mythology and was conversant in Sanskrit. His *khanqa* was thronged by people of all creeds and cults.
38. Ibid., p. 191.
39. Ibid. See also Nazir Ahmad, 'Language and Literature' (Persian), in *History of Medieval Deccan (1295–1724)*, ed. H.K. Sherwani and P.M. Joshi, 2 vols., Hyderabad: Print and Publication Bureau, Government of Andhra Pradesh, 1973–4, pp. 76–8.
40. Hussaini Shab, 'Deccan, Deccani Zeban aur Uska Adab', *Sabras*, Hyderabad: Idaari-Adibiyat Urdu, June–August 1974, pp. 48–59.

    > The reciprocity of relationship between the *khanqas* of north and south and the Pan-Indian organization pattern and the perspective of some of the spiritual orders helped in bringing the north closer to south and initiated a new phase of reproachment between religious creeds and cultures. The eagerness of Sufis to establish a direct contact with the common man and share the joys and sorrows of his life led to the growth of a new medium of communication called proto Urdu.

    See H.K. Sherwani, *Islamic Culture*, vol. XII, p. 50. See also H.K. Sherwani, *Cultural Trends in Medieval India*, Bombay: Asia Publishing House, 1968, pp. 96–101.
41. Hussaini Shab, 'Deccan, Deccani Zeban aur Uska Adab', *Sabras*, Hyderabad: Idaari-Adibiyat Urdu, June–August, 1974 pp. 7–10.
42. Ibid., pp. 5–10.
43. Ibid. See also H.K. Sherwani, 'Bahmani Sultans of Deccan', in *Deccan ke Bahmani Saltain*, tr. Rahim Ali Al Hashmi, New Delhi: Urdu Bureau, 1978, pp. 323–30.
44. Ibid.
45. Nazir Ahmad, 'Language and Literature', p. 78.
46. Abdul Hague, *Urdu ke Ibtidai Nashu-u-nama me Sufiya-i-Kiram Ka Kam*, Delhi: Anjuman-K-Taraque Urdu, 1961, pp. 19–40; and Nazir Ahmad, 'Language and Literature', p. 82.

47. Anniemarie Schimel, 'The Influence of Sufism on Indo-Muslim Poetry', in *Anagogic Qualities of Literature*, ed. J.P. Strelka, University Park: Pennsylvania State University Press, 1971, pp. 183–202.
48. The motivation power of Sufi saints was so strong and effective that Amir Khusro says, 'The people of the areas of Devagiri and Tilang were all believers in him [Sufi Kamalud-din].' Amir Khuordro, Siyar-ul-auliya, Muhibbe Hind publishers Delhi. 1885, p. 158; Nizami, 'Sufi Movements in the Deccan', p. 178.
49. Ibid.
50. Ahmad, 'The Sufi and the Sultan in pre-Mughal India', pp. 142–53.
51. Nizami, 'Sufi Movement', pp. 173–99.
52. Nizami, *Aspects of Religion and Politics*, pp. 230–9.
53. Ibid.
54. M.S. Siddiqi, 'Syed Mohammad Al-Hussani Gesu Daraz', in *Islamic Culture*, Hyderabad: Islamic Culture Board; Academic and Cultural Publications Charitable Trust, July 1978, vol. 52, pp. 173–283.
55. Nizami, *Aspects of Religion and Politics*, pp. 230–9; Victor Babu, *Popular Culture and State in Medieval Andhra: 14th to 17th Century*, PhD thesis, University of Hyderabad, 1998.
56. Nizami, *Aspects of Religion and Politics*, pp. 211–16.
57. Ibid.
58. Nizami, 'Sufi Movement', p. 183; see also for details Hazrat Sayyid Muhammad Akbar Hussaini Hazarat Banda Nawaz, *Jawamiul-Kalim (1321–1422)*, Hyderabad: Anis -ul- Ushshaq; Urdu translation by Captain Wahid Bakhsh Siyal Chishti Sabri, Lahore: Al-Faisal Nashiran, Tajran-i-Kutub, 2010, pp. 29–55.
59. Tabattabai, 'Burhān-i Ma'āsir', p. 44; Ferishta, *Tarikh-i-Ferishta*, vol. I, p. 316. For details see Report of Hyderabad Archeological Department, 'On the Administration of H.E.H. the Nizam's Dominions for the Year 1347 Fasli (6 October 1939 AD to 6 October 1940 AD)', published by the Order of Government, Hyderabad: Deccan Government Central Press, 1942–9, pp. 4–6.
60. Yusuf Husain Khan, P. Sitapati and M.A. Nayeem, eds., *Farmans and Sanads of Deccan Sultanates (1408–1687 AD)* Hyderabad: A.P. State Archives, 1980; Eaton, *Sufis of Bijapur*, pp. 211–16.
61. Ibid.
62. Ghauri, 'Muslims in the Deccan', pp. 162–3.
63. Eaton, *Sufis of Bijapur*, pp. 210–42. See also Saiyid Ali Tabattabai, Burhān-i Ma'āsir (Persian), ed. Majlis Khatutat Farsi, Hyderabad: Deccan, 1936, p. 12; J.S. King, 'The History of the Bahmani Dynasty', London: Luzac, 1900, pp. 121–4.

64. The *Shattari khanqas* had big *madrasas* attached to them. Sheikh Muhammad of the *Shattari* Sufi order set up a seminary along with hospice because of his teaching interests. See Nizami, *Some Aspects of Religion and Politics*, p. 66.
65. Eaton, *Sufis of Bijapur*, pp. 205–35.

CHAPTER 7

Early State Formation in Kashmir

Nor can religion be stable without royalty,
Nor can royalty be permanent without religion,
They are two foundations interlaced with one another,
which intelligence hath combined in one.

—FIRDOUSI, *Shahnama*

THE STRONG AND positive allegiance that was engendered by popular religious beliefs and practices for a number of ruling dynasties has rightly come to be seen as one of the basic issues towards understanding the nature of the state in medieval Kashmir. From early times, along with other factors, religion enabled rulers in Kashmir to uphold the view that they were the sovereign rulers of the region. Initially, the social expressions of Brahminism—the popular belief system and its carefully designed ritual apparatus—were the dynamic, pertinent and creative means in manufacturing inequalities, and in shaping political ideas to maintain and perpetuate the authority of state. The political inspiration of Brahminism extended over law, justice, administration, and economic organization. Through these processes, it became a privileged instrument and over a period of time, increasingly allowed royal intervention. In the process of providing appropriate social conditions for gaining and maintaining the absolute power of Kashmir's kings, the patronization of Brahminism gradually evolved a hierarchical landed aristocracy of both religious and secular nature. While elaborating administrative organization and governability, the state's allocation of these religious and secular grants of land and their revenues—a practice which became essential on a wide scale—led to the growth of exploitative structures which consumed a large proportion of the state's income. The state's efforts to contain these tendencies led to a perpetual tension between the state and the religious institutions on the one hand, and the state and other dominant social groups on the other. In these circumstances, it was not the state's authority alone which suffered with the growth of private power, but Brahminism—the bulwark of social, cultural, economic, and political order—also developed the cracks and fissures of decay. The process of state formation, which had enjoyed a long life by this time, tried to cover all these developments with a veil of apparent unity and political stability in the region. This veil had been in tatters from the ninth century, but the political disorder and social discontent became clearly visible only from the beginning of the eleventh century.

Different historical circumstances shaped the process of state formation in medieval Kashmir. During this process, various societal institutions facilitated certain class interests and alliances which underpinned and reinforced the patterns of power and domination. The nature of this early state formation cannot be understood in isolation from those processes which led to the evolution of complex relationships between the region's economic forces and the role of the political elite in the functioning of the state. Regarding the origins of early state formation, most of the historians generally believe that there was a transition of human civilization from the hunter-gatherer way of life to the cultivation of land, also referred to as Neolithic Revolution, which gradually resulted in the growth of complex social relations, sometimes associated with progression in terms of political organization from band level to tribal-level formation.[1]

In Kashmir, the first complex formation stemmed from the tribal foundations of Nagas among whom two conflicting and collaborating classes of warrior chiefs and peasants, pastoralists, and craftsmen formed the state's structure. The seats of these chiefs became the first centres of political power. These warrior chiefs acquired legitimacy for their authority through kinship lineages and singular ethnicity, to command the resources and loyalty of their subjects.[2] In the case of Kashmir, too, the Naga tribal formation appears to have been the earliest political formation, from where the early state emerged. The growth of private property and the accumulation of surplus by the Naga tribal chiefs, which led to the increasing social differentiation, seems to have brightened the prospects of socio-political dominance of a particular group, which strengthened the Nila Nagas' power over other chiefs in the valley. Much before the Christian era, the territories of Kashmir were inhabited by various tribes among whom the Nagas were the most prominent stock. The *Nilmata Purana* records, 'Thus devoid of grief thousands and hundred millions of Nagas dwell there without the fear of TARKASAYA.'[3] It is true that these estimates of the *Nilmata Purana* cannot be considered exact because the author has at times circumvented proof and is prone to such poetic exaggerations. Though plausible at times, a critical sensibility of his information does indicate the predominance of Nagas as autochthonous elements in Kashmir with whom evolved the basic preliminaries of socio-political formation. The *Nilmata Purana* was written in the seventh century AD. Ved Kumari Gai attributes the authorship of this Purana to Nila Naga, the chief of the Naga tribe in early Kashmir. But a careful study of this Purana reveals that it is a case of pseudo-epigraphy. It is very likely that the *Nilmata Purana* was written by a Brahmin to advance the ritual apparatus among tribes inhabiting Kashmir as part of the process of Sanskritization, and to popularize the *Purana* among the tribes, the authorship was attributed to Nila Naga.[4] The bulk of tantric literature, produced during the post-Mauryan period, also indicates the existence of Naga tribal formation which was gradually absorbed and influenced by *Agamas* (Shaivite tantricism) at the hands of Brahmins and led to a relatively advanced stage of state formation.[5] *Nilmata Purana* states that there were 592 clan settlements of Nagas sparsely spread over the entire Kashmir Valley. The chiefs of these settlements acknowledged the authority of their super-chief Nila Naga by payment of regular tribute and obedience to him.[6] The

Nilmata Purana refers to Nagas as the progeny of Kashapa and his wife Kadaru.[7] But scholars have different views regarding their ethnicity and origin. James Fergusson takes them as Turanians.[8] Alexander Cunningham describes them as Tarkhas who descended from the Naga chief Takshaka.[9] James Todd mentions them as Toorskas who ruled Arverm in Sakadipa.[10] However, a critical survey of literature establishes the fact that they were among the indigenous tribes inhabiting various parts of northern India since early times.

One of these chiefs, Sadhangula, was even dismissed by Nila for having carried away the wives of other chiefs to satisfy his terrible lust.[11] Evidence suggests that this vaguely defined tribal formation was protected by various chiefs from external threat. The Naga chief Bindusara protected the valley from the east, chief Srimadhaka from the south, and another chief Uttaramansa from the north. The super-chief Nila Naga was thus helped by various subordinate chiefs to hold his co-tribesmen in subjugation and in restricting the intrusion of non-Naga tribes into his domain.[12] It is necessary to mention that the superiority of the Naga chief Nila over others was natural because it was based on lineages and kinship ties, the ideology of power at this stage having no need to look beyond this justification. Such a structure would have based itself on specific polity, but that does not necessarily identify the politically structured ruling class as such. The protection of the Kashmir Valley by various chiefs not only indicates the nature of their relations with the super-chief Nila, but also points to the loosely structured territorial organization which formed an essential element in the process of state formation from early times. This evidence defines the tentative boundaries of the Naga kingdom in Kashmir. These territorial limits of the Kashmir Valley were never stagnant but kept on changing as indicated by literary and numismatic evidence. The nucleus was always the main valley which provided the bulk of its resources and manpower to the state. However, compared with the fully developed models of the early state, this formation does not seem to have grown to that scale in the pre-Mauryan period.

The structural model of the early state, which is derived from a number of empirical case studies establishes that it is a socio-political organization with its definite territorial limits, a centre of governance sustained on agrarian economy, pastoral products, tribute, and taxes derived from trade. It has a two-tier social format comprising: (a) the sovereign and his relations and the aristocracy, and (b) peasants, tenants and craftsman as their subjects. The position of the ruler in the early state is supported by mythical charters and fake genealogies connecting him to supernatural forces. The administration is carried out by numerous functionaries.[13] But it had certainly attained the features of an organization to enforce its authority. It was from these elements that the structure of the future state was derived.

This tribal-level state formation could not possibly remain unaffected by internal and external forces forever. The various forces which helped to break the isolation of Kashmir from the rest of the world included: (a) the penetration by the non-Naga tribes of Madras, Tanganas, Darvas, Abhisaras, Gandharas, Juhundaras, Sakas, Khasas Madaras, Antagiris, Bahiragiris, Kaulindras, Yavanas, and Piscas[14] (the session of these tribes played a highly significant role in de-tribalizing the Naga tribal formation); (b) the extension of Mauryan rule and spread of Buddhism; and (c) the growth of *Agamas* at the hands of the Brahmins.

The tribe was only a commonsensical notion, being a political community based on singular ethnicity and kinship ties. With the increasing interaction and mixing of various other tribes, the existing organization now sought to organize its members (people) by means of concepts which were not familiar from personal experience. It is most likely that the people's recourse to demands believed to be supernatural helped the growth of the early state-formation process. The tantric literature that emerged after the dissolution of tribal formation evolved around religious institutions and ritual apparatus at the hands of Brahmins and Buddhist monks, who generated new social and political role. All these forces significantly influenced the process of state formation. The intrusion of various non-Naga tribes led to a competition to procure the necessities of life and gradually started reproducing the basic structure. The advent of the Kushanas, Yavanas (Greeks), Pahalvas (Parthians), Tukharas (Tocharians), Hunas and Mauryas between 200 BC and AD 300 integrated tribal formation into more complicated socio-economic formation of the mainstream type with the partial development of class and *jati* (caste) differences and alienation within the community.[15] As a result, the tribal formation witnessed endless disintegration into various settlements growing and spreading over river valleys and hills in a widely dispersed manner. In their early writings (1846–86), Karl Marx and Friedrich Engels also noted that only within the community has each individual the means of cultivating his gifts in all directions; hence personal freedom becomes possible only within the community.

Consequently, the community broke up into various groups based on their social positions. Instead of viewing others as helping co-equals, they viewed them as potential rivals for scarce goods. With the division of community into exploiting and exploited classes came the full alienation of its harmony.[16] The old structure began to be expressed in what David Laibman calls 'the gradual dissolution of primitive kinship forms and appearance of rudimentary division of labour accompanied by slow differentiation, the appearance of hereditary priesthoods and invidious ranking of customary status'.[17] On the one hand, these developments destroyed[18] the strength derived until then from the earlier singular ethnicity and kinship lineages, and on the other hand, posed serious problems to the extending of Mauryan rule in Kashmir. The growth of sparse settlements with varied cults and cultural forms restricted the physical interaction between the central structure and these areas, particularly when the means of communication (which formed an effective means of keeping the centre's authority intact in these areas) was of a primitive nature. At this stage, the Buddhist monks and the Brahmins came to the rescue of regional rulers of the Mauryan state in Kashmir. They provided ideological materials for absorbing these varied cults into a culturally and religiously homogenous population and rendered acceptance of the new rulership possible. There has always been a close connection between religion and polity because the state was always in need of justifying inequalities, power, differentials, heavy taxes, and tribute. For this purpose, invocation of the supernatural or the promise of a better life after death offered powerful legitimation. Herbert Frey rightly observes that the ruling class obtained its rents and services by exercising tight control over all the avenues of communication with so-called extra-human belief systems of their own manufacture. Class division appeared as a differentiation of mental from physical work. While the former by use of religion gave the right to supervising the process of production, the latter enforced the inexorable routine performance of labouring tasks.[19] The rulers patronized Buddhism and Brahmins for legitimizing purposes. The foundation of the town of Srinagara in 250 BC and various stupas are attributed to Ashoka.[20]

Regarding Ashoka's measures in Kashmir, considerably more meaningful details are provided by Hiuen Tsang.[21] The Kushana kings Hushka, Jushka and Kanishka are said to have constructed various *viharas*, *mathas*, and *chaityas* to patronize Buddhism.[22] There are also references to an exchange of ambassadors between Kashmir and China much before the sixth century AD.[23] Even before that, there are references to Kashmir in the account of Fa Hien, who spent more than a year in Kashmir during his journey to India. The import of Kashmiri saffron by China dates back to the third century AD.[24] With the growth of Buddhism, a majority of Kashmiris also turned towards it. At this point of time, most of the Kashmiris accepted Buddhism at the popular level and many among the Kashmiri religious elite became *bhikshus* (monks) voluntarily and many among them voluntarily travelled to distant lands including various parts of Central Asia, China and Japan to preach Buddhism. Some of them combined the preaching of Buddhism with their trading activities on the Silk Route. Buddha himself was quite impressed by Kashmiris' proclivity to pursue spirituality and religion. He said, 'The kingdom of Kashmir is where it will be easiest to lead the religious life. For contemplation and meditation, will that be the best place.'[25]

Although Buddhism overwhelmed the religious life of Kashmiris for centuries, unfortunately not much literature on early Buddhism in Kashmir has survived. Whatever has survived is available in repositories of Tibet which was aggressively taken over by China, and one does not know what happened to that vast treasure of information in Tibetan language. There is a lot of untouched literature on early Buddhism in Sri Lanka and that, too, remains untranslated and inaccessible to scholars. Therefore, our discussion on early Buddhism in Kashmir remains miserably brief. However, that does not belittle the contribution of Kashmiris to Buddhism. The *Mahavibasha* (Great Exegesis) which was prepared by various monks under Samghabhadra, a great Kashmiri scholar, mentions:

> Having become the holy land of Buddhism, the high Himalayan Valley, in its twin, had to contribute to the 'gift of Law'. It did so with honour. Its [Kashmir's] geographical situation, at the boundaries of India, of Persia, and of Central Asia, was destining it to play a great role in the spreading of Buddhism.[26]

A Kashmiri monk Gunavarman (431–367 BC) was delighted after visiting Java, when he received an official invitation from the emperor of the Southern Song dynasty of China and travelled by ship through the port of Guangzhou and arrived at the song capital at 431 BC.[27] G. Coedes says that the Indianized communities of South-East Asia became more Hinduized as well, but the commerce and Buddhist missionary zeal were the initial impulses that drove this expansion of Indic culture.[28] In AD 458, five Kashmiri *bhikshus* arrived from Kashmir and introduced Buddhism in China.[29] Interestingly, along with Buddhism, the patronization of *Agamas* is also associated with Ashoka's successor Jaluka in Kashmir. He is said to have transformed base metals into gold, arresting the waters of lakes, his queen Isnadevi placing circles sacred to mothers (*matrikas*). These practices cannot be dismissed outright. They contain a grain of truth regarding the synthesis of tantric Buddhism and Shaivite tantra. The foundation of the shrine of Jyesthrudra and Agrahara of Varabala (Barawul in Wangath area) is also attributed to him.[30]

All these measures reveal that there were periods of constant interaction between Kashmir and China, and Kashmir and the Indian mainland from very early times. Before the emergence of the Brahmins as a resident nobility, the state was helped in its formative process by Buddhist monks. It would be interesting to investigate, in as detailed a manner as possible, if and to what extent Buddhism and state formation accompanied and reinforced each other. But the limitations of sources and their chronological unreliability poses some serious problems. Even if this was counterchecked with whatever evidence has survived, some drawbacks would still remain in the argument. According to D.D. Kosambi:

> The Brahmins were not the only ideological and priestly imports of use to the state. Buddhist monks are supposed to have become powerful from the time of King Jaluka [son of Ashoka] who is further credited with having introduced the four caste class system, legal procedure and central administration headed by eighteen officials which continued as a standard form throughout the Kashmirian history. With later modifications, the monks nearly extinguished the tribal Naga units which would have obstructed any central rule unless wiped out or assimilated by state religion. The later step was taken by the Brahmans who had been reduced to helplessness at the time of *Bodhisattva Nagarjuna*. These priests gained a solid base among the people by writing the (still extant) *Nilmata Purana* which gives official sanction to Naga cult ritual, readjusted comfortably to standard Brahman practice and observances with royal patronage from the time of Gonda III.[31]

The evolution and application of Buddhist and Shaivite tantricism at the hands of priests made the natural forces appear not only as belonging to an extra-human sphere, but accessible only through human prayer, sacrifice, rituals, and veneration. With developing complexities of social formation, religion became the most important instrument for legitimation. For the subordination of the majority also a religious explanation was sanctified. All these attempts were directed to control the primary producers and ensure their complete subjection to perpetuate the authority of the state.

From the literary and archaeological evidences, it appears that the worship of the mother goddess and phallic rituals were the principal forms of devotion among the autochthonous tribal population of Kashmir from very early times. The various art objects obtained from excavation at Harappa and Mohanjodaro provide us with clear evidence regarding the earliest existence of the mother goddess cult. The female figures among these objects are adorned with profuse jewellery and pannier-like management on each side of their heads, pointing to the worship of mother goddess in third millennium BC.[32] Kalhana also refers to worshipping the mother goddess in the form of *Matrika* as early as the Mauryan rule. Under Ashoka, they are associated with queens or the sorceress.[33] The phallic rituals were supposed to be the means of attaining material objectives. Basically, in the pre-state society of Kashmir, people believed that the collective performance of these rituals would help them overwhelm the forces of nature. But with the commencement of the process of transition to early state formation in Kashmir, these rituals were transformed into the esoteric art of the dominant elements in society.

Interestingly, the rituals and symbol of power have never been more incidental ephemeras but are always central to the structure and working of any society. In fact, various rituals were deployed and transformed by ruling elements as a means of ordering their territorial realms and to sustain their earthly dominance.[34] The varied rituals they performed always played a very vital role, as they do in every religion even today. Among Kashmiri Pandits, the traditional element in their religion is represented by a host of rituals, and that ensures the continuity of its form from generation to generation. Interestingly, no single religion is perfect; all religions have their own specificities in terms of rituals, morality, philosophy, ideas of God, and priesthood. It is people's need that gave birth to these different cults, religions, cultures, and languages. Like other human societies, religion was needed by Kashmiris, too, from very early times, even before they evolved as a community of Pandits or adopted and accepted Buddhism and Kashmir Shaivism, popularly referred to as *Trika Shaivism* or *Agama*. They required religion for their spiritual satisfaction.[35]

The evolution of theistic ideas among Kashmiri Pandits has a long and complex history. Its journey from antiquity to the consolidation of Shaivite philosophy, which continues even today as a predominant religious form among them, is not devoid of various stages, from the vague divine sprits of primitive times to fetishism, totemism, animism, ancestor and mother-goddess worship, tantricism, *Shakta*, *Reshi Pratha* (order of saints), and other cult-worshiping traditions and myths. In the early stages of societal development, Kashmiris did worship nature and supernatural forces, such as death, which were not under their control. It is said that fear of death, above all, was the first mother of gods and it was followed by the fertility-goddess cult.[36] Kashmiris indulged in practising all these things when they were deeply embedded in tribal social formation. Primitive Kashmiris regarded the ways of nature as mysterious. In the course of time, Kashmiris became increasingly aware of the advantages of procreation. Man and woman befriended each other. Woman took the initiative and this was not only aimed to satisfy sexual/biological needs but, more importantly, it was also to respond to the everyday challenges posed by material culture in this region and the continuous evolution of life surrounding it, despite several geographical and ecological handicaps. The women took the lead, which led to the development of matriarchy. As a result, in early times, Kashmiris had a matriarchal society with women as more powerful. B. Bhattacharya observes:

> The caveman regarded the ways of Nature as mystery. As soon as man had time to notice something beyond the ken of the immediate, he became increasingly aware of the sweetness of beauty, and of a type of rewarding and charming thrill which was not associated just with satisfaction of the demands of the flesh. Eve's demand was impulsive. She just wanted to know more. She refused to be mystified by life.[37]

In its early stages, people viewed and perceived nature's working as an expression of procreation. In Rig Veda, there is a beautiful description of this phenomenon when a bridegroom says to the bride, 'I am the sky, and you are the earth ... I shall cast seed unto thee, to mix with your juice and so shall we procreate.'[38]

Therefore, phallic worship also dates back to the second millennium BC. The earliest evidence of phallic worship in Kashmir is provided by the stone images at Burzoham. These were later incorporated into the Shiva–Shakti cult by Shaivite Acharyas.[39] The phallic emblems were replaced by the symbolic representation of Shiva–Shakti and the installation of *lingam* in a *yantra* type of *yoni* indicating continuous growth and regeneration of the universe. The assimilation of various mother goddesses into *Bhairava* and *Bhairavi* was accomplished by means of rituals which while reducing the number of *Kauladevis* led to an increase in sacrifice and *chakrapuja* forcing the clientele to surrender their social surplus to those Brahmins who acquired a monopoly in performance of highly tantricized rituals and the *mantras* connected with them.[40]

Therefore, the evolution of the installation of the stone *lingam* in a *yantra* type of *yoni* is not an indication of eroticism in Kashmir but symbolises a continuous process of regeneration of universe and is worshipped in many other ancient societies as well. Bhattacharya further writes:

> The quiescent aspect of Siva is by definition inert.... Activity is the nature of nature (*Prakriti*). For this reason is the female form represented in esoteric sexual union figures as an active partner riding above (*Viparta*) the male. When the Devi is shown as the active power over and above the lying Shiva, it also represents the living aspect of mother.... We call ourselves civilized according to a code of behaviour fixed by us. But these people who lived in the past and were mystified by the wonders of sex, stood in an awesome grand regard for its mysteries.[41]

The Neolithic culture in Kashmir was also dependent on hunting. With the decline of Neolithic culture and transition to food production, women retained their dominant position.

This dominant position goes back to the third to second millennium BC. The end of Neolithic culture in Kashmir gave birth to agricultural revolution. In this region, because of geographical limitations, good going of agriculture was not possible throughout the year. Therefore, there was an increasing tendency to possess land, plants, trees, sheep, cattle, and large pasturage. Development of agriculture and craft-making had the tendency to split up early Kashmiri tribal social formation into clans and towards individualism. Domestication of animals was necessitated by sacrifice to deities and spirits; besides, animals provided protein, clothing, and were a source of transport to Kashmiris in early times.[42] Since agriculture did not flourish throughout the year, dependence on cattle wealth required a large number of family, women and children to care for animals, and with change of time, even slaves like other ancient societies.

Thus, Kashmir had a strong matriarchal society that is not only attested by the fact that Kashmiris were primarily mother goddess worshippers even after the growth of Shaivism. In early tribal societies, while men had to hunt for daily food, women were guardians of fire and makers of pottery, apart from producing children. They evolved the knowledge of plants and have made significant contribution to agricultural cultivation, caring of flocks, herds, and cattle rearing after the animals were domesticated. Women facilitated the upgradation of men from hunter to producer of food. Besides, in primitive societies with the practice of polyandry, women emerged as a predominant force because they transmitted the lifeblood of tribes and clans.[43] Will Durant also supports this view when he says that women were more healthy in primitive societies and equal in stature and endurance to men. According to him:

> The difference in strength which now divides sexes, hardly existed in those days, and is now environmental rather than innate in nature. Woman apart from her biological disabilities was almost equal to man in stature, endurance, resourcefulness and courage; she was a robust animal able to perform arduous work for long hours, and if necessary to fight to death for her children or her clan. The most economic advantages were made

> by women rather than men. While for centuries he clung to these ancient ways of hunting and herding, she developed agriculture near the camp and those busy arts of the home which were to become the most important industries of the later days. It was apparently she who developed sewing, weaving, basketry, pottery, woodworking and building and in many cases it was she who carried primitive trade.[44]

In ancient Kashmir, women also directed affairs in society and were thus raised to priesthood, and finally became goddesses like many other early societies. As active participants in agriculture and in the course of further evolution, both men and women encountered various challenges and mysteries like other societies. People began to pay obeisance to earth, water, fire, the rivers, the trees, and mountains. As a consequence, stone symbols of gods and goddesses came up as emblems for worship and a medium of expression of reverence to them and other deities. *Nilmata Purana* is full of details on many of these aspects. The author of this valuable work has assembled and presented interesting information from a wide range of sources. It states, 'Men possessed of horses should worship Revanta, the son of Aditya. Persons possessing cows should worship Surabhi and those who have got goats should worship fire. Shepherds should worship the god (Varuna), the lord of waters, and those who own elephants should worship the lord of Ganas.'[45]

Likewise, each tribe or group or *jati* had its own set of gods and deities, some of them continued to be worshipped till our contemporary times after they got assimilated and incorporated into different village settlements, irrespective of varied social and economic changes and growth of knowledge systems. People who had been powerful during their life or belonged to a powerful clan/tribe, family or group or *jati* and, therefore, were feared or revered, were especially worshipped after their death.[46] This also becomes clear from the megaliths that were raised in different sizes and shapes on their graves in Kashmir.[47] The practice of worshipping the sun exists from the earliest times in Kashmir. This becomes clear from the archaeological evidence from Gufkral, Martand Sun Temple and other archaeological sites in early Kashmir.[48]

In such circumstances, when Kashmiris were in the early stage of tribal social formation, the religious myths were a source to convey a kind of knowledge by explaining natural phenomenon that could not be understood by everyone. Obviously, whatever little rational learning people had at that time only provided them with distorted information that had plentiful gaps. Such mythification was accompanied by pseudoscience, magic, and false information. This was the only method to provide answers to questions of the fear of death, excessive rain and windstorms, suffering and the desire to preserve human society, and give reasons (false or otherwise) for the natural or manmade crises which stuck early Kashmiri society very often. Bhattacharya rightly says:

> Death not in ordinary sense of decay, degeneration and disintegration, but a complete fade out, going out of existence, following by the decaying life, lingering gradually, but inevitably; the withering flesh, losing its charm of youth, flow of warmth; these as experiences had long since been tolerated and accepted. But the other kind of death; the sudden death of new born; of the growing twaddling; of lovingly young, through accidents, floods, disease and attacks. Such deaths created terror, made man look foolish, helpless. And the apparent unreasonableness of such a treatment, such a scheme of things was felt to be out of line, out of joint. Man got suspicious of some lack of order; some miscalculation, some want of arrangement. This aggravated an unacceptable situation; and man wanted to know, to master, to control this hated, horrid, unknown power, an entirely uncertain antagonist whose spell was final. These mysterious powers of nature, life and death and the urge of these had to have, they were sure, a source a beginning, a central control somewhere. Urge for life's knowledge led to the search for the Divine. Divinity has a rude beginning, in mating, multiplying and separation. Life and the phallic were inseparable both bristled with mystery. Divinity had a phallic start.[49]

With this kind of framework, the self-styled spiritual elite who emerged in early Kashmiri society organized people or groups, monitored their collective thinking, controlled their social relationships, and articulated their dominance the way they wanted. On one of the occasions, the people were instructed by the priestly thus:

> With their bodies anointed and well adorned, they should worship the Brahmanas and feast themselves in the company of friends, servants, wives and children. Since then the Brahmanas should keep the fire kindled in their houses, at night, for a period of six months.... On the eleventh night of bright half of the month, the man observing fast should wake up God Hari with songs and dances.... On the Pournamasi, nothing should be eaten during the day time. After the rising of moon, Krttikas, Karttikeya, Khadga and Varuna along with Hutasana should be worshipped with garlands, scents, incenses, eatables of various kinds such as rice boiled in milk, vegetables, preparations of sugarcane, half ripe barley, cakes of sugar covered with seeds, beautiful trees of lamps and worship of the twice born [*sic*].[50]

The dialectic that linked the emergence of various developments in early Kashmiri society to new myths, and their diffusion among the general public for the stratification of people and then their subjugation by the dominant who ultimately claimed the position of Brahmins, is a very complex relationship. There are many such intervals in the history of evolution of religions life in Kashmir which involved destruction, innovation, adaptation, distortion, patient work, creativity and the behaviour of dominance and subjection by Kashmiri Pandits within their own community. The *Nilmata Purana* and other Sanskrit texts of Kshemendra, Kalhana and others are full of such details on this subject.

We must remember that it was out of such an environment that the religious outlook of Kashmiri Pandits evolved for perceiving the world around them; their institutions of worship and their beliefs grew, and rituals evolved. Generally speaking, religion was not born in Kashmir out of analytical reasoning and needed no proof of its veracity. It was only when people's interaction with various other communities and their cultures grew, which led to the evolution of another religion and began to undermine the previous one, that people began to look for rational grounds. Hence, religion was not a set of propositions deriving its sense from a criterion of reference or from its verifiability. Whether that god existed or not was hardly a religious issue.

At this stage, both the Buddhist monks and the Brahmins realized that there were similarities between the tribal tantric rituals and Buddhist and Shaivite practices. They found them very useful for evolving the Buddhist tantric rituals. However, in the long run, Buddhism failed to triumph over Shaivism because Buddhism simply turned its back on social Durkheimian aspects of religion. It offered no real guidance while Shaivism succeeded, due to its capacity and with the state's patronage, to organize social relationships. The Shaivite Acharyas responded to challenges of the state and Buddhism by extending and regularizing the services they performed on every occasion in the life-cycle, and their presence became firmly anchored in the locality.[51]

From the Mauryan period onwards, when the interaction of Buddhist monks and Brahmins with the tribal population of Kashmir increased, the Brahmins learned the tantric lore of Buddhism and Shaivism, and absorbed the religious beliefs, deities, and cults of tribes in the Shiva–Shakti cult and Buddhism.[52] This superimposition of Buddhist and Shaivite practices over the tribal rituals was encouraged by the ruling elements in order to appropriate to their growing needs the monopoly of political power by influencing the religious life of the people.[53] This relationship between the royalty and the priests is very old. Even in the *Rig Veda*, the nature of the *purohita's* duties and functions indicates this indispensability to royalty. He is said to have accompanied the king and his army to the battlefield and prayed there to ensure the king's victory.[54] Perhaps they (the priests) realized that religiosity was an important force which ideologically bound people together in a society. The state's hegemonic abilities and capacity to structure its socio-economic and political institutions and behaviour always depended on the type of its legitimacy. Therefore, the state had to base its functioning on a certain degree of acceptance or agreement of its subjects, and to achieve such a situation, the royalty had to act more or less in accordance with the existing expectations of the people. At this juncture, the state needed an agency to present its functioning and actions as being in agreement with the people's expectations. In medieval societies, one finds that it is the priestly class who generally played a significant role in engineering the consent of the masses, and the state, in turn, lavishly rewarded this class. Sometimes, this feature is common to most of the early states.[55] In medieval Kashmir, too, the Brahmins began to evolve a bulk of *Agamas* revealing a widespread tendency to extract surplus in the form of gifts from the common people; *dana*, *dakshina*, *pratigraha* became ritual practices in which both men and women participated.[56] With this kind of structure, the self-styled spiritual elite who emerged in early Kashmiri society organized people or groups, monitored their collective thinking, controlled their social relationships, and articulated their dominance the way they wanted.

Given the nature of Kashmir's geography and the availability of labour, the participation of women was most essential even in a one-crop economy which was supplemented by the pastoral and craft produce. Due to climatic conditions, very little time was left for regular agriculture between May and August every year. Everything had to be carried out during this short period. Thus, the labour of women assumed great significance and was essentially needed to cope with the situation. In early tribal formation, the role of women in the raising of crops and in tending cattle was highly significant. Religious texts also emphasized their role of persistence in various social activities.[57] Therefore, the Brahmins continuously exploited all tantric rites and other rituals to ensure regular labour and the services of men and women for the supply of social surplus. They knew that women were that most dependable source of labour and were given equal status with men in *Saivagamas* as well. According to *Saivagamas*, the worshipping of Shakti is the key to success, and a woman occupies equal place with man; she is mentioned as one-half of the man. Like other matriarchal societies, in Kashmir, the general notion about women as coequals of men has in course of time shaped and promoted the organization of social relations between the two sexes.[58]

From tantric literature and other sources, it becomes amply clear that gradually the Shaivites or the Brahmins as acharyas came to closely involve themselves in various fields of human activity. Efforts were made to wean the dominant elements among Nagas from their tribal past so that the superiority of the Brahminical elements could be asserted. To this effect, there are frequent references in the *Nilmata Purana*: 'O Nila, the Vedas have sung about you the eternal one, the essence of Vedas, the object of worship in fire, the fulfiller of desires of those who seek salvation and those who are ambitious of material gain.'[59]

A temple, *matha* or a shrine with the Brahmin *parsada* (corporation) soon became the centre of all religious action. Apart from conducting all ceremonies from birth to the disposal of the dead, Brahmins consented to marriages, scheduled dates for sowing and harvesting of crops and raising of new structures, dispensed justice, and waived the law.[60] Kashmiri kings always acted according to *Smritis* where Brahmin is always given the key role. Both Kalhana and Khemendra have held Brahmins in high esteem in their works. Kalhana says that even the royal fortune could be lost by showing disrespect to Brahmins. He attributes to them a high degree of spirituality, but it was also a manipulating tactic which Brahmins cloaked in religion and spirituality.[61] On all such occasions, giving of gifts and sacrificial fee (*dakshina)* was an important aspect of the socio-economic life of the people. Though initially it started with rituals and symbolism, it soon acquired socio-economic importance. The *dakshina* to the gods and deities may have been symbolic, but to the Brahmins it had to consist of actual objects.

On one occasion, it was laid down that 'having made a fish of sand, one should fill it with milk, provide it with jewels and then give it to a brahmana'.[62] On another occasion, the demand was that 'food preparation of half ripe barley along with purified butter should be given to the Brahmins'.[63] The rituals of *sradha* for the deceased had to be held with offerings of vegetables, meat, cakes, and flour.[64] People were asked to worship the Brahmins with varied forms of wealth on all occasions. Thus, through the bulk of *Agamas*, the Brahmins laid down a general scheme which would ensure that the ritual and sacrificial observances would result in the well-being and reproduction of social groups, environment and crops. Peasants were asked to commence cultivation only after obtaining prior permission of a Brahmin, for he alone practised austerities through which he gained the power to endorse or bestow auspiciousness on time, space, and action.[65]

The *Malinivijayuttara Tantra* while referring to *vastu-yaga* (the household sacrifice and image worship) indirectly indicates the actual motive behind this ritual. It was the perfect way to exploit the resources of household worshippers by a Brahmin guru. This ritual left the householder with bare sustenance. The *sadhakas* were bound to serve their spiritual teachers, make provision for their food and surrender their right to property dedicated to the deity and the guru. Household implements like mull, stone, mortar, pestle, etc., used in the worship of gods should never be touched with feet. The feudal obligation of complete loyalty was ensured by rituals designed to maintain the unassailable authority and property rights of the guru. This explains the emphasis laid on the performance of *yaga*, *homa*, and *japas* in one's home to achieve all *siddhis*.[66]

Although the ideology of *Vimarsha* and *Prakasha* was evolved by the Brahmins, people were subjected to social inequalities through the ethics of *varna*. All this evidence lays bare the fact that the application of *Agamas* shifted the ground from haphazard and fortuitous conditions of society to a well-organized body knit together by an elaborate ritual apparatus. The social implications of these rituals reveal just how intense were the attempts at shaking the foundations of human existence and conditions which determined the material level of people. The main aim of these various examples is to illustrate the role played by the *Agamas* in resting the society on new practices and beliefs produced by the priestly class so that it was to these practices and beliefs that they had recourse to when problems arose.

People were deprived of their basic needs and the ritual apparatus supported only those groups who dominated the forces of production. Among those dominant elements were *gramdhyakas* (heads of villages) and *desadhyakas* (heads of *deshas*—localities or areas) who looked for patrons and allies to seek protection and to mediate their relations with the peasants,[67] because they occupied important places in the social and political hierarchy of the early state. The state had direct control over manpower and resources through these agents at different levels of its functioning from pre-Gupta times till the end of the second Lohara dynasty (AD 1101–71). The *Agamas* flourished under healthy patrons and helped the Brahmins play an effective role in supervising the social and political situation with unrestricted objectives. Not only were they effective in facilitating the exercise of paramount influence by kings and other socially dominant elements over the socio-economic and religious life of Kashmir, but they also provided a rudimentary machinery for the perpetuation of state control and authority. It is, therefore, scarcely surprising that the Brahmins were in a position to draw considerable personal and group advantages from the inability of the early state to control the situation without their help. They fulfilled the functions of an ideology for the early state. This is shown even more convincingly by the dictum: 'For those who shall act according to the instructions of Nila (King) as far as their means permit there shall be health, long life, much wealth. After death those people shall go to the world of gods and their sons and grandsons shall share the heaven.' This was one of the principal ways through which the ruling elite tried to maintain social order and sustained their own earthly dominance.[68] On the occasion of the coronation of kings, the Brahmins are said to have performed special sacrifices, recited *mantras* for the long life of the king, his fearlessness and prosperity.[69] This was how the Brahmins, after committing themselves to the defence of their roles as ritual legitimizers, helped the state to maintain social order. There is rich evidence to show that the Brahmins supplied the necessary technical materials in the shape of doctrines or religious support by underpinning and propping up the exploitative system. Their role was perhaps the most direct structural link between Kashmir's polity and religion but it was by no means the sole link. The kings and other landed elements representing the state also reciprocated by honouring the Brahmin community with large tax-exempt *agraharas*.

The earliest *agraharas* granted to them were those of Levera, Kuruhara, Khagi, and Khonmusa. The *agrahara* of Levera was granted by King Lava. This is identified with modern Lever village on the right bank of River Lidder in present-day Pahalgam tehsil. The *agrahara* of Kuruhara was founded by King Kusa and is the present-day Kular village in the western part of the Lidder valley. The other two *agraharas* of Khagi and Khonmusa were granted by King Khagendra. Khagi is the present-day Khag area near Biru, and the *agrahara* of Khonmusa is the Khonmoh village a few miles to the northwest of Pampore.[70]

From the Mauryan period up to the end of Harsha's reign (AD 1089–1101), a large amount of land was granted to the Brahmins for the maintenance of *mathas*, shrines, temples, and *viharas*. King Godhara granted the *agraharas* of Godhara and Hastisala. These have been identified with the modern villages of Gudar and Asthihel in Kulgam.[71] King Janaka (who succeeded Suvarna, the tenth king of the Gonda dynasty) gave the *agrahara* of Jalora, which is the present-day village of Zollur, a few kilometres from Awantipura.[72] The *agraharas* of Samangasa and Sanara are attributed to King Sacinara. Samangasa is the modern Shangas village in the Kuthar area in district Anantnag. *The agrahara* of Sanara is the village Kother near Achabal town. King Sacinara also belonged to the Gonda dynasty.[73] Jaluka, the successor of Ashoka, granted the *agrahara* of Varbala and also endowed lands to the shrine of Jyesthrudra for its upkeep.[74] The *agrahara* of Kantkotsa was granted by Abhimanyu I (the last king of Gonda dynasty).[75]

Mihirakula (AD 515–50), who destroyed the Buddhist *viharas* on a large scale, granted one hundred *agraharas* to Kashmiri Brahmins out of Gandhara land.[76] King Akasa gave the *agraharas* of Aksavala, which is the modern village of Achabal 8 km. from Anantnag proper enroute the Breng area,[77] while King Gopaditya endowed the *agraharas* of Khola, Hadigrama, Skandpura, and reaffirmed the grant of Khagika and Samangasa. Kalhana attributes five *agraharas* to King Gopaditya but the latter actually gave only three *agraharas* of Khola, the Khull village near Volur area. Hadigrama is the village of Aregam near Nagam, and Skandpura is identified with Khundur village in Kuthar area. In case of the *agrahara* of Samangasa and Khagika, the grant was only reaffirmed because they were given by King Khagindra and Sacinara respectively.[78] The Brahmins associated with the shrines of Shiva Buteshvara were granted *agraharas* by King Narendraditya.[79] The *agraharas* of Katimusa and Ramusa were granted by King Tunjana and his queen Vakpushtha. Katimusa is modern Kaimuh near Adhvin on the left bank of River Vishav, and Ramuh is a place on the high road from Srinagar to Shopian. The lands around Ramuh were till recently the *jagirs* of the Dhar family of Srinagar.[80] King Megvahana granted *agraharas* to the Brahmins of Meghamatha.[81] His queen Amrit Prabha founded the *agraharas* with Amrit Bavana, donating large and fertile tracts of land to maintain them. The villages assigned to this shrine were later appropriated by Mamma, uncle of Cippatayapida, for maintenance of his other temples.[82]

A Brahmin minister of Vikramaditya also founded *mathas* and *viharas* along with the *agraharas* so that the Brahmins could maintain them.[83] The *agrahara* of Bedra was granted by King Baladitya. Bedra is the modern Bidder village in Breng area. The village is presently known for the shrine of Man Reshi who is referred as Manshah in the post-conversion period and is revered by both Muslims and Hindus of Kashmir.[84] Regarding Lalitaditya (AD 725–53), it is said that in practically every town or village, he granted *agraharas* to the Brahmins. Prominent among these were Suvarna Parsva, Phelpura and Locantsa.[85] King Avantivarman's (AD 855/6–83) brother and minister Samkarvarman gave the villages of Suryakunda and Panchata as agraharas to the Brahmins. Panchata is the village Panzath near Devasar area in district Anantnag[86] on the banks of Vitasta (River Jhelum). A number of villages were endowed with as many as 55 *agraharas* by King Yasaskara (AD 939–48). Here it should be noted that the kings in the early state had recourse to religious elements to justify royal authority. Therefore, royal power did not appear as an arbitrary imposition on the subjects, but the growth of *agraharas* would have certainly appeared as seizure of their territory to the *agraharas*.[87] Queen Suryamati also granted 180 *agraharas* to the Brahmins. Her son Haldra also founded *agraharas* when he became the prime minister.[88] These grants strengthened the financial foundations of the Brahmins besides providing security to the donors.

Interestingly, the pattern that was set by these *agraharas* in various parts of Kashmir should not be taken as an isolated phenomenon, but as an essential element in the relations and processes of production. The patronage to the priestly sector and the maintenance of the establishments which allowed them material strength should be considered more specifically as the function of a presiding legitimacy in the existing state of affairs of the rule by a given class. The absolute accumulation of the *agrahara* surplus by the priestly class, beyond certain limits, inevitably resulted in not only social but economic class development. And in the course of time, it was this class which emerged as the main link between the state and the subjects because the state rested on society which had a fundamental grounding in the religion (tantricism) preached and practised by the Brahmins.[89] Unfortunately, information on the exact amount of land that each of these *agraharas* occupied is not available, but it was indeed from these religious and secular *agraharas* that the first landed aristocracy made its appearance in Kashmir. *Svacchanda Tantra* shows clearly how much interest the gifting of land had acquired in value as compared with other objects of *dana* during the period. The *desadhyakas* had to gift away 100 villages, the *mandalesa* (head of the mandala) of 100 villages had to give five, the owner of twenty villages had to give one, and the owner of one *ksetra* (a single plot of land), had to give away a twentieth part of his land, along with ownership rights as *dana* or *dakshina*.[90] It will not be out of place to indicate, though firm evidence is still not available, even an approximate casual connection perhaps establishes that there was a considerable area of commonality of interests between the ritual and economic overloads. Given the primitive levels of development of social formation at that stage, the consolidation of the ritual supremacy does hold a significant key to the understanding of a political formation in general and state formation in particular. However, such a perspective needs to be blended with socio-economic dynamics at work at the same time. For the ruling classes, religion had a useful function; the formation of the priesthood and the maintenance of their establishments contributed to strengthening the beliefs which were unconsciously present in the minds of people. The *agraharas* preserved the people's religious craving for a god and supernatural forces. They emphasized that sacrificial observations were necessary to prevent chaos in society. Life was hard and constantly menaced by disasters; people only looked for religion that would give them support in these conditions and compensate for their suffering in the other world after death. As a result, the growth of the social awareness among people was restricted to perpetuating the domination of power.[91] Since the Brahmins had the advantage of having acquired intellectual hegemony, they tried to put forth these beliefs and rituals in such a manner that they had beneficial consequences for the ruling classes. The Brahmins projected their patrons (kings) as people who possessed divine powers, and any form of protest against them was deemed a sin, since this was an effective mechanism in undermining the magnitude of any social protest. By emphasizing that kings were part of the divinity, Brahmins ideologically conceived changes conditioning the position of various elements in society, thus necessarily involving a change in the conception, structure, and purpose of the existing political institutions. Besides, when the structures of a social ensemble are transformed, for any reason whatsoever, the ideology is also affected. Nevertheless, the differential dynamics which rule the structures of social inter-relationships on the one hand, and the symbolic systems on the other hand, will usually result in these changes not occurring simultaneously.[92]

Brahmins also tended to emphasize the gulf between the producers and non-producers. Since an *agrahara*-based economy was important for their sustenance, Brahmins perceived land as an essential part of their dignity. Their authority tended to be legitimized by their training in literary and religious texts. This also lent special credence to their roles in states or areas where there was secular functioning. Basically, the gradual increase of various grants would have necessitated the need for scribes, record-keepers, and other officials connected with the maintenance of records. This provided another opportunity for the Brahmins to occupy secular positions as well. In fact, under King Jaluka, the number of the offices of state rose from seven to eighteen. With this expansion of the state's apparatus, the number of people in the organization of state also increased and led to the furtherance of specialization in societal format.[93] The most striking development came with the state's reliance on these Brahmins as advisors, law-givers, ministers, and as members of its administrative machinery. With gradual expansion, the number of these people in administration also increased.

The Brahmin Mitrasaraman was the *samdivigrahika* (foreign minister) of King Lalitaditya.[94] Devasarman was the minister of King Jayapida.[95] Bhatphalguna was the courtier of King Semgupta (AD 950–8).[96] Canpaka was the *Dharpati* (Lord of the Gate) of Harsha.[97] Ajaka was the minister of King Salhana (AD 1111–12).[98] Manka, the author of *Srikantha Charita*, belonged to a family of ministers. His brother Alamkara was *brahadganja* (superintendent of the treasury) and later also held the post of *rajasthania* (chief justice).[99] Judicial positions were mostly the prerogative of the Brahmins. Sringara was the *brallentrpati* (judge) under King Sussala (AD 1112–20).[100] During King Sangramraja's reign (AD 1003–28), there were a number of Brahmin councillors.[101] King Yasaskara (AD 939–48) was helped by a Brahmin in his political ascendancy.[102] Keshva, a Brahmin from Trigarhata, was King Ananta's (AD 1028–63) minister.[103]

Brahmin Raka rose to the position of the prime minister from that of an ordinary soldier.[104] Kalhana mentions that even Brahmins in humbler positions were appointed to very important posts.[105] Khemendra uses the word *samanta* as a synonym for Brahmins. He has shown how the Brahmins practically monopolized the power of the state.[106] The outcome of this close relationship of state and the Brahmins was the direct exploitation of lands consolidated into compact *agraharas*, both religious and secular in nature. By taking charge of the state's administrative machinery, they directly transferred control over the region's economic surplus into their own hands. Particularly at a stage when production relations were based on arbitrary appropriation of the means of production, the kings often submitted themselves to the guidance of the Brahmins and spent their countries' resources on both secular and religious establishments. Some structures and the ruins of others suggest that almost everyone in Kashmir must have contributed materials and manpower to these establishments. The structures of Martand, Vijeshvara, Avantipura, and others would have been impossible without creating harsh conditions for the peasants and craftsmen who expended the major portion of their labour on these *agraharas* attached to various temples and *mathas*.

For the rural society, the cultivation of the holdings of Brahmins was an act of reverence towards the deity. Apart from labour services of the peasants and craftsmen, Brahmins, as the members of the landed aristocracy, were also entitled to receive gifts and customary obligations. In the secular functioning of the world, people would generally believe that their life was in fact protected by divine wisdom. Thus, working on such establishments had, according to them, a hidden meaning which was a bond to be recalled in heaven.[107] Since cultivation of land was possible for only half the year due to geographical and ecological limitations, such labour assumed great economic importance. There must have been periods during which it can easily be said that the demand for labour and other services by religious and secular grantees would have led to a serious labour shortage. This, in the course of time, led to the evolution of forced labour which is revealed in recorded information from King Samkarvarman's time (AD 883–902). Kalhana states that forced labour (*rudhabarudi*) of thirteen categories was in practice. Villagers who abandoned the carrying of loads are said to have been fined the value of the load, calculated according to prices prevailing in that area.[108] There is ample evidence that people were reduced to the lowest depths of poverty. On the pretext of offering sacrificial rituals to the images of innumerable deities and gods, for building and rebuilding of various structures of both a secular and religious nature, a large proportion of peasant surplus in the form of labour and produce was extracted on various occasions. *Netra Tantra* gives a detailed description of various items offered to the Shaiva Acharyas and other priestly people on different occasions. He says that deities were offered clothes, gold, metals, precious stones, and various kinds of grains on various occasions to avert the effect of evil spirits.[109] This was done largely for reasons which were not economic.

The rights to these *agraharas* came directly from the state and this affected the proportions of cultivable waste—from above, setting the degrees of decline in the state's share of revenue, and from below, the peasants. Samkarvarman levied special contributions for the pay of village clerks, *gramkayasthas* and *skandkas* as well as other taxes.[110] Khemendra is also very critical of the role of *skandkas* in the revenue administration at the village level.[111] Kalhana mentions that at the instigation of the Kayasthas, only breathing was exempt from taxation.[112] King Samgram Raja himself admitted to obtaining such resources by unlawful means. In King Harsha's time, even Brahmins were made to render *rudabarudi* (forced labour).[113] To maintain the income of the state's treasury, Sussala deprived various officers of the state of their living by dismissing them from service.[114]

The state needed to derive additional taxes to support its existence. Therefore, it created harsh conditions for those working on these *agraharas*. The Brahmins provided justification for their dominance by exploiting people who were steeped in superstition, blind belief, and fear of the supernatural in an archaic manner. These Brahmins could effectively put across their indispensability to the rulers since they claimed themselves to be the creators of divinity. This is a classic case of the ruling classes selling ruling ideas as the ruling reality. Not surprisingly, therefore, contradictions developed between the non-producer ritual legitimizers (whose claims to social dominance did not last long) on the one hand, and the king, who was burdened with the task of not allowing the centre to fall apart, on the other hand. While pointing to the situation in medieval Europe, I. Wallerstein rightly remarks that a crisis is a situation in which the restitutive mechanisms of systems are no longer functioning well and therefore the system will either be transformed fundamentally or disintegrate.[115] But in the case of Kashmir, except in the case of religious change, there was no thorough transformation in terms of the politico-economic structure. Yet the system was in crisis. At times, the state did not hesitate in using the crisis for its sustenance.

From Samkarvarman's time, one finds a marked decline in the state's grants to these religious establishments. It was now that the state realized how untenable the claims of the Brahmins to the large wealth locked up in these religious establishments were.

However, it was not for long that the alliance of the Brahmins and the state remained intact. The Brahmins acted no more as the ideologues of the state, becoming the prophets of time, trying to cloud the strong consciousness of the masses to legitimize the state's authority. Soon, however, this ritual and economic domination came to be subjected to intra-class contradictions. The phenomenon of this interplay of contradictions was clearly manifest in its logical consequence of the decline of the Brahminical monopoly and the subsequent emergence of relatively more secular economic forces in the form of domination by Damaras and Tantrins. Apart from Kalhana, the term Damara has been used by Khemendra to denote the members of landed groups. There would have been some ranking system among Damaras on the basis of their wealth and power.[116] Khemendra used terms like Damaravisaya, Damara, Damarapati, Dammradhipati, and Tantrapati.[117] However, it was only during the twelfth century AD that the Damaras emerged as a dominant power.

The various areas associated with the Damaras are Lohara, Selyapura (modern Silput), Devasara (modern Divsar), and Nilasva (modern Nilav). All these areas are located on the trade routes and also are fertile zones for the good of agriculture.[118]

The Damaras were not in receipt of any land grants and, therefore, did not owe their position to the state. The main source of their power was land. Their estates were mostly located in the fertile regions of the valley.[119] Kalhana's description of Jayaka Damara in the seventh book of *Rajatarangini* throws some light on the material base of Damaras. Jayaka, a resident of Selyapura, is supposed to have acquired great wealth from the revenue of his land and by the sale of victuals as a trader to distant regions.[120] King Lalitaditya also puts special emphasis on the role of agriculture in the augmentation of Damara power. While addressing his ministers, he says:

> Those who wish to be powerful in this land must guard against internal dissensions. Because of foreign enemies (*parloka*) they are as little in fear of the world beyond (*parloka*) as the *Carvakas*. Those who dwell there in the mountains, and are not easily accessible should be punished even if they commit no offence. Because they are sheltered by their fastness, they are difficult to break up, even if they have accumulated wealth once. Every care should be taken that food for more than one year's consumption should not be left with villagers, because if they should keep more wealth, they would become very formidable *Damaras* in a single year, strong enough to neglect the commands of the King.[121]

Another factor which facilitated the emergence of the dominance of the Damaras was their frequent forays into activities of loot and plunder. They could always replenish their exhausted finances by resorting to robbery on the various trade routes cutting across the main valley. In fact, one of the opinions expressed is that the Damaras were the descendants of Udambaras who lived on the fertile Karewas (*uddars*) in Kashmir from very early times. They were endowed with such zones on these Karewas which produced commercial crops such as pulses, oilseeds, saffron, etc. Besides, most trade routes within the valley and outside Kashmir cut across these *uddars*, and the Damaras benefited from trade and also from the commercial crops which helped them to accumulate and multiply their wealth.[122] Kalhana records, 'then the citizens and Damaras striking at each other with unpraised weapons, plundered the treasures and other valuables of the burning palace'.[123] On another occasion, Kalhana refers to the looting of the autumn harvest by the Damaras.[124]

Whatever the nature of their activities, the Damaras certainly developed as a potential force for the medieval state to contend with. The nature of their response to the state was to create a perpetual tension. They felt that the opportunity for their political ascent had been progressively narrowed down by the Brahmins, who had been running the affairs of the state for a long period. By this time, the state had become aware of the unholy nature of its alliance with the Brahmins, but this did not help resolve the crisis. V.N. Drabu feels that the King Jayapida and Samkarvarman adopted various measures to curb the growing power of Damaras but; this was because these two kings extended the apparatus of the state to enforce the collection of revenue, which was falling due to the political turmoil and also to bring the *agrahara* lands under the direct network of taxation.[125] The Damaras attacked both the secular and religious establishments to undermine the political influence of the Brahmins. Damara Dhanva is found expropriating the villages endowed to the temples by kings. One of the temple priests on being asked by King Avantivarman to explain the poor state of offerings in the temple replies, 'In the Lohara district, O King, there lives a powerful Damara, Dhanva by name who is attached to minister Sura and is treated by him like a son. The Damara, whose power is unrestricted, has taken away the villages (belonging to shrine) and thus we can offer to *buttesha* only the oblation.' This shows that the Damaras seem to have been confident enough to enter into an open confrontation with the royal power. Kalhana says, 'When that fierce Damara came out at last before Sura, he made the earth shake with the tramp of his foot soldiers and did not bend his back.'[126]

Drabu considers the Damaras to have been local chiefs who had their own followers and private armies to cooperate and sometimes to confront the authority of the state in Kashmir.[127] He also mentions the existence of the tradition of *kottarajas* or lords living in fortified castles, the remnants of which are still there. This clearly establishes the fact that Kashmir was at that time divided into small chieftaincies of Damaravisayas and Damarapatis.[128] There are lots of references to the civil strife which took place among various claimants to the throne, revealing the active intervention of the Damaras. These interventions in various incidents of turbulent civil strife offered the Damaras excellent opportunities to enhance their power by resorting to various manipulative practices. Samgram Damara, while entering into a pact with the king says, 'If you promise to look upon us at all times in kindness I march before you with my troops on the very morrow.'[129]

Consequently, the Damaras came to exercise a decisive influence on the polity of Kashmir. During King Avantivarman's reign, the fierce confrontation took place between the Damaras and the state forces.[130] During the tenth century AD, the power of Damaras was so well acknowledged that the deposed King Cakravarman (AD 935–6) entered into an alliance with Samgram Damara to seek the help of Damaras against Tantrins to secure the throne.[131] Queen Dida (AD 980–1003) of the first Lohara dynasty in AD 981 tried to reduce the formidable power of the Damaras in the functioning of the state. She had to take varied measures for this. Kalhana writes, 'Hardened by the continuous cruelty, the Queen resolved to kill the sons of Sangrama, who had shown prowess, while they were stopping near her.'[132] They fled to Ghasa in Uttara, their own place and killed Kayyaka, the lord of the gate and others who attacked them. Then the queen feared a rebellion and began to appease them.[133] These Damaras frequently aligned themselves with one pretender or the other and had established their complete control over the political developments of that period. They made and unmade kings through their manipulative tactics and perpetuated civil strife in Kashmir. Therefore, the relations of the Damaras with the state were that of perpetual conflict, although some of them were coopted by the state by giving them powerful administrative positions.[134] Kalhana says that the kind-hearted King Uccala (AD 1101–11) allowed *dasyu* (robbers) Damaras to rise to high posts in remembrance of their past services just as the sandalwood allows the snakes to climb upon it.[135]

Kalhana is very critical of the Damaras. Keeping their nature in view, he refers to them as robbers. Kosambi is right when he says that because of a weak state, the kings were not able to maintain a regularly paid strong army. As a result, Damaras became all powerful by their cooperation and confrontation with state.[136] While writing about the Damaras, Kalhana says, 'Trillaka, who was gathering place for all robbers (*dasyu*, i.e. Damaras) just as the pit is for the owls, consumption for diseases, hell for demons and the ocean for the seamonsters, the, great in deceit got the prefect of Devasarasa (district) (modern Devsar) over to his side and raised a rebellion [sic].'[137] Damaras had become too powerful to be ignored by the state. They also entered into matrimonial alliances with ruling families. A powerful Damara Gargacandra was offered matrimonial alliance by King Salhana, but the Damaras considered him too weak for such alliance.[138] Damaras became very powerful and were fully participating in power struggles in the state. There was persecution of Damaras at the hands of some rulers, but by and large, the kings adopted a policy of conciliation and appeasement towards the Damaras. King Kalasa (AD 1063–89) persecuted some of the Damaras. But when he realized their strength, he reversed his policy and tried to secure his position by posting Ksirabhupa and many other Damaras as guards at their respective places.[139]

During the reign of Ananta (AD 1028–63), Tribhuvana, the powerful commander-in-chief, sought the help of Damaras to deny the throne to the king.[140] King Harsha indulged in persecuting the Damaras. From *Rajatarangini*, it becomes clear that Harsha excluded Damaras from the benefits of lavish gifts and positions of power. Kalhana writes, 'Then furious like another death, he ordered the governor to slay all Dammaras who had become so powerful.' He first attacked all the Damaras of Holada in Madavarajya and killed them like birds in their nests. At the gate of the king's palace, there were seen everywhere rows of triumphal arches with Damara skulls which appeared like cups. Indeed, whoever brought the head of a Damara received bracelets, dresses, and other rewards which were hanging at the gate at the royal palace. After totally exterminating Damaras in Madvarajaya, he hurriedly went to Karamrajya to adopt the same policy.[141] But the Damaras in Karamrajya rose in rebellion and stopped the governor taking any action aganist them. This let to anarchy which was further precipitated by worsening economic conditions in Kashmir. Krishna Mohan says, 'Harsha's rule, though initially witnessing a period of consolidation, later due to heavy fiscal exactions necessitated by luxurious curt and cruel persecution of Damaras saw the rise of grave rebellion under the leadership of Uccala and Sussala, both relations of Harsha from a side branch of Lohara dynasty.'[142]

According to Kalhana, during the tenth century AD, the Tantrins, Lavanyas, and the Ekangas also came to exercise their influence in the political affairs of the medieval state. Hosts of Tantrin foot soldiers formed a confederacy strong enough to punish or favour any ruler of the land.[143] The kings became mere puppets in the hands of the Tantrins and sought their help like village officials, by offering bribes.[144] Kalhana lamented, 'In this land the rulers of which had conquered Kanyakubja and other countries, the kings now maintained themselves by giving bills of exchange (*hundika*) to the Tantrins.'[145] There were plenty of such signs of hostility within the Kashmir nobility at this time. But the obvious division was between the Damaras and the Tantrins. The former believed that they were the key to the state's prosperity and tried to stress their social pre-eminence while the latter thought that their positions could easily be justified along military lines. But in reality, at the political level, the dominance of both was determined not only by their participation in the active political life of the medieval state, but was made more explicit by the official recognition and enlistment of their support by the state for suppressing the other social orders. Since the ideological apparatus of the state had become secure with the decline of the power of the Brahmins, the state continued to patronize the warrior and aristocratic elements in turn in order to safeguard its authority. This is highlighted in *Rajatarangini*. The deposed Chakravarman sought the help of the Damaras to combat the Tantrin power.[146] Damara Sangarama while aware of his own powers, discounts the strength of the Tantrins with utter contempt in these words, 'Tantrins are blades of grass, are they counted in battle, which is a last in which I could not help you.'[147] In fact, the analysis of the nature of the Damaras' and the Tantrins' relations with the king and various offices of state that worked in the shadow of that power, and the nature of their attitude towards each other, is a prerequisite for understanding the strong social and political significance of the state in the pre-Sultanate period in Kashmir's history.

One finds that there was a transition from a system produced by singular ethnicity and kinship lineages, to one depending on priestly sanction for legitimization of the political system. The new political system gave autonomy to the priests with regard to productive land and the surpluses produced. In these circumstances, the growth of the state's apparatus and its dependence on the sustenance obtained by appropriation of the produce, which was by right that of the peasants, was but natural. But the increasing need to transfer production to the priestly class and the monopoly of surplus to the state to support its expanding structure began to affect the positions of the secular economic forces. Consequently, these forces tried to assert their position by forcibly taking over the processes of production. This became necessary as the priests realized that hereditary occupations in the production processes determined the quantum of political power.

Thus, through the evolution of early state formation till the establishment of the Sultanate, a definite pattern of alignments and readjustments is seen among various classes in Kashmir. Two constants, however, persist through this troubled history. These are the institutions of kingship and the royal domination which persisted *pari passu* due to the blind obedience of fearful masses. The kings have changed but not their hierarchical positions. The masses have been taken on a royal ride through this whole process of the legitimization of Shaivite tantricism without its substantially affecting their socio-economic conditions for a better existence. Classes began to emerge in the process of internal disturbances as well as external intrusions during the resolution of this contradiction. The principal manifestation of such a change lay in the gradual conversion from Shaivism to Islam on a large scale. The game has all along been one not of restructuring power relations, as much as it has been of access to power.

NOTES

1. M. Mann, *Sources of Social Power: A History of Power from the Beginning to* AD *1760*, 2 vols., London: Cambridge University Press, 1986, vol. I, p. 10.
2. *Nilmata Purana* (Sanskrit; henceforth *NP*), tr. Ved Kumari Gai, 2 vols., Srinagar: Jammu and Kashmir Cultural Academy, 1973, vv. 986–7, p. 251.
3. *Tārkṣya* is the name of a mythical being in the *Rig Veda* described as a horse with the epithet *āriṣṭa-nemi* 'with intact wheel-rims' but alternatively taken to be a bird and later identified with Garuda (*Mahabharata*, Harivamsha) or Garuda's father. See Ramesh Menon, *Bhagavata Purana*; repr., Delhi: Rupa, 2018, hymns 6.6.2, 21, counted among the offspring of Kashyapa in the *Mahabharata*, 1.2548, 4830 and 12468. It is also the name of the hymn ascribed to *Tārkṣya Ariṣṭanemi*. I think it refers to Aryans here because they were more powerful and aggressive in the neighbouring regions. See *The Complete Rig Veda* (The Vedas Book 2), tr. Ralph T.H. Griffith, Kindle edn., London: Classic Century, 1896, hymns RV 189.6, RV 10.178.1, RV 5.51, RV 10.178.
4. D.D. Kosambi, 'Origins of Feudalism in Kashmir', *Journal of the Bombay Branch of Asiatic Society*, 115th Anniversary Volume, Bombay: Asiatic Society, 1957, pp. 110–11.
5. *Mrgendratantra*, Kashmir Series of Texts and Studies (Sanskrit) (henceforth KSTS), Bombay: Nirnaya Sagar, 1930, no. 1, pp. 32–47.

See also *Gandharva Tantra* (Sanskrit), KSTS, ed. R.C. Kak and Hari Bhatta Shastri, Srinagar: Pratap, 1934, pp. 6–22.

6. *NP*, vol. II, vv. 915–83, pp. 232–50. James Todd refers to them as Toorskas who ruled Arverm in Sakadipa. See Alexander Cunningham, *Archaeological Survey Report*, vol. II, Delhi: Government Central Press, 1863–4, p. 10.
7. *NP*, vol. I, p. 49.
8. James Fergusson, *Tree and Serpent Worship*, London: W.H. Allen, 1873, pp. 60–1.
9. Cunningham, *Archaeological Survey Report*, vol. II, p. 10.
10. James Todd, *Annals and Antiquities of Rajasthan*, edited with an introduction by William Crooke and Humphrey Milford, London: Oxford University Press, 1914, p. 45.
11. *NP*, vol. II, vv. 1–92, 1000, pp. 1–27, 252–5.
12. Ibid.
13. Henri J.M. Classen and Peter Skalnik, *The Early State, Models and Reality*, Hague: Mouton, 1978, pp. 367–650. See also Henri J.M. Classen, 'The Internal Dynamics of Early State', *Current Anthropology*, vol. XXV, no. 4, August–October 1984, pp. 365–76.
14. *NP*, vol. II, pp. 58–76.
15. V.N. Drabu, *Saivagamas: A Study of Socio-Economic Ideas and Institutions*, Delhi: Indus, 1990, p. 36; S.C. Ray, *Early History and Culture of Kashmir*, Calcutta: U.N. Dhur and Sons, 1957, pp. 1–20.
16. Karl Marx and F. Engels, *Selected Works*, 3 vols., Moscow: Progress, 1969, vol. I, pp. 17–24; see also James W. Russel, *Modes of Production in World History*, London: Routledge, 1989, pp. 44–5.
17. David Laibman, 'Modes of Production and Theories of Transition', *Science and Society*, vol. XLVIII, no. 3, Fall 1984, p. 268.
18. Ksemaraja, *Svacchanda Tantra* (Sanskrit), ed. Paṇḍit Madhusudan Kaul Shastri, KSTS, nos. 31, 38, 44, 48, 51, 53, 56, 1921–35, pp. 23–45 See also *Netra Tantra* (Sanskrit), with commentary by Ksemaraja, ed. Paṇḍit Madhusudan Kaul Shastri, KSTS, nos. 46, 61, 1926, pp. 18–27.
19. Herbert Frey, 'Religion as an Ideology of Domination', in *Religion and Revolt*, London: Manchester University Press, 1984, p. 16.
20. Kalhana, *Rajatarangini* (Sanskrit), English translation with notes by M.A. Stein, 2 vols., Westminster, 1900, vol. I, book I, vv. 101,107, pp. 19–20; vol. II, pp. 239–41 (henceforth *RT*).
21. Hiuen Tsang, *Si-yu-ki*, tr. S. Beal, *Buddhist Records of the Western World*, 2 vols., London: Trubner, 1884, vol. I, pp. 148–9. See also G.M. Bongard Levin, *Mauryan India*, Delhi: Sterling, 1985, pp. 21–33.
22. Wieber Reinard, *Memoirs Surt Inde* (French), Paris, 1849, p. 189.

23. Kalhana, *RT*, vol. I, book IV, vv. 102–4, p. 9.
24. P.C. Bagchi, *India and China, Interactions through Buddhism and Diplomacy: A Collection of Essays*, Calcutta: China Press, 1944, pp. 72–3; Kosambi, 'Origins of Feudalism in Kashmir', pp. 108–12.
25. Jean Naudou, *Buddhists of Kashmir* (French), Presses Universitaries de France, 1968, tr. Joel P. Brereton and Claudine Picron, Delhi: Agam Kala Prakashan, 1980, p. 1.
26. Ibid., pp. 2–3.
27. Ibid.
28. G. Coedes, *The Indianised States of South East Asia*, (first edition of this work appeared in Hanoi [Imprimerie d'Extreme-Orient] in 1944, under the title *Histoire ancienne des etats hindouises d'Extreme-Orient*), ed. Walter F. Vella, tr. Susan Brown Cowing Canberra: Australian National University Press, 1968, pp. 19–21, 23, 50, 51, 63–4.
29. Liang Shu, *Dynastic History of Liang* by Yao Silian (AD 557–637) Beijing Zhonghua shuju 1973.25.256. As a result, Shaivism did not receive much patronage and remained in infancy for centuries during the predominance of Buddhism from almost the beginning of the seventh century BC to early fourth century AD.
30. Kalhana, *RT*, vol. I, p. 23; vol. II, book I, pp. 110–12, 114, 122, 312, 316; book III, vv. 348, 350, 458, pp. 21, 23, 46, 47, 102, 112; M. Marcell, *The Gift*, London: Cohen & West, 1954, p. 45, fn. 53–71.
31. Kosambi, 'Origins of Feudalism in Kashmir', pp. 108–20.
32. Sir John Marshall, *Mohanjodaro and the Indus Civilisation*, 3 vols., London: Arthur Probsthain, 1931, vol. I, pp. vii, 49–52. See also Plate nos. XII, XCIV–XCV of the same book. We have a bulk of evidence regarding this form of worship in Kashmir. The earliest evidence is that of *Sapta Matrika* preserved in Devasar and Pandrenthan (Purana Adhisthana) Panels in Sri Pratap Museum in Srinagar. *Nilmata Purana* also mentions various river goddesses. *NP*, vol. II, vv. 82, 145, 159, pp. 22–4.
33. Kalhana, *RT*, vol. I, book I, vv. 122, 123, 333, 335, 348; book III, 99; book V, v. 55. See also T.A.G. Rao, *Elements of Hindu Iconography*, 2 vols., Madras: The Law Printing House, 1914, vol. 1, part 2, pp. 379–85.
34. C. Greertz, 'Centres, Kings, and Charisma, Reflections on the Symbolics of Power', in *Culture and its Creators*, ed. J. Ben David and T.N. Clark (*Essays in Honour of E. Shills*), Chicago: Chicago University Press, 1977, pp. 34–72.
35. B.N. Pandit, *History of Kashmir Saivism*, Srinagar: Utpal, 1989, p. xii.
36. Will Durant, *Story of Civilization: Our Oriental Heritage*, New York: Simon and Schuster, 1963, p. 58.

37. B. Bhattacharya, *Saivism and the Phallic World*, vol. 1, New Delhi: Oxford & IBH, pp. 68–72.
38. Ibid.
39. Drabu, *Saivagamas*, pp. 166–70.
40. Ibid., pp. 167–8.
41. Bhattacharya, *Saivism and the Phallic World*, pp. 270–1.
42. Aijaz Ahmad Bandey, *Prehistoric Kashmir: Archaeological History of Palaeolithic and Neolithic Cultures*, Delhi: Dilpreet, 2008, pp. 34–56.
43. In ancient Iran, the matriarchal tradition was very strong and was even passed on to Aryans. R. Ghirshman, *Iran: A Volume in the Pelican Archaeological Series*, London: Penguin, 1954, pp. 27–8.
44. Durant, *Story of Civilization*, pp. 33–43.
45. *NP*, vol. I. pp. 102–3.
46. Herbert Spencer, *Sociology*, vol. I, New York: D. Appleto, 1910, p. 406.
47. *Indian Archaeology: A Review*, ed. A. Ghosh, Director General of *Archaeology* in India, Archaeological Survey of India, 1962–3, 1966, 1967, 1969 and 1970.
48. B.M. Pande, 'Neolithic Hunting Scene on a Stone Slab from Burzahom, Kashmir', *Asian Perspective*, vol. XIV, 1971, pp. 134–8.
49. B. Bhattacharya, *Shaivism and the Phallic World*, New Delhi: Oxford and IBH, 1975, pp. 69–70.
50. *NP*, pp. 116–17. 'Having made a fish of sand, one should fill it with milk, provide it with eyes of jewels, and then give it to a Brahmana.... Then a nice white bull, clothed and endowed with all scents and bearing all sorts of grains, should be given to the twice born.' Ibid. pp. 116–17.
51. John A. Hall and C. John Ikenberry, *The State*, Milton Keynes: Open University Press, 1989, pp. 29–30. For dominance of Hindu rituals over the Buddhist ones, which also was a cause for failure of Buddhism to create a stable political process, see David N. Gellner, *Monk, Householder and Tantric Priest*, Cambridge: Cambridge University Press, 1992; 1st Indian edn., 1993, pp. 83–4.
52. *NP*, vol. II, vv. 1175, 1191, 1315, 1316, 1386, 1393, pp. 297–347. See also J.N. Farquhar, *An Outline of Hindu Religious Literature*, Oxford: Oxford University Press, 1919, pp. 165–7.
53. Ksemaraja, *Svacchanda Tantra*, KSTS, vol. II, pp. 326–9; D.D. Kosambi, *Introduction to the Study of Indian History*, Bombay: Popular Book Depot, 1956, p. 275. See also J.P.S. Oberoi, *Politics of Kaula Kings*, Manchester: Manchester University Press, 1962, pp. 27–33.
54. S.D. Singh, 'The Early Development of Kingship in PreMuslim India', in *Pattern of Kingship and Authority in Traditional Asia*,

ed. Ian Mabbett, London: Croom Helm, and Melbourne: Monash University, 1985, p. 88.

55. Jean-Claude Gaily, ed., *Kingship and the Kings*, London: Laurence & Wishart, 1989, pp. 220–49.

56. Somananda, *Sivadrsti, Kashmir Sanskrit Granthavali*, ed. Madhusudan Kaul Sastri, KSTS, vol. 54, Srinagar, 1934, VII, vv. 121–5. See also *Socchanda Tantra*, KSTS, X, pp. 61–6, II, pp. 535–6. See Abhinavagupta, *Tantraloka* (Sanskrit), KSTS, ed. Pandit Mukunda Rama Shastri and Pandit Madhusudan Kaul Shastri, 12 vols., KSTS, nos. 23, 28, 29, 30, 35, 36, 41, 47, 52, 57, 58, 59, vol. VIII, 155–61; and *Malinivijayottara Tantra*, ed. Pandit Madhusudan Kaul Shastri, KSTS, no. 37, Bombay: Nirnaya Sagar, 1922, vol. I, p. 697; *NP*, vol. II, vv. 461, 480, pp. 118–24.

57. The study of Kashmir's early geography has rarely been the subject of specialized research. The efforts of M.A. Stein on the subject indicate probable boundaries, seasonal variation, and crop patterns. Stein has based his description on Kalhana's *Rajatarangini* and *Nilmata Purana*. See M.A. Stein, *Ancient Geography of Kashmir*, Calcutta: Baptist Mission, 1899. Some useful literature on Kashmir's geography is also provided by Somadeva's *Kathasaritsagara*, English translation under title *Ocean of Stream of Stories and Notes*, ed. N.M. Penzer and E.H. Tawney, 10 vols. privately printed for subscribers only by Chas J. Sawyer, London: Grafton House, 1924. The literature in the works of F. Drew, *Jammu and Kashmir Territories*, London: Edward Stanford, 1895; Peer Hassan Shah, *Tarikh-i-Hassan* (Persian), 3 vols., Research Department Library, Srinagar: Govern, 1885, is significant in detail and should prove rewarding in scrutinizing some traditional analysis which has been uncritically accepted so far.

58. *Malinivijaya Tantra* (Sanskrit), ed. Pandit Madhusudan Kaul Shastri, KSTS no. 31, vv. 22, 24, 28.

59. *NP*, vol. II, 359, p. 93.

60. There are plentiful references of this nature in early Sanskrit texts on Kashmir. For example see *Katyayana Smriti*, ed. P.V. Kane, Poona: Aryasamskriti Press, 1933, pp. 55–6.

61. Kalhana, *RT*, book VII, vv. 12, 13, 15; book VIII, vv. 768–5, 900–94, 2076. Khemendra, *Lokaprakasha* (Sanskrit), ed. Pandit Jagadar Zadoo Shastri, KSTS, no. 75, Srinagar: The Research and Publication Department, Jammu and Kashmir Government, 1947, p. 17. See also *NP*, vol. II, pp. 147–212.

62. *NP*, vol. II, v. 454, p. 117.

63. Ibid., v. 480, p. 124.

64. Ibid., pp. 189–91.

65. Ibid., vv. 560–3, p. 143.
66. Drabu, *Saivagamas*, p. 99. For details see also J.N. Banerjee, *Development of Hindu Iconography*, Calcutta: University of Calcutta, 1956, pp. 220–l.
67. Drabu, *Saivagamas*, pp. 185–8. For details see Kalhana, *RT*, vol. I, books IV and V, pp. 120–235.
68. *NP*, vol. II, vv. 507, 653, 901, pp. 130–66. The answers to important questions arising out of this type of analysis have been provided by J.R.F. Price, *Rituals and Power, the Roman Imperial Cult in Asia Minor*, Cambridge: Cambridge University Press, 1984.
69. *NP*, vol. II, pp. 13–166.
70. Kalhana, *RT*, vol. I, book I, vv. 87–93, pp. 15–17.
71. Ibid., vol. I, book I, v. 96, p. 17. Kalhana does not give the exact period of his rule but places him as the ninth ruler of the Gonda dynasty. The date of accession of the first ruler of the Gonda dynasty is assumed to be *Kali Samvat* 653, *Laukika Samvat* 628.
72. Ibid., book I, v. 98, p. 18
73. Ibid.
74. Ibid., pp. 124–6. *Agrahara* of Varabals is the Barawul area near Wangath. Except Kalhana no other sources mention Jaluka as the son of Ashoka. See also Bishop Cowie, *JASB*, 1866, p. 10 l.
75. Ibid., vol. I, book I, vv. 174–6, pp. 31–3. The *agrahara* of Kantkotsa is modern Kondur village near Biru.
76. Ibid., book I, vv. 307–11, p. 46.
77. Ibid. Aksa ruled for 60 years, the year of his succession according to *Laukika* is 2587-6-13.
78. Gopaditya also ruled for sixty years from *Laukika* 2707-6-19. See Kalhana, *RT*, vol. I, book I, vv. 89–90, 100, pp. 18, 50–1.
79. Ibid., p. 52.
80. Tunjana ruled for 36 years from *Laukika* 2960. Ibid., book II, v. 55, p. 60.
81. Ibid., pp. 72–80.
82. Ibid.
83. Ibid., book III, p. 14. His calculated date of accession is *Laukika* 2599-2-1. He ruled for 35 years.
84. Ibid., vol. I, book I, vv. 480–1, p. 115.
85. He ruled from *Laukika* 3772-6-25 for 36 years. Ibid., vol. I, book IV, vv. 126–32, pp. 130–1.
86. Ibid., book V, vv. 23–5, pp. 187–8. Panchta is the village Panzath near Devasar area in the district Anantnag.
87. Ibid., book VI, vv. 180–207, pp. 282–6.
88. Ibid.
89. *Malinivijayottara Tantra* (Sanskrit), ed. Pandit Madhusudan Kaul Shastri, KSTS, no. 37, p. 697.

90. *Svacchanda Tantra*, vol. II, pp. 535–6.
91. Abhinavagupta, *Tantra sara* (Sanskrit), ed. Pandit Mukundram Shastri, KSTS, no. 17, Srinagar: Pratap, 1918, pp. 60–5, for details see also *NP*, vol. II, pp. 117–80.
92. *NP*, vol. II, vv. 507, 653, 655, 900, 903, pp. 113–16, 228.
93. Kalhana, *RT*, vol. I, book I, v. 120, p. 22.
94. Kalhana, *RT*, book IV, vv. 137–8, p. 132. He was the fifth king of Karkota dynasty.
95. Ibid., book IV, vv. 469, 551, 583, pp. 171, 173, 463.
96. Ibid., book VI, vv. 168, 194, 195, pp. 248–52, later he rose to the position of the prime minister but was soon ousted by Abhimanyu in AD 958–72.
97. Ibid., book VII, vv. 1177–8, pp. 361–90.
98. Ibid., vol. II, book VIII, v. 472, p. 39.
99. Manka, *Srikanthacarita* (Sanskrit) with Jonaraja's commentary, ed. Pandit Durga Prasad and K.P. Parab, Bombay: Tukaram Javaji, 1900, canto XXV, pp. 40–1; Kalhana, *RT*, book VIII, v. 2423.
100. Kalhana, *RT*, book VIII, v. 2422. The *Smritis* also refer to preferential treatment to Brahmins for appointment to judicial and other offices of state; see P.V. Kane, *History of Dharmasastra*, 4 vols., Pune: Bhandarkar Oriental Research Institute, 1960, p. 271.
101. Kalhana, *RT*, book VIII, vv. 576–90, pp. 130–3. See also Krishna Mohan, *Early Medieval History of Kashmir*, AD 1003–1171, Delhi: Meharchand Lachhmandas, 1981, pp. 211–25.
102. Kalhana, *RT*, vol. II, book VII, pp. 242–5.
103. Ibid., vol. II, book VII, p. 278.
104. D.D. Kosambi, 'Origins of Feudalism in Kashmir', *JASB*, p. 111.
105. Ibid.
106. Khemendra, *Lokprakasha*, ed. Pt. Jagaddhar Zadoo Shastri, KSTS, no. 75, Srinagar: Partap, 1947, pp. 7–12.
107. David Cannadine and S. Price, *Rituals of Royalty: Power and Ceremonial in Traditional Society*, Cambridge: Cambridge University Press, 1987, pp. 1–19.
108. Kalhana, *RT*, vol. I, book V, vv. 172–5, pp. 209–10.
109. *NP*, vol. II, pp. 122–70.
110. Kalhana, *RT*, vol. I, book V, v. 175, p. 210.
111. Khemendra, *Samayamatrika* (Sanskrit), ed. Durga Prasad and K.P. Parab, Bombay: Nirnaya Sagar, 1925, canto VI, p. 15.
112. Kalhana, *RT*, vol. I, book V, v. 184, p. 211.
113. Ibid., book VII, vv. 1089–90, p. 352.
114. Ibid., book VIII, vv. 563–7, 1949, 1951, 1961, pp. 151–2.
115. I. Wallerstein, *The Politics of the World Economy, the State, the Movements and the Civilization*, Cambridge: Cambridge University Press, 1984, p. 23.

116. Khemendra, *Lokprakasha*, p. 60.
117. Ibid.
118. Kalhana, *RT*, vol. I, book VII, v. 122; vol. II, book VIII, vv. 15, 17, 424, 591, 733, 1430, 1637, 3115, 2749, 3115, pp. 2, 36, 48, 59, 112, 129, 216, 245.
119. Kalhana, *RT*, vol. I, book VII, v. 494, pp. 307–8.
120. Ibid.
121. Ibid., book IV, vv. 345–8, p. 154.
122. Ibid.
123. Kalhana, *RT*, vol. II, book VII, v. 1572, p. 389.
124. Ibid., vol. II, book VIII, v. 795, p. 64.
125. V.N. Drabu, *Kashmir Polity*, New Delhi: Bahri, 1986, Appendix I, p. 341; Kalhana, *RT*, vol. I, book IV, v. 628, p. 177.
126. Kalhana, *RT*, vol. I, book V, v. 57, p. 194.
127. Drabu, *Kashmir Polity*, Appendix I, p. 336.
128. Khemendra, *Lokprakasha*, p. 60.
129. Kalhana, *RT*, vol. I, book V, v. 324, p. 225.
130. Kalhana, *RT*, vol. I, book V, pp. 51–7.
131. Ibid., book VI, pp. 280–1, 354.
132. Ibid, pp. 280–2.
133. Ibid.
134. Ibid., vol. II, book VIII, vv. 520, 627, 960, 1640, 1681.
135. Ibid., vv. 2750.
136. Kosambi, 'Origins of Feudalism in Kashmir', p. 139.
137. Kalhana, *RT*, vol. II, book viii, vv. 2731–2, p. 215.
138. Ibid., book VIII, vv. 441–2
139. Ibid., book VII, v. 266.
140. Ibid., book VIII, v. 154.
141. Ibid., book VII, vv. 1228–40.
142. Krishna Mohan, *Early Medieval History of Kashmir*, Delhi: Meharchand Lachhmandas, 1981, p. 202.
143. Kalhana, *RT*, vol. II, book V, vv. 304–31, pp. 224–5.
144. Ibid.
145. Ibid., vol. I, book V, v. 266, p. 221.
146. Ibid.
147. Ibid.

Conclusion

THE FORGOING DISCUSSION of these various aspects of medieval period is an illustration of the fact that despite a plethora of work on this period, there is still lot of scope to unearth its contribution to Indian history and society. A variety of opinions has been expressed in characterizing this period in specific timeframes in the Indian context, but it does broadly extend from the eighth to the nineteenth century AD, though not uniformly in each region of India. The variations of regional specificities were not only facilitated by the geographical characteristics, but also by the speed with which medieval developments embraced these regions and continued to inhibit the features and process of modernization from touching them. Therefore, the features of the medieval and the modern coexisted till the transition was complete when the economy and technology entered into a colonial and capitalist mode, but in certain regions, certain characteristics had not fully disappeared. Therefore, periodization of Indian history should not be viewed from a narrow frame of chronology alone, but should also incorporate the broad contours of political, social, cultural, geographical, and changing historical variants that impact any region's life and times.

It was during the medieval period that the linkages between India and Central Asia were strengthened firmly. There are varied elements that played a significant role in these processes and that provided the social basis for non-Indian forces to extend their area of influence in India. Like any other medieval civilization, medieval India also can never be determined on the basis of whether or not all people shared a common origin. The Turkomans were one of early ethnic groups that laid firm foundations for this long lasting relationship. Gradually they acquired political power. The new political community, therefore, could not expect its members to develop a sense of belonging to India unless the new state valued and cherished them all equally. This got reflected in the state structure, policies, conduct of public affairs, self-understanding, and self-definition. This involved patronizing the ruling elements with a decent standard of living, and the opportunity to develop the nobles while they participated in making their respective contributions to their collective life in the new environment. It was then that the Afghans and Mughals played a dominant role in shaping medieval India's ideas and institutions.

People from outside used to migrate to India earlier as well, but thirteenth century onwards, migrants from Persia and the Arab world brought in new religion and religious elements, artisans, traders, warriors, technology, and a variety of craftsmen to India. Religion and trade played a significant role in medieval India. Medieval Indian rulers were fully aware of the fact that politics alone was not sufficient to promote pluralism and give them stability on Indian soil. They felt that political doctrines were ways of structuring political life and did not offer a comprehensive philosophy of life. They structured medieval Indian polity around religious and ceremonial events. They seriously indulged in encouraging ceremonies and symbolism of great Persian and local rulers. The ceremonial at the court of the sultans and the Mughals was a living thing. They adopted multiple ideological mechanisms to seek legitimacy and tried to undermine violence and establish order in the Indian society.

The promotion of trade and building of towns and cities was one of the major tasks that medieval rulers accomplished not only to get revenues and settle people, but also to perpetuate their rule. The flourishing of commerce provided further revenues that allowed the rulers to fund expeditions targeting locations that brought more resources and opportunities and aided the expansion of the empire. The truth remains that the ideas, themes, and stories connected with these ventures travelled through the highways and were spread by travellers, merchants, pilgrims, and the accompanying traders and armies. This trend led to the broadening of minds with new images, new challenges and concepts and technology. The cities and towns became centres of economic, social, cultural, and political interaction and facilitated mobility in a variety of scales that interfered to a large extent with the age old institution of caste. Though the caste system did not totally disappear, the growth of artisans and other professionals working in cities and towns strengthened the horizontal mobility. This was of great significance for medieval rulers as it strengthened their political position. Their well-trained bureaucracy oversaw the efficient administration of day to day affairs of state.

The ideal ruler in medieval period was a timeless necessity and the virtues expected of him are well documented in our Persian chronicles. Undoubtedly, Akbar was one of the greatest rulers in the medieval world; for him the protection and welfare of subjects was a prime concern. Not only in the context of the medieval period, but even in future, if India wishes to justify its present through its past, it cannot ignore such rulers as Akbar, irrespective of any ruler's loyalty to prejudice for petty ideological reasons. There is no country without its past history. The role of this history is to uphold the pride of all people by calling to mind the unfailingly glorious foundations that were laid in medieval times. It is on those firm foundations that our modern nation state rests. Be it the roots for Indian multiculturalism, pluralism, varied practices for syncretic culture or institutions, medieval India has remarkably enriched us.

In the medieval Indian environment, these developments and the kind of willingness to adopt new cultural practices was an important item in the scheme of enabling Turks, Persians, Afghans, Uzbeks, and Mughals to build the medieval Indian system. The medieval Indian state worked for its political ambitions and promoted cultural synthesis, thus assimilating each other's traditions and cultural practices. This also resulted in new cultural trends that were an integral part of medieval India in its expansion and legitimacy. With the good going of all these processes, the ruling elements presented themselves as the beacon of stability and fairness, and crushed revolts and uprisings to establish order. Medieval India was deeply shaped by various forces. Dependent predominantly on an agrarian economy, no state could advance beyond a certain limit. Therefore, once the expansion of the medieval Indian state also outran its resources, there was a broad disjunction during which new forces intervened and incorporated it into a colonial state. Although new imperial experiments dotted the Indian landmass, medieval India shall always continue to be a great reference point in Indian history, the dimensions of which are wider and need the attention of scholars for exploring the best part of India's past.

Bibliography

Abhinavagupta, *Tantraloka* (Sanskrit), ed. Pandit Mukunda Rama Shastri and Pandit Madhusudan Kaul Shastri, 12 vols., KSTS, nos. 23, 28, 29, 30, 35, 36, 41, 47, 52, 57, 58, 59, Srinagar: Pratap, 1918–38.

———, *Tantrasara* (Sanskrit), ed. Pandit Mukundram Shastri, KSTS, no. 17, Srinagar: Pratap, 1918.

Ahmad, Aziz, 'The Sufi and the Sultan in pre-Mughal India', *Der Islam*, vol. 38, 1962, pp. 142–53.

Ahmad, Nazir, 'Language and Literature', in *History of Medieval Deccan (1295–1724)*, ed. H.K. Sherwani and P.M. Joshi, 2 vols., Hyderabad: Government of Andhra Pradesh, vol. II, 1973–4.

Ahmad, Salma, *Islam and Mughal State*, New Delhi: Sundeep Prakashan, 2005.

Ahmed, Akbar S., *Discovering Islam: Making Sense of Muslim History and Society*, London: Routledge, 1988.

Aijaz, Ahmad, *Lineages of the Present: Political Essays*, Delhi: Tulika Books, 1996.

Alam, Javed, 'The Composite Culture and its Historiography', in *Islam in History and Politics: Perspectives from South Asia*, ed. Asim Roy, Delhi: Oxford University Press, 2006.

Al-Ghazali, Abu Hamid, *Ihya-ulum-ul Din*, vol. 2, extract translated in *Islamic Society and the West*, ed. H.A.R. Gibb and H. Bowen, 1950; repr., London: Oxford University Press, 1960.

Ali, M. Athar, 'Encounter and Efflorescence: Genesis of the Medieval Civilisation', Presidential Address, *Indian History Congress Proceedings*, Golden Jubilee Session, Gorakhpur, Delhi, 1989.

———, 'Recent Theories of Eighteenth-Century India', *Indian Historical Review*, vol. 13, nos. 1–2, 1986–7, pp. 102–8.

———, *Mughal Nobility under Aurangzeb*, Delhi: Asia Publishing House, 1966.

———, *The Apparatus of Empire: Awards of Ranks, Offices and Titles to the Mughal Nobility (1574–1658)*, Delhi: Oxford University Press, 1985.

Ali, Musawi al-Qadiri, 'Mishat-i-Nabuwat' (Persian MS), *Tazkira*, no. 21, Asafiya Library, Hyderabad, 1983.

Ali, Sayyid, *Tarikh-i-Kashmir*, Persian MS, folio 16a, Research Department Library, Srinagar, Jammu and Kashmir.

Ali, Syeed Ameer, *The Spirit of Islam*, London: W.H. Allen, 1931.

Altman, Irwin and Martin M. Chemers, *Culture and Environment*, Cambridge: Cambridge University Press, 1984.

American Historical Review, vol. 65, no. 3, April 1960.

Ashraf, K.M., *Life and Conditions of the People of Hindustan*, 2nd edn., Delhi: Munshiram Manoharlal, 1969.

Aziz, Ahmad, *Studies in Islamic Culture in Indian Environment*, Oxford: Clarendon, 1969.

Aziz, Mahmud Abdul, 'The Deccan in Fifteenth Century', *Journal of Asiatic Society of Bengal*, vol. 21, 1925, pp. 569–71.

Azzaroli, A., *An Early History of Horsemanship*, Leiden: Brill, 1985.

Babu Victor, *Popular Culture and State in Medieval Andhra: 14th to 17th Century*, PhD thesis, University of Hyderabad, 1998.

Babur Padshah Ghazi, Zahir-ud-din Muhammad, *Babur Nama*, tr. A.S. Beveridge, London: Luzac, 1922, repr., Delhi: Low Price, 1989.

Badauni, A.Q., *Muntakhab-ut-Tawarikh*, ed. George S.A. Ranking, W.H. Lowe and Sir Wolseley Haig, 3 vols., Calcutta: Bibliotheca Indica, 1925; repr., Delhi: Low Price, 1986.

Bagchi P.C., 'India and China', *Interactions through Buddhism and Diplomacy: A Collection of Essays*, Calcutta: China Press, 1944.

Bandari, Shujan Rai, *Khulasat-ul-Tawarikh*, tr. J.N. Sarkar, under the title *India of Aurangzib*, Calcutta: M.C. Sarkar & Sons, 1912.

Bandey, Aijaz Ahmad, *Prehistoric Kashmir: Archaeological History of Palaeolithic and Neolithic Cultures*, Delhi: Dilpreet, 2008.

Banerjee, J.N., *Development of Hindu Iconography*, Calcutta: University of Calcutta, 1956.

Barani, Zia ud-din, *Tarikh-i-Firuzshahi*, ed. Syed Ahmad Khan, W.N. Less and Kabiruddin, Calcutta: Bibliotheca Indica, 1862.

Barfield, Thomas J., *The Perilous Frontier: Nomadic Empires and China*, Cambridge, Mass.: Basil Blackwell, 1989.

Barthold, V.V., *Four Studies on History of Central Asia*, tr. V. and T. Minorsky, Leiden: Brill, 1962.

Basham, A.L., ed., *Cultural History of India*, Oxford: Clarendon, 1975; repr., Delhi: Oxford University Press, 1998.

Battuta, Ibn, *Kitab-ur-Rahla of Ibn Battuta*, vol. 2, Cairo, 1870.

———, *Rehla*, tr. Agha Mahdi Hussain, Baroda: Oriental Institute, 1953.

———, *Safarnama*, tr. H.A.R. Gibb, *The Travels of Ibn Battuta*, AD *1325–1354*, published for the Hakluyt Society, London: Cambridge University Press, 1958.

Bennett, Lance W., 'Myth, Ritual and Political Control', *Journal of Communication*, vol. 30, no. 4, 1980, pp. 166–79.

Bhattacharya B., *Saivism and the Phallic World*, New Delhi: Oxford & IBH, vol. 1, 1975.

Bongard-Levin, G.M., *Mauryan India*, Delhi: Sterling, 1985.

Braudel, Fernand, 'History and Social Sciences: The Long Duree', in *Review: A Journal of the Fernand Braudel Centre for the Study of Economies, Historical Systems, and Civilizations at Binghamton University, State University of New York*, vol. 32, no. 2, 2009, pp. 171–203.

———, *On History*, tr. Sarah Matthews, London: Weidenfeld and Nicolson, 1980.

Browne, E.G., tr., *Chahar Maqala: ('Four Discourses') of Nizami-i-Arudi of Samarqand, Followed by an Abridged Translation of Mirza Muhammad's Notes to the Persian Text*, London: Luzac, 1921.

Bull, Marcus, *Thinking Medieval: An Introduction to the Study of the Middle Ages*, New York: Palgrave Macmillan, 2005.

Bustami Ali bin Taifur, 'Tuhfatulk Gharib and Anwarul Tahqiq', unpublished Persian MS, Hyderabad: Salarjung Museum Library, n.d.

Cannadine, David and Simon Price, eds., *The Rituals of Royalty: Power and Ceremonial in Traditional Societies*, Cambridge: Cambridge University Press, 1987.

Carpenter, C.R., 'Territoriality: A Review of Concept and Problems', in *Behavior and Evolution*, ed. Anne Roe and George G. Simpson, New Haven: Yale University Press, 1958.

Chand, Tara, *Influence of Islam on Indian Culture*, 2nd edn., Allahabad: Indian Press, 1976.

Chandra, Satish, 'Some Religious Grants of Aurangzeb to "Maths" in the State of Marwar', *Proceedings of the Indian History Congress*, Jabalpur, vol. 32, 1970.

Chattopadhyay, B.D., *Making of Early Medieval India*, Delhi: Oxford University Press, 1994; repr., 2012.

Claessen, Henri J.M. and Peter Skalnik, *The Early State, Models and Reality*, The Hague: Mouton, 1978.

Claessen, Henri J.M., 'The Internal Dynamics of Early State', *Current Anthropology*, vol. XXV, no. 4, August–October 1984, pp. 365–79.

Coedes G., *The Indianised States of South East Asia*, 1st edn. under the title *Histoire ancienne des etats hindouises d'Extreme-Orient*, Hanoi: Imprimerie d'Extreme-Orient, 1944; ed. Walter F. Vella, tr. Susan Brown Cowing, Canberra: Australian National University Press, 1968.

Cunningham Alexander, *Archaeological Survey Report*, vol. II, Delhi: Government Central Press, 1863.

Dalrymple, William, *The Last Mughal: The Fall of a Dynasty, Delhi 1857*, Delhi: Viking, 2006.

Davies, Elsepth, *The Years of Barbarians, Edinburgh:* Pentland, 1988.

Delvoye, Francoise 'Nalini', ed., *Confluence of Cultures: French Contribution to Indo-Persian Studies*, New Delhi: Manohar, 1995.

Derrett, J.D.M, *The Hoysalas*, Oxford: Oxford University Press, 1957.

Drabu, V.N., *Kashmir Polity*, New Delhi: Bahri, 1986.

———, *Saivagamas: A Study of Socio-Economic Ideas and Institutions*, Delhi: Indus, 1990.

Drew, F., *Jammu and Kashmir Territories*, London: Edward Stanford, 1895.

Dughlat, Mirza Haidar, *Tarikh-i-Rashidi*, tr. N. Elias and E. Denison Ross, London: Sampson, Low, Marston, 1895.

Durant Will, *Story of Civilization: Our Oriental Heritage*, New York: Simon and Schuster, 1963.

Dwivedi, S.D., *Relation of Rajputs with Delhi Sultans,* AD *1206–1526*, Agra: Sriram Mehra, 1978.

Eaton, Richard M., *Essays on Islam and Indian History*, Delhi: Oxford University Press, 2000.

———, *Sufis of Bijapur*, Princeton: Princeton University Press, 1978.

Elliot, H.M. and John Dowson, *The History of India, as Told by its Own Historians*, 8 vols., London: Trübner, 1867–77; repr., Delhi: D.K. Publishers, 2001.

Erskine, William, *History of India*, London: Longmans, 1854, cited in H.G. Knee, *Turks in India*, London: W.H. Allen, 1879.

Farooqui, Salma Ahmad, *Islam and the Mughal State*, New Delhi: Sundeep Prakashan, 2005.

Farquhar, J.N., *An Outline of Hindu Religious Literature*, London: Oxford University Press, 1919.

Faruki, Zahiruddin, *Aurangzeb and His Times*, Delhi: Idarah-i Adabiyat-i Delli, 1972.

Fazl, Abul, *Ain-i-Akbari*, tr. and ed. Henry Blochmann and H.S. Jarrett, 3 vols., 2nd edn., Calcutta: The Asiatic Society, 1927.

———, *Ain-i-Akbari*, tr. Henry Blochmann (vol. 1) and Col. James (vols. 2 and 3), Calcutta: Bibliotheca Indica, 1867.

Fergusson James, *Tree and Serpent Worship*, London: W.H. Allen, 1873.

Ferishta Abdul Qasim Hindu Shah, *Tarikh-i-Ferishta*, tr. John Briggs, *History of the Rise of Muhammadan Power in India*, 3 vols., Lucknow: Nawal Kishore, 1864–5.

Forster, William, *The Embassy of Sir Thomas Roe to the Court of the Great Mogul, 1615–1619*, London: Hakluyt Society, 1899.

Forsyth, T.D., *Report of a Mission to Yarkund in 1873, under Command of Sir T.D. Forsyth, with Historical and Geographical Information*

Regarding the Possessions of the Ameer of Yarkund, Calcutta: Foreign Department, 1875.

Fragner, Bert G., 'Social and Internal Economic Affairs', in *The Cambridge History of Iran*, vol. 6, ed. Laurence Lockhart and Peter Jackson, Cambridge: Cambridge University Press, 1986.

Frank, Andre Gunder, 'The Centrality of Central Asia', *Comparative Asian Studies*, no. 8, Amsterdam: V.U. University Press, 1992.

Frey, Herbert, 'Religion as an Ideology of Domination', in *Religion and Revolt*, Manchester: Manchester University Press, 1984.

Gaborieau, Marc, Muzaffar Alam, Francoise 'Nalini' Delvoye, eds., *The Making of Indo-Persian Culture: Indian and French Studies*, New Delhi: Manohar and Centre de Sciences Humaines, 2000.

Gaily Jean-Claude, ed., *Kingship and the Kings*, London: Laurence & Wishart, 1989.

Gandharva Tantra (Sanskrit), Kashmir Series of Texts and Studies (KSTS), ed. R.C. Kak and Hari Bhatta Shastri, Srinagar: Pratap, 1934.

Gellner, David N., *Monk, Householder and Tantric Priest*, Cambridge: Cambridge University Press, 1992.

Ghauri, Iftikhar Ahmad, 'Muslims in the Deccan in Middle Ages: An Historical Survey', *Islamic Culture*, July 1975.

Ghirshman, R., *Iran: From the Earliest Times to the Islamic Conquest*, London: Penguin, 1951.

Gimbutas, Marija, *The Early Civilization of Europe*, Indo-European Studies Centre, Los Angeles: University of California Press, 1980.

Gordon, Stewart, ed., 'Introduction: Ibn Battuta and a Region of Robing', in *Robes of Honour: Khil'at in Pre-Colonial and Colonial India*, Delhi: Oxford University Press, 2003.

Goswami, B.N. and J.S. Grewal, *The Mughals and Jogis of Jakhbar*, Simla: Indian Institute of Advanced Study, 1967.

Greertz, C., 'Centres, Kings, and Charisma, Reflections on the Symbolics of Power', in *Culture and its Creators (Essays in Honour of E. Shills)*, ed. J. Ben David and T.N. Clark, Chicago: Chicago University Press, 1977.

Grewal, J.S., *The Sikhs of Punjab*, The New Cambridge History of India, vol. 3, Cambridge: Cambridge University Press, 1990.

Grover, B.L. and Alka Mehta, *A New Look at Modern Indian History: From 1707 to the Modern Times*, revd. edn., New Delhi: S. Chand, 2011.

Gupta, Ishwar Prakash, *Urban Glimpses of Mughal India: Agra, the Imperial Capital, 16th & 17th Centuries*, Delhi: Discovery, 1986.

Habib, Irfan, 'Agrarian Economy', ed. Tapan Raychaudhuri and Irfan Habib, *The Cambridge History of India*, 2 vols., Delhi: Orient Longman, 1987.

———, 'Formation of Sultanate Ruling Class of the Thirteenth Century', *Medieval India I: Researches in the History of India, 1200–1750*, ed. Habib, Delhi: Oxford University Press, 1992.

———, 'Technology and Social Change', *Presidential Address, Indian History Congress*, Varanasi, 1969.

———, 'The Eighteenth Century in Indian Economic History', in *The Eighteenth Century in India*, ed. Seema Alvi, Delhi: Oxford University Press, 2002.

———, *Essays in Indian History: Towards a Marxist Perception*, Delhi: Tulika, 1995.

———, *Interpreting Indian History*, Shillong: North Eastern Hill University Publication, 1988.

———, *The Agrarian System of Mughal India, 1556–1707*, Bombay: Asia, 1963; repr., Delhi: Oxford University Press, 2013.

———, *The Economic History of Medieval India*, Delhi: Tulika, 2001.

Habib, Mohammad, *Politics and Society during the Early Medieval Period*, vol. 1 of *Collected Works of Professor Mohammad Habib*, ed. K.A. Nizami, 2 vols., Delhi: People's Publishing House, vol. 1, 1974; vol. 2, 1981.

———, *Sultan Mahmud of Ghaznin*, 1951; repr., Delhi: S. Chand, 1967.

Habibullah, A.B.M., *The Foundation of Muslim Rule in India: A History of the Establishment and Progress of the Turkish Sultanate of Delhi, 1206–1290 A.D.*, 2nd revd. edn., Allahabad: Central Book Depot, 1961.

Haig, Wolseley, ed., *The Cambridge History of India*, 5 vols., Cambridge: Cambridge University Press, vol. 3, 1987.

Hall, John A. and C. John Ikenberry, *The State*, Milton Keynes: Open University Press, 1989.

Hambly, Gavin, *Central Asia*, Weidenfeld and Nicholson Universal History, vol. 16, London: Wedenfeld and Nicholson, 1969.

Hangloo, Rattan Lal, 'Kashmir under Sultan Zain-ul-Abidin', *NEHU, Journal of Humanities and Social Sciences*, vol. 1, 1998, pp. 21–30.

———, 'Sufism in Medieval Deccan: Politics and Worship', Presidential Address (Medieval Section), *Proceedings of Andhra Pradesh History Congress*, 24th Annual Session, Rajahmundry, Andhra Pradesh, January 2000.

———, 'Mass Conversion in Medieval Kashmir: Academic Perceptions and Peoples Practices', in *The Valley of Kashmir: The Making and Unmaking of Composite Culture?*, ed. Aparna Rao and T.N. Madan, Delhi: Manohar, 2008.

———, *The State in Medieval Kashmir*, Delhi: Manohar, 2000.

Haque, Abdul, *Urdu ke Ibtidai Nashu-u-nama me Sufiya-i-Kiram Ka Kam*, Delhi: Anjuman-K-Taraque Urdu, 1961.

Harawi, Khawaja Nimatullah, *Makhzan-i-Afghana* (also known as *Tarikh-i-Khanjahan Lodi*), in *A History of India, as Told by its Own Historians: The Muhammadan Period*, ed. and tr. H.M. Elliot and John Dowson, vol. 5, London: Trübner, 1867–77.

Hardy, Peter, 'Islam and Muslims in South Asia', in *The Crescent in the East Islam in Asia Major*, ed. R. Israeli, London: Humanities Press, 1982.

———, 'Modern Muslim Historical Writing on Medieval Muslim India', in *Historians of India, Pakistan and Ceylon*, ed. C.H. Philips, London: Oxford University Press, 1961.

———, 'Some Studies in Pre-Mughal Muslim Historiography', in *Historians of India, Pakistan and Ceylon*, ed. C.H. Philips, London: Oxford University Press, 1961.

Hasan, Ibn, *The Central Structure of Mughal Empire and Its Practical Working up to the year 1657*, London: Oxford University Press, 1936; repr., Delhi: Munshiram Manoharlal, 1970.

Hassan, Amir, *Fawaid Al-Fawad*, ed. Latif Malik, Lahore: Amir Ali Sijzi Dehlvi, 1966.

Herzfeld, E., *Archaeological History of Iran*, London: British Academy, 1935.

———, *Iran in the Ancient East*, London: Oxford University Press, 1941.

Hiuen Tsang, *Si-yu-ki*, tr. S. Beal, *Buddhist Records of the Western World*, 2 vols., London: Trübner, 1884.

Hockett, C.F. and R. Ascher, 'The Human Revolution', *Current Anthropology*, vol. 5, no. 3, June 1964.

Hunter, W.W., *A Brief History of the Indian Peoples*, London: Trübner, 1882; 23rd repr., Delhi: Vikram Jain, 1990.

Husain, Yusuf, *Indo-Muslim Polity (Turko-Afghan Period)*, Simla: Indian Institute of Advanced Study, 1971.

Hussain, Agha Mehdi, *Tughlaq Dynasty*, Calcutta: Thacker Spink, 1933; revd. edn., Delhi: S. Chand, 1976.

Hussain, Syed Ata, *Maktubat* (Persian), Hyderabad: Anis-ul-Ushshaq, 1901.

Hussaini Hazrat Sayyid Muhammad Akbar, Hazarat Banda Nawaz, *Jawamiul-Kalim (1321–1422)*, tr. Captain Wahid Bakhsh Siyal Chishti Sabri, Lahore: Al-Faisal, 2010.

Inden, Ronald, 'Introduction: 'From Philogical to Dialogical Texts', in *Querying the Medieval Texts and the History of the practices in South Asia*, ed. Ronald Inden, Jonathan Walters and Daud Ali, New York: Oxford University Press, 2000.

Indian Archaeology: A Review, ed. A. Ghosh, Director General of Archaeology in India, Archaeological Survey of India, 1962–3, 1966, 1967, 1969 and 1970.

Isami, Khwaja Abdul Malik, *Futuh-us-Salatin (Persian)*, ed. A. Mahdi Husain, Delhi: Educational Press, 1938.

Izzatullah, Mir, 'Safar-Nama (AD 1812–13)', unpublished MS, Research Department Library, Kashmir University, Srinagar.

Jahangir, Nooruddin, *Tuzuk-i-Jahangiri*, tr. Alexander Rogers, ed. Henry Beveridge, 1909, 2 vols., London: Royal Asiatic Society, 1909.

Jalibi, Jamil, *Tarikh-i-Adab-k-Urdu*, vol. I, *Agaz se 1750 tak* (Urdu), Lahore: Majlis Taraki Urdu Adab, 1975.

Jones, Sir William, *Dissertations and Miscellaneous Pieces Relating to the History and Antiquities, the Arts, Sciences, and Literature of Asia*, 4 vols., London: G. Nicol, J. Walter, and J. Sewell, 1792.

Kalhana, *Rajatarangini*, tr. M.A. Stein, under the title *River of Kings*, 3 vols.; repr., Delhi: Motilal Banarasidas, 1979.

Kane, P.V., ed., *Katyayana Smriti*, Poona: Aryasamskriti Press, 1933.

———, *History of Dharmasastra*, 4 vols., Pune: Bhandarkar Oriental Research Institute, 1960.

Kertzer, David, *Ritual, Politics, and Power*, New Haven: Yale University Press, 1988.

Kessler, Clive S., *Islam and Politics in a Malay State: Kelantan 1838–1969*, Ithaca: Cornell University Press, 1978.

Khan, Iqtidar Alam, 'Akbar's Personality Traits and World Outlook, A Critical Reappraisal', *Social Scientist*, vol. 20, no. 9, September–October 1992, pp. 16–30.

Khan, Yusuf Husain, P. Sitapati and M.A. Nayeem, eds., *Farmans and Sanads of Deccan Sultanates (1408–1687 AD)*, Hyderabad: A.P. State Archives, 1980.

Khemendra, *Lokaprakasha* (Sanskrit), ed. Pandit Jagadar Zadoo Shastri, KSTS, no. 75, Srinagar: Research and Publication Department, Jammu and Kashmir Government, 1947.

———, *Samayamatrika* (Sanskrit), ed. Durga Prasad and K.P. Parab, Bombay: Nirnaya Sagar, 1925.

Khusrau, Amir, *Qiran-us-Sadain*, ed. Muhammed Faizullah and Mirza Sher Ali Beg, Lucknow: Newal Kishor, 1845.

Khusro Amir, 'Khazain-Al-Futuh', MS, British Museum, 1838; tr. H.M. Elliot and John Dowson, *History of India, as Told by Its Own Historians*, 8 vols., London: Trübner, 1871.

———, *Siyar-ul-auliya*, Delhi: Muhibbe Hind, 1885.

Kosambi, D.D., 'Origins of Feudalism in Kashmir', *Journal of the Bombay Branch of Asiatic Society*, 115th Anniversary Volume, Bombay: Asiatic Society, 1957.

———, *Introduction to the Study of Indian History*, Bombay: Popular Book Depot, 1956.

Krader, Lawrence, *Peoples of Central Asia*, Bloomington: Indiana University Press, 1971.

Ksemaraja, *Svacchanda Tantra* (Sanskrit), ed. Pandit Madhusudan Kaul Shastri, KSTS, nos. 31, 38, 44, 48, 51, 53, 56, Bombay: Nirnaya Sagar, 1921–1935.

Kulke, Hermann, ed., *The State in India, 1000–1700: Themes in Indian History*, New York and Delhi: Oxford University Press, 1995.

Kuzmina, Y.Y., and K.F. Smirnov, 'The Origin of Indo-Iranians in the Light of Recent Archaeological Data', *Journal of Central Asia*, vol. 1, no. 1, 1978, pp. 68–70.

Labh, Vijay Lakshmi, *Researches on Economics of Delhi Sultanate: Collection of Some Challenging Historical Concepts in Reinterpretations*, Delhi: Abhijeet, 2015.

Lahori, Abdul Hamid, *Padshah Nama*, ed. Moulvi Kabiruddin and Moulvi Abdurahim, Calcutta: Bibliotheca Indica, 1878, vol. 2.

Laibman, David, 'Modes of Production and Theories of Transition', *Science and Society*, vol. 48, no. 3, 1984, pp. 257–94.

Lal, Ruby, *Domesticity and Power in the Early Mughal World*, New York: Cambridge University Press, 2005.

Lambton, A.K.S., 'Reflection in Iqta', in *Arabic and Islamic Studies in Honour of Hamilton A.R. Gibb*, ed. George Makdisi, Leiden: Brill, 1965.

Lane-Poole, Stanley, *Babar*, London: Fischer Unwin, 1914; repr., Delhi: Low Price, 1990.

———, *Mediaeval India Under Mohammedan Rule, 712–1764, London:* Haskell House, 1903; repr., Delhi: Low Price, 1990.

Lapidus, Ira M., 'State and Religion in Islamic Societies', *Past and Present*, vol. 151, no. 1, May 1996, pp. 3–27.

Larson, Gerald James, *India's Agony over Religion*, Delhi: Oxford University Press, 1997.

Lemercinier, Genevieve, *Religion and Ideology in Kerala*, Delhi: D.K. Agencies, 1984.

Lewis Bernard, *The Arabs in History*, 4th edn., London: Oxford University Press, 1966.

Lockhart, Laurence and Peter Jackson, eds., *The Cambridge History of Iran*, 7 vols., Cambridge: Cambridge University Press, vol. 6, 1986.

Ludden, David, *India and South Asia: A Short History*, London: Oneworld, 2006.

Machiavelli, Nicolo, quoted in Edward Muir, *Civic Ritual in Renaissance Venice*, Princeton: Princeton University Press, 1998.

Mahmud, Mahmud Khan, *Tarikh-i-Junubi Hind* (Urdu), Bangalore: Government Press, 1967.

Majumdar, R.C., 'Nationalist Historians', in *Historians of India, Pakistan and Ceylon*, ed. C.H. Philips, London: Oxford University Press, 1961.

———, ed., *The History and Culture of the Indian People: The Delhi Sultanate*, 4th edn., 11 vols., Bombay: Bharatiya Vidya Bhavan, 1990, vol. 6.

Malinivijayottara Tantra, ed. Pandit Madhusudan Kaul Shastri, KSTS, no. 37, Bombay: Nirnaya Sagar, 1922.

Malkapuri, Abdul Jabar, *Tazkira-i-Aulaiya-i-Deccan* (Urdu), 2 vols., Hyderabad: Hassan, 1912.

Mamalbery, I., *Human Territories*, Amsterdam: John Benjamins, 1977.

Manka, *Srikanthacarita* (Sanskrit), with Jonaraja's commentary, ed. Pandit Durga Prasad and K.P. Parab, Bombay: Tukaram Javaji, 1900.

Mann, D.N., 'Symbolism in Ritual Context', in *Handbook of Social and Cultural Anthropology*, ed. John J. Honigmann, Chicago: Rand McNally, 1973.

Mann, M., *Sources of Social Power: A History of Power from the Beginning to AD 1760*, 2 vols., Cambridge: Cambridge University Press, 1986.

Marcell, M., *The Gift*, London: Cohen & West, 1954.

Marshall, Sir John, *Mohanjodaro and the Indus Civilisation*, 3 vols., London: Arthur Probsthain, 1931.

Marx Karl and F. Engels, *Selected Works*, 3 vols., Moscow: Progress, 1969.

Masson, V.M. and V.I. Sarianidi, *Central Asia: Turkmenistan before the Achaemenids*, London: Thames and Hudson, 1972.

Masson, V.M., *Turkmenistan in Mirror of World History*, Ministry of Foreign Affairs of Turkmenistan Republic in the frame of International Scientific Conference, St. Petersburg, 2000.

McNeill, William, *Rise of West: A History of Human Community*, Chicago: Chicago University Press, 1963.

Menon, Ramesh, *Bhagavata Purana*; repr., Delhi: Rupa, 2018.

Mill, James, *The History of British India*, London: Baldwin, Cradock and Joy, 1817.

Minhaj-i-Siraj, *Tabaqat-i-Nasiri*, ed. Nasu Lees, Khadim Hussain and Abdul Hai, 2 vols., Calcutta: Bibliotheca Indica, 1864; repr., Delhi: Low Price, 1981.

Mohan, Krishna, *Early Medieval History of Kashmir, AD 1003–1171*, Delhi: Meharchand Lachhmandas, 1981.

Moorcroft, William, *Tour Diary*, MS EURD-265, Jammu University Library, Jammu.

Moreland, W.H., *Agrarian System of Muslim India*, 2nd edn., Delhi: Oriental, 1968.

Moreland, W.H. and Pieter Geyl, eds. and trs., *Jahangir's India: The Remonstrantie of Francisco Palesart*, Cambridge: W. Heffer, 1925.

Moreland, W.H., *India at the Death of Akbar: An Economic Study*, London: Macmillan, 1920.

Mrgendratantra (Sanskrit), KSTS, no. 1, Bombay: Nirnaya Sagar, 1930.

Mukherjee, S.N., *Sir William Jones: A Study in Eighteenth-Century British Attitudes to India*, Cambridge: Cambridge University Press, 1968.

Mukhia, Harbans, 'Medieval India an Alien Conceptual Hegemony', in *The Medieval History Journal*, vol. 1, no. 1, January–June 1998, pp. 91–106.

Mukhia, Harbans, 'Peasant Production and Medieval Indian Society', in *Feudalism and Non-European Societies*, ed. Harbans Mukhia and Terry J. Byres, London: Frank Cass, 1985.

———, *Historians and Historiography during the Reign of Akbar*, Delhi: Aakar, 1976; repr., 2017.

———, *Perspectives on Medieval History*, Delhi: Vikas, 1993.

———, *The Mughals of India*, London: Blackwell, 2004.

Nadvi, Maulana Syed Suleman, *Arab-o-Hind Ke Talluqat*, Allahabad: Hindustan Academy, 1930.

Naqvi, Hameeda Khatoon, *Urbanisation and Urban Centres under the Great Mughals, 1556–1707*, Simla: Indian Institute of Advanced Study, 1971.

Nasir-al-din Hashami, *Dakan mein Urdu*, 6th edn., Lucknow: Kitab Mahal, 1963.

Naudou, Jean, *Buddhists of Kashmir* (French), Presses Universitaries de France, 1968; tr. Joel P. Brereton and Claudine Picron, Delhi: Agam Kala Prakashan, 1980.

Nayak, Prasanta Kumar, *Periodisation of History: Arunachal Pradesh*, Delhi: Kalpaz, 2017.

Nazim, M., *The Life and Times of Sultan Mahmud of Ghazna*, Delhi: Munshiram Manoharlal, 1971.

Netra Tantra (Sanskrit), with the commentary by Ksemaraja, ed. Pandit Madhusudan Kaul Shastri, KSTS, nos. 46, 61, Bombay: Nirnaya Sagar, 1926–1939.

Nieburg, H.L., *Culture Storm: Politics and Ritual Order*, New York: St. Martin's, 1973.

Nilmata Purana (Sanskrit), tr. Ved Kumari Gai, 2 vols., Srinagar: Jammu and Kashmir Cultural Academy, 1973.

Nizami, Hasan, *Taj-ul-Masir*, in *The History of India, as Told by its Own Historians*, tr. Elliot & Dowson, vol. 2, London: Trübner, 1867–77; repr., Delhi: D.K., 2001.

Nizami, K.A., 'Sufi Movement in Deccan', in *History of Medical Deccan (1295–1724)*, ed. K.K. Sherwani and P.M. Joshi, Hyderabad: Government of Andhra Pradesh, 1974.

———, *Akbar and Religion*, Delhi: Idarah-i-Adabiyat-i-Delli, 1989.

———, *Some Aspects of Religion and Politics in India during the Thirteenth Century*, Delhi: Idarah-i Adabiyat-i-Delli, 1961; repr., Delhi: Oxford University Press, 2002.

O'Bannon, George W., *The Turkoman Carpet*, London: Duckworth, 1974.

Oberoi, J.P.S., *Politics of Kaula Kings*, Manchester: Manchester University Press, 1962.

Pande, B.M., 'Neolithic Hunting Scene on a Stone Slab from Burzahom, Kashmir', *Asian Perspective*, vol. XIV, 1971, pp. 134–8.

Pandit, B.N., *History of Kashmir Saivism*, Srinagar: Utpal, 1989.

Panikkar, K.N., *Communal Threat and Secular Challenges*, Chennai: Earthworm, 1997.

Philips, C.H., 'James Mill, Mountstuart Elphistone and The History of India', in *Historians of India, Pakistan and Ceylon*, London: Oxford University Press, 1961.

Philips, E.D., *The Royal Hordes, Nomadic People of Steppes*, London: Thames and Hudson, 1965.

Pirenne, Henri, 'A Problem of Transition', *Mohammed and Charlemagne*, Allen & Unwin, (in) *Economic History Review*, vol. 10, no. 1, 1939, pp. 60–2.

Prasad, Beni, *History of Jahangir*, Allahabad: Indian Press, 1930.

Prasad, Ishwari, *A Short History of Muslim Rule in India*, Allahabad: *Indian* Press, 1965; repr., Delhi: Abhijeet Publications, 2016.

———, *History of Medieval India from 647 A.D. to the Mughal Conquest*, 2nd edn., Allahabad: Indian Press, 1931.

Price, J.R.F., *Rituals and Power, the Roman Imperial Cult in Asia Minor*, Cambridge: Cambridge University Press, 1984.

Pye, L.W., *Asian Power and Politics: The Cultural Dimensions of Authority*, London: Belknap, 1985.

Qanungo, K.R., *Life and Times of Sher Shah*, Calcutta: Orient Longman, 1965.

Qureshi, I.H., *The Administration of the Mughal Empire*, Delhi: Oriental, 1979.

Rampuri, Maulvi Abdul Gafur Khan and Moulvi Mir Kazim Ali Khan, eds., *Tarikh-i-Deccan* (Urdu), Hyderabad: Azam Steam Press, 1941.

Rao, T.A.G., *Elements of Hindu Iconography*, 2 vols., Madras: The Law Printing House, 1914, vol. 1, part 2.

Ray, S.C., *Early History and Culture of Kashmir*, Calcutta: U.N. Dhur, 1957.

Rees, J.D., *The Muslim Epoch*, London: Longmans, Green, 1894; repr., Delhi: Asian Publication, 1978.

Report of Hyderabad Archaeological Department, on the Administration of H.E.H. the Nizam's Dominions for the Year 1347 Fasli (6 October 1939 AD to 6 October 1940 AD), published by Order of the Government, Hyderabad-Deccan.

Rizvi, S.A.A., *History of Sufism in India*, 2 vols., Delhi: Munshiram Manoharlal, 1978.

Rousseau, Jean Jacques, *Discourse on the Origin and Foundation of Inequality among Mankind*, New York: P.F. Collier, 1976.

Roy, Asim, ed., *Islam in History and Politics: Perspectives from South Asia*, New Delhi: Oxford University Press, 2006.

Russel, James W., *Modes of Production in World History*, London: Routledge, 1989.

Sacchanda Tantra (Sanskrit), with commentary by Ksemaraja, ed. Pandit Madhusudan Kaul Shastri, KSTS, nos. 31, 38, 44, 48, 51, 53, 56, Bombay: Nirnaya Sagar, 1921–35.

Sahlins, Marshall, *Historical Metaphors and Mythical Realities: Structure in the Early History of the Sandwich Islands Kingdom, Ann Arbor:* University of Michigan Press, 1981.

Saletore, B.A., *Ancient Indian Political Thought and Institutions*, Bombay: Asia, 1963.

Salim, Mohammad, 'The Attitude of Chisti Saints towards Political Power', *Proceedings of Pakistan Historical Conference*, vol. 3, 1952, pp. 183–9.

Sardesai, G.S., *The Main Currents of Maratha History*, Bombay: K.B. Dhalve, 1933.

Sarkar, J.N., *A Short History of Aurangzib*, Delhi: Orient Blackswan, 1979.

———, *Mughal Polity*, Delhi: Idarah-i Adabiyat-i Delli, 1984.

———, *Thoughts on Trends of Cultural Contacts in Medieval India*, Calcutta: OPS, 1984.

Sarma, M.S., *History of the Reddi Kingdoms, circa 1325 AD to circa 1448 AD*, Waltair: Andhra University, 1948.

Sayer, Andrew, 'The Difference that Space Makes', in *Social Relations and Spatial Structures*, ed. Derek Gregory and John Urry, *London:* Macmillan, 1985.

Schimel, Anniemarie, 'The Influence of Sufism on Indo-Muslim Poetry', in *Anagogic Qualities of Literature*, ed. J.P. Strelka, University Park: Pennsylvania State University Press, 1971.

Shab Hussaini, 'Deccan, Deccani Zeban aur Uska Adab', *Sabras*, Hyderabad: Idaari-Adibiyat Urdu, June–August 1974.

Shaban, M.A., 'The Origins of Iqta', in *Islamic History of New Interpretation (AD 75–1055)*, ed. Shaban, Cambridge: Cambridge University Press, 1976.

Shah Peer Hassan, *Tarikh-i-Hassan* (Persian), 3 vols., Srinagar: Government Press, 1885.

Sharma, R.S., *Advent of Aryans*, Delhi: Manohar, 1999.

Sharma, S.R., *The Religious Policy of the Mughal Emperors*, London: Asia Publishing House, 1940; repr., Delhi: Munshiram Manoharlal, 1972.

Shaw, Robert, *Visit to Higher Tartary, Yarkand and Kasghar (Formerly Chinese Territory) and Return Journey over the Karakoram Pass*, London: John Murray, 1871.

Sherwani, H.K., 'Bahmani Sultans of Deccan', in *Dakan ke Bahmani salatin*, tr. Rahim Ali Al Hashmi, New Delhi: Urdu Bureau, 1978.

———, Cultural Trends in Medieval India, Bombay: Asia, 1968.

———, *The Bahmanis of the Deccan*, New Delhi: Munshiram Manoharlal, 1953.

Shu, Liang, *Dynastic History of Liang by Yao Silian, (557–637)*, Beijing: Zhonghua shuju 1973.

Siddiqi, M.S., 'Syed Mohammad Al-Hussani Gesu Daraz', *Islamic Culture*, vol. 52, July 1978, pp. 173–84.

Siddiqi, S. Suleiman, *Bahmani-Sufis:* Delhi: Idarah-i-Adabiyat-i Delli, 1989.

Singer, B.M., 'Emblems of Identity: A Semiotic Exploration', in *On Symbols Anthropology: Essays in Honor of Henry Hoijer, 1980*, ed. J. Maquet, Malibu: Undena, 1982.

Singh, S.D., 'The Early Development of Kingship in PreMuslim India', in *Patterns of Kingship and Authority in Traditional Asia*, ed. Ian Mabbett, London: Croom Helm, and Melbourne: Monash University, 1985.

Sinor, Denis, *Inner Asia, History–Civilization–Languages: A Syllabus*, Uralic and Altaic Series, vol. 96, Bloomington: Indiana University and The Hague: Mouton, 1969.

Siraj, Afif Shams, *Tarikh-i-Firuz Shahi*, ed. Wilayat Hussain, Calcutta: Bibliotheca Indica, 1964.

Skrine, F.H. and Edward D. Ros, *The Heart of Asia, London: Methuen, 1888.*

Smith, Adam, *An Inquiry into the Nature and Causes of the Wealth of Nations*, London: Strahan and Cadell, 1776; repr., New York: Scholars' Press, 1980.

Somadeva, *Kathasaritsagara*, English translation under the title *Ocean of Stream of Stories and Notes*, ed. N.M. Penzer and E.H. Tawney, 10 vols., privately printed for subscribers only, London: Chas J. Sawyer Grafton House, 1924.

Somananda, *Sivadrsti, Kashmir Sanskrit Granthavali*, ed. Madhusudan Kaul Sastri, KSTS, no. 54, Srinagar, 1934.

Spear, Percival, *A History of India*, 2 vols., London: Penguin, vol. 2, 1990.

Spellman, John W., *Political Theory of Ancient India*, Bombay: Oxford University Press, 1980.

Spencer, Herbert, *Sociology*, vol. I, New York: D. Appleto, 1910.

Sperber, Dan, *Rethinking Symbolism*, tr. Alice L. Morton, Cambridge Studies in Anthropology, Cambridge: Cambridge University Press, 1975.

Srivara, Pandit, *Jain Rajatarangini*, tr. J.C. Dutt, Calcutta: I.C. Bose, 1898; repr., Delhi: Low Price, 1990.

Stein, Burton, *Peasant State and Society in Medieval South India*, Delhi: Oxford University Press, 1985,

———, *Vijayanagara: The New Cambridge History of India*, 2 vols., Cambridge University Press, 1993.

Stein, M.A., *Ancient Geography of Kashmir*, Calcutta: Baptist Mission, 1899.

Tabattabai, Saiyid Ali, 'Burhān-i Ma'āsir', in *The History of the Bahmani Dynasty*, ed. J.S. King, London: Luzac, 1900.

Tchitcherov, Alexander I., *India: Changing Economic Structure in the Sixteenth to Eighteenth Centuries: Outline History of Crafts and Trade*, Delhi: Manohar, 1998.

Teelock, Vijayalakshmi, *Mauritian History: From Its Beginning to Modern Times*, revd. edn., Moka, Mauritius: Mahatma Gandhi Institute, 2009.

Thapar, Romila, *A History of India*, 2 vols., London: Penguin, vol. 1, 1966.

Thapar, Romila, Harbans Mukhia, Bipan Chandra, 'Communalism and the Writing of Indian History', *Economic and Political Weekly*, vol. 5, no. 19, May 1970; also published as a book, Delhi: People's Publishing House, 1969.

The *Rig Veda* (in Sanskrit); [unabridged English translation] *The Complete Rig Veda*, book 2, Kindle edn. by Ralph T.H. Griffith, London: Classic Century, 1896.

Todd, James, *Annals and Antiquities of Rajasthan*, edited with an introduction by William Crooke and Humphrey Milford, Oxford: Oxford University Press, 1914.

Topa, Ishwar, *Politics in Pre-Mughal Times*, Delhi: Idarah-i Adabiyat-i Delli, 1938; repr., 1976.

Umar, Muhammad, *Urban Culture in Northern India during the Eighteenth Century*, Delhi: Munshiram Manoharlal, 2001.

Vatikiotis, P.J., *Islam and the State*, London: Croom Helm, 1966.

Vovelle, Michel, *Ideologies and Mentalities*, tr. Eamon O'Flaherty, Oxford: Polity Press, 1990.

Wallerstein, I., *The Politics of the World Economy, the State, the Movements and the Civilization*, Cambridge: Cambridge University Press, 1984.

Walzer, Michael, 'On the Role of Symbolism in Political Thought', *Political Science Quarterly*, no. 82, June 1967, pp. 191–205.

Watson, G., 'Interpretations of Central Asian Influence of Mughal India: The Historical Debate', *Journal of South Asia*, vol. 18, no. 2, 1995, pp. 1–22.

Weber, Reinhard, *Memoirs Sur Inde* (French), Paris, 1849.

Yesoda, Devi V., 'Social and Economic Structure in Andhra Desh in Reddi Age', *S.V. University Oriental Journal*, vol. I, 1972, pp. 51–2.

Zore, Muhi-ud-din, *Deccan Adab-ki-Tarikh (1350–1750)* (Urdu), Karachi: Karachi Urdu Academy, 1960.

Index

CPSIA information can be obtained
at www.ICGtesting.com
Printed in the USA
LVHW101543010522
717570LV00042B/988/J

9 789355 721846